$\mathcal{T}$o the
MOUNTAIN

To the MOUNTAIN

ONE MORMON WOMAN'S SEARCH FOR SPIRIT

PHYLLIS BARBER

QUEST
BOOKS

Theosophical Publishing House
Wheaton, Illinois * Chennai, India

Cover images: Author photo by Catherine Hope. Morning landscape of Mt. Pandim by Pallab Seth/Getty Images
Cover design by Mary Ann Smith
Typesetting by DataPage, Inc.

Earlier versions of chapters 1, 5, and 8 were published as "Dancing with the Sacred, Three Parts," in *Numero Cinq Magazine* (March 2012).
Chapter 2 was published as "The Knife Handler" in *Agni Magazine*, no. 71 (Spring 2010).
Chapter 3 was published as "The Precarious Walk Away from Mormonism, All the Time with a Stitch in My Side," in *Dialogue: A Journal of Mormon Thought* 29, no. 3 (Fall 1996).
Part of chapter 4 was published as "With the Goddesses in Quintana Roo" in *Exponent II* (Winter 2012).
Chapter 7 was published as "In the Body of the Serpent" in *Tiferet: A Journal of Spiritual Literature* (September 2012).
Chapter 9 was published as "Sweetgrass" in *upstreet*, no. 5 (2009).
Chapter 11 was adapted from "The Gift of a Broken Heart," published in *Sunstone: Mormon Experience, Scholarship, Issues and Art*, no 118 (April 2008).
Chapter 12 was published as "At the Cannery" in *Dialogue: A Journal of Mormon Thought* 42, no. 2 (Summer 2009).

"Out of the Mouths of A Thousands Birds" is from *The Subject Tonight is Love: 60 Wild and Sweet Poems of Hafiz* (New York: Penguin, 1996), translated by Daniel Ladinsky and used with his permission.

Some of the names in the essays have been changed to protect the privacy of the individuals.

Library of Congress Cataloging-in-Publication Data

Barber, Phyllis.
    To the mountain: one Mormon woman's search for spirit / Phyllis Barber.—First Quest edition.
        pages   cm
    Includes index.   X, 258
        ISBN 978-0-8356-0924-1
    1. Barber, Phyllis.   2. Spiritual biography.   3. Spirituality.
    4. Religions.   5. Mormons—United States—Biography.   I. Title.
    BL73.B365A3 2014
    289.3092—dc23
    [B]   2014001204

        5 4 3 2 1 * 14 15 16 17 18 19 20

Printed in the United States of America

For Bill and his brand of spirituality

The spiritual life is the life of man's real self, the life of that interior self whose flame is so often allowed to be smothered under the ashes of anxiety and futile concern. . . . Without a life of the spirit our whole existence becomes unsubstantial and illusory. The life of the spirit, by integrating us in the real order established by God, puts us in the fullest possible contact with reality—not as we imagine it, but as it really is.

—Thomas Merton, *No Man Is An Island*

The word religion *is based on the root* lig, *meaning "to bind or connect together" (as in* ligament*), so* religion *means reconnecting or rebonding broken relationships—with God, with neighbor, with stranger and enemy, with nonhuman life, with all creation.*

—Brian D. McLaren, *Why Did Jesus, Moses, the Buddha, and Mohammed Cross the Road?*

CONTENTS

Acknowledgments

To those who helped with the inception, creation, and production of this book, I would like to give my thanks.

To Richard Smoley, editor of Quest Books, for recognizing the worth of this manuscript and bringing it to fruition; and to Sharron Dorr and Will Marsh for their enlightened editorial comments. To the writer friends I first met with in Denver after moving back to Colorado in 2007—Mary Domenico and Harrison Fletcher—who shepherded these essays in their earliest incarnation and reassured me with their enthusiasm.

Always to my sister, Kathryn Gold, and her son, Jay, who read through many of the essays and suggested that I keep working when I was ready to say, "This is done." To David Jauss, my colleague from the Vermont College of Fine Arts MFA in Writing Program, and Dan Wotherspoon, founder of Mormon Matters and former editor of *Sunstone*, who read through the entire manuscript and offered not only their expert opinion, but their encouragement. To Lance Larsen, who, with his well-trained eye for the poetic line, helped me refine the text of many of these essays.

To Gladys Swan and Leslie Ullman, my longtime writing colleagues, who have sustained me through the years with their appreciation, critiquing, praise, and friendship; to Shirley Smith of Meander Adventures, who helped open the doors of the international world for me; to Virginia and the late Jim Pearce for their assurance that they did not want to change me; to David Barber for his curious mind that jolted me out of any complacency in which I might have been tempted to bask; to my many writing students at VCFA and our lively interchange about writing and life; to Barry Sharcot, Rick Posner, and Elyse Hughes, three of my Lighthouse writing students who helped me find a title for this book; to Janice Roetenberg, Sylvia Milanese, and Andrea Doray and other members of my writing classes in Denver for their thoughtful editorial observations; to Karen

ACKNOWLEDGMENTS

Taylor for her helpful suggestions regarding "Sweetgrass"; to Emma Lou Thayne for her friendship and wholehearted support of this manuscript; and to the VCFA MFA in Writing Program, where I first gave a lecture on "Spirituality in Writing"—the origination of this collection.

Last, but not least, to my three sons, Christopher Jon, Jeremy, and Brad, and their families, for the joy and sustenance they give, and to my husband Bill Traeger, for his forbearance, his respect for the fact that I write and want to keep writing books, and for his love and generous support.

SEARCHING FOR SPIRIT

May thy Spirit be with and guide us this day.

—Phrase from my childhood's family prayer

Ever since I fell off the precipice of knowing, I have been searching for places where Spirit resides—those ineffable places where I feel connected to others, to nature, and to the ethereal. I find that as I have given up trying to file answers in my "I Know" box, I more than ever before want to capture the essence of Spirit and keep it in a cricket basket where it can breathe, yet be examined. Yet I know that captivity is folly. If one pursues Spirit with determination and a basket, it turns away. It recedes. It hides.

Even an exact definition is evasive, though I still have antennae out searching for it much of the time. Nevertheless, I have learned to trust Spirit— the spirit of being alive, the spirit of a song, the spirit that has whispered to me when I have been faced with a difficult choice. I find myself longing for conversations in which language transcends the ordinary and for moments of awareness of something alive in addition to the "normal" world.

Like the time I walked in snow boots and a hooded parka in the Colorado Rockies, witnessing a white rainbow arching through ice crystals over Lake Dillon—a perfect rainbow with no color, blowing snow dancing across the top—and feeling a dramatic shift in what is real. Like the time I danced with the head shaman of the Shuar tribe in Ecuador's Miazal jungle or the night I sang with Goddess worshipers at Uxmal under a battlefield of shooting stars. Like the times at Mormon meetings when

I have felt the presence—a burning in the throat and a quickening of the heart—of Spirit, of the feeling of being in a river-like flow that carries all of us forward through our lives. And like the time the elderly Chinese fortune-teller—a round-shouldered man dressed in loose trousers and a worn gray cotton jacket with faded stripes—took my hand in Lijiang, studied lifelines, and then, with an enigmatic smile, pronounced me the owner of a kind heart. We bowed to each other, Spirit circling us with its threads of connection.

All of this may be subjective . . . perhaps.

What of parallel worlds, being in this world but not totally of it? Is there a spirit world side by side with the human world where a metaphorical hand can reach out of the clouds to tap people on the shoulder and remind them of what they can't see or know? Is there a nest within a nest within a nest—matter, mind, and soul held by the large hands of Spirit? Some say that Spirit is in the wind, in the air we breathe to take in life itself before releasing it to the next inhalation. Is Spirit the essence that animates our bodies and our material substance?

I am intrigued by words such as *God*, *Allah*, and *Creator*, though the idea of Spirit feels closer, more intimate. After all I was raised with God, the Father, at the helm, his name invoked daily. For Mormons, God is an embodied God who is always progressing. But for me, behind this embodied God I sense an energy field running through all and everything, a subliminal hum vibrating against the scrim.

I am fully aware that the word *God* makes some people nervous and fails to comfort. Many people shout about the right God—their God—with absolute surety and a deadeye, fist-pumping, even trigger-happy confidence. They say they know who God is and who his children are (and are not), who are the infidels, who are the gentiles, the Other. In my opinion, there is too much shouting about who is right and who is wrong, about what is true and what is false.

I have no desire to add to this cacophony, but I do know that threads of connection can be found in unexpected places. Many seek the Ineffable, the Force, the I Am Self, the Great Spirit, Divine Power, Higher Power, the Great Architect, or, in simpler terms, a connection to Spirit, be it through religion, holy scripture, music, nature, beauty, visual images, prose, poetry, team sports, even "sex, drugs, and rock and roll."

One Friday afternoon, I found myself in the midst of men dressed in embroidered prayer caps and loose trousers with cloth strings tied in front. Among women who were strangers wrapped in long, colorful scarves. Me, wrapped in the green scarf that must have been a curtain panel once upon a time, the one I borrowed at the front desk from a woman I had met a few minutes before.

In the summer of 2008, I had met the Imam of the Denver Muslim Society in an interminably long line in the parking lot of Invesco Field, home of the Denver Broncos (after it was Mile High and before it was Sports Authority), while thousands waited to hear Barack Obama accept his nomination as a candidate for president. After exchanging a number of words with this elegant man and his equally elegant and refined wife, I said with some caution, "The terrorists associated with Islam have to be fanatics at the fringes of your culture. I wish I knew more about the mainstream of your religion."

An inscrutable shadow passed through his eyes, a hint of a bird flying overhead and patching out the sun. "These times have been troubling to all of us," he said. "If you are genuinely interested, you might come to one of our services," he added, handing me a card on which he had written, "Friday, 1:00 p.m."

I waited longer than I had intended, hesitant to step into this unknown milieu by myself, and a month later, on this particular Friday afternoon, he was nowhere in sight. When I asked the woman at the front desk, the one who lent me the scarf, she said he was away on a business trip. Suddenly,

I felt presumptive, invasive, like the dreaded sore thumb among these strangers, most of them speaking foreign languages, all of them Muslim.

A few men in bare feet kept changing places at the front of the room—talking softly, then loudly, straightening their mats, prostrating themselves, then standing in a cluster for a discussion in a language I did not understand. They occupied the back of the narrow storefront and seemed to be deciding what to do next. The women were clustered near the front door—the official back of the room. Someone in another time and place had told me that the men did not want to be distracted by a woman bowing in front of them. This explanation made common sense, so I did not get upset about being relegated to the back of the congregation with the women, none of us wearing shoes.

While I waited for the service to begin, a dozen or so women with their young children—a mix of Sudanese, Ethiopian, and Middle Eastern believers—straggled at the last minute into the space beside me, giggling softly, adjusting their scarves, looking at me with curiosity, even amusement. My silver hair and Scandinavian face were not fully covered by the bulky head scarf. I was a stranger here, a foreign body, or possibly a spy or an enemy.

The meeting started abruptly. No speeches. No introductions. Before I was ready to do such a thing, I was following the lead of the women: bending down onto my knees, trying to sit back on my thighs. Because I had had two knee surgeries, I bluffed and sat back halfway before we lunged into a bow that I could not hold long enough to show my respect for this mode of worship. When we stood again, we repeated words spoken by the man conducting the service. Then we repeated all of this again, and then again.

The thing I remember most was the light-green scarf—its smell especially. No hint of perfume or hair spray. One sniff of the polyester reminded me of something crumpled in a cardboard box and left in a corner. I had draped it over my head and crossed it over my shoulders, but its synthetic nature did not allow my body heat, increasing in intensity every second, to escape. Uncontrollably perspiring in that cramped space among the crowd of women and children, I bent again to the linoleum floor in the middle of downtown Denver, stretched into yet another bow, stood, only to repeat the process yet another time.

The ritual seemed closer to a demanding fitness regimen and was definitely foreign to my mode of worship. But, as if I were learning a dance, I settled into the rhythm and followed the choreography. We moved in concert in this temporary mosque, otherwise a barren commercial space in a tired strip mall. As we repeated the ritual, I became a singular thread in the warp and weft of this new-to-me-yet-old fabric. There was a yearning in this room for the infinite, not unlike my own. I felt delicately connected to these women gathering to praise God, even if they were strangers in a strange land themselves, even if I was raining sweat onto the linoleum floor, trying to keep up with them, up and down, on our knees, on our feet.

When we had finished the prayers and I lifted the see-through green scarf off my head and shoulders and felt the breeze from the pedestal fan on my arms and face, I turned to catch a glimpse of a broad smile full of abundant, uneven teeth. A young African woman tipped her head to one side, welcome written on her face. She did not know why I had visited the Muslim Society on a Friday afternoon, but she smiled as if we had met on a playground a long time ago—two young girls who had decided to balance the teeter-totter.

In the mirror of her eyes, I saw devotion and playfulness. I saw history, questions, answers, and a hint of mischief. She was seeing something in the mirror of my eyes, too, and for a few brief seconds we were sisters.

Born into a Mormon family, I could say that I was hijacked by religion at birth: taken to The Church of Jesus Christ of Latter-day Saints every Sunday; held on my mother's knee while members spoke of repentance, salvation, and the Spirit; taken by the hand to interminable Sunday School classes to learn about the restoration of the gospel.

Morning prayers, evening prayers—always asking for Spirit to guide us. Stories about brave pioneers persecuted for their religious beliefs. Covered wagons. Handcarts. Babies buried in shallow graves on wind-swept prairies. More stories of angels, golden plates, and God himself appearing to Joseph Smith. Parental instructions: God will help you in a jam if you knock on his door and ask for help; you will be blessed if you listen to the prophet; you will have a better life if you tithe and keep the Word of Wisdom: no coffee, tea, or alcohol. The Latter-day Saints claim to know the answers to the Big Questions—why people are here on earth, where they are going, and how you can turn aside your own will for God's. Each of us is a child of God. This was the language of the tribe into which I was born. This was how the world worked. End item.

But there were hybridizing factors.

In Boulder City, Nevada (the town created to build Hoover Dam), Grace Community Church, the oldest church in town with its peaked roof, whitewashed adobe walls, and stained-glass windows, tempted me. Most townspeople joined that congregation, and I did not like being left out of anything. One summer my mother said I could go to Bible School at Grace Community, where they would be studying knights and Crusaders, but only if I did not miss the weekly Primary meeting for Latter-day Saint children on Wednesdays and never asked for such per-mission on Sundays.

In 1932, the small building used to house our Mormon ward had been brought by a tractor trailer from Las Vegas to Avenue G—a square wooden church with a steeple, a place that seemed commodious to me as a child, but that, in truth, would fit into the corner wing of the Grace Community complex. Our family flourished in the warmth and acceptance of our small community of faithful Mormons, but we were small potatoes compared to Grace Community and such other mystical abodes as St. Christopher's Episcopal Parish at the intersection of Utah and Arizona Streets. Looking back, I wonder, how could we say we were the "only true church" if we didn't have more real estate in town?

Most of the week, the Foursquare Gospel Church sat quietly down the block from our home on Fifth Street. On days when we felt daring (never on Sunday), my brother and I peeped into our reflections glaring back from covered windowpanes. We listened for strange and exotic sounds (who knew what Holy Rollers did and on what days of the week?) but never heard anything to satisfy our voyeurism. Some of our friends went to catechism after school at St. Andrew's, whose priest was famous for "drowning in his cups" at Railroad Pass, the closest casino outside the boundaries of the federal reservation where we lived. And then there were the US rangers who watched over our town. These reflective-sunglasses-wearing men smacked of vigilantes I had seen onscreen at the Saturday matinee, the way they peered over the steering wheels and out the windows of Ford sedan cruisers, wearing soft felt hats, beige shirts, and neckties. These overseers would get you if you did not obey the law.

Put all of this together with the sun, which could burn your skin in three minutes and fry eggs on asphalt. When I heard in church that mortals could not take even a quick glimpse of God or they would faint dead away, I decided that God must be something like the blazing sun into which we must not look directly for fear of going blind. I was also convinced that he was something like the mammoth Hoover Dam, that gigantic concrete plug in the Colorado River about fifteen miles down the road, where turbines and electric transformers hummed at all hours. So, even though my parents were adamant that our family never miss a church meeting and labored diligently to teach us from holy scripture, these other things made their mark on my theology.

After moving to Las Vegas, which felt stranger than the topography of Mars, I finished my schooling and graduated from Las Vegas High School. My parents urged me to attend Brigham Young University (dubbed Breed 'Em Young by gentiles) with instructions to get an MRS degree above all else. I married a returned missionary in a Mormon temple and gave birth to four sons. After they graduated from high school, I finally faced the inevitable upheaval of my marriage, largely caused by our differing opinions regarding our religion. My husband and I filed for divorce, and I chose to look elsewhere for spiritual solace. Looking to other religions / spiritual practices for comfort, however, I still felt marooned and disconnected without my family around me, without the sustenance from familiar church meetings. Where could I find that sense of community, of harmony and connection that I had experienced with the Mormons?

I looked for a new home at Catholic mass, at Pentecostal / Second Calvary Baptist meetings, megachurch meetings, charismatic Christian, Episcopalian, Methodist, Lutheran, Unitarian, Congregational, and African Methodist Episcopalian services. In the jungles of Ecuador and the mountains of Peru I chanted with shamans in their ceremonies and drank their potions. In the remote hills of the Ozarks inside a tiny Baptist church, I witnessed a young boy in black-and-white oxfords being saved. In the Yucatan, with a group of goddess-in-embryo devotees, I climbed stone-carved steps built for feet half my size to the top of towering Mayan temples. In the Indian state of Sikkim at Rumtek Monastery, I sat across from a monk from Bhutan for lessons on Tibetan Buddhism 101. For several years on Wednesday nights, I studied what I considered to be esoteric Christianity in a nonsmiling, nonemotive Gurdjieff study group. Sometimes I wondered if I had merely become a tourist of the exotic in my longing for connection, but I still wanted to find that something that inspired me, enlarged my heart and mind, and made me feel an integral part of the whole.

Whatever that answer to connectivity might be, while I circled the earth looking for it, not unlike a spiritual but low-flying astronaut, I grew deeply uncomfortable with any generic term used to describe a particular person: a Muslim, a Buddhist, a Catholic, a Jew, a Hindu, a Baptist, a Seventh-day Adventist, even a Mormon. I could not dismiss anyone carte blanche and say they were this or that. No one is ever an exact replica of another. And, regardless of their leanings, the people I met in these settings seemed tuned to this thing called Spirit.

But, again, what does it mean to be spiritual, to be connected?

I think of music. Before I decided to take my insufferable perfectionism to the blank page and the task of writing prose at age thirty-two, I aspired to be a concert pianist. I had given numerous recitals, played solos and piano duets, accompanied many vocalists, trios, quartets, trumpeters, violists, flautists, etc., in talent shows, church meetings, school assemblies, nursing homes, and at political fundraisers. When I worked with an ensemble, in rare instances everything and everyone became greater than the individuals playing their instruments. Once in a great while the musicians let go of self and lifted the music off the notated page into something unspeakably harmonious, even luminous. There is a taste of supreme satisfaction when musicians follow the direction of *spiritoso*, crossing borders toward the Divine.

Music experienced in this way is similar to making love. It is like rising to that summit of feeling sometimes too powerful to withstand. Call it consonance out of dissonance—migrating birds that all change direction at the same moment, all of them listening to some innate music and manifesting it against the backdrop of sky.

A month after I attended the Denver Muslim Society meeting, I visited the Denver Art Museum to see an exhibit of the Gee's Bend quilts made by women from a historically isolated African-American community in Alabama. I noticed a posted quote from Mary Lee Bendolph, born in 1935, that summed up the vitality, the life force that spoke from that wall: "Now I can have it [new cloth], but I see the value of the leftover cloth. Old clothes have the Spirit and I can't leave the Spirit out. The Spirit is all we had to lead and guide us, back in the day, and it still is."

In its broadest connotation, spirituality has been called the purest of the moral, artistic, and intellectual aspirations of humanity. In the abstract, it can be found in the ethics and philosophy of peoples and their nations. In the concrete, it may be said to affect the enlightened ways human beings treat each other, connect with nature, and create their art. Something brought to life by a writer, composer, painter, or sculptor, for instance, can be called spiritual if it offers insight, a new perception, an uplift for one's heart and mind, and if it takes the observer to an "aha" place or widens one's heart. Anything created to open the self to the beauty inherent in every small thing, even to the beauty in a particular ugliness, such as Lucy Grealy's perception of her deformed face in *Autobiography of a Face*, can be called spiritual.

In its stricter connotation, spirituality can be found in the deep-inside-the-seashell realm of a religious life in which a person or a gathering of people seeks to live in harmony with God. This is not to say that organized religion is the only way to Spirit, but religion has taken some hard knocks in recent years, has been held suspect and discounted wholesale by many observers. There is beauty that can be witnessed in a body of worshipers attempting to explain, understand, and be moved by God. Many writers approach the topic of spirituality with specificity, including St. Augustine, Thomas Merton, Hildegarde of Bingen, C. S. Lewis, Graham Greene, Marcus Borg, Pema Chödrön, Paramahansa Yogananda, and Chögyam Trungpa, among hundreds of others.

"At its best, religion can reconnect its followers not only to God, but with neighbor, with stranger and enemy, with nonhuman life, with all creation," as Brian McLaren says in *Why Did Jesus, Moses, the Buddha, and Mohammed Cross the Road?*[1]

Ultimately, I discovered that I was a mere beginner in the ancient business of understanding God or Spirit or the Divine. So many had gone before me. So many had walked the path, some limping on crutches, some crawling on their knees. So many had proclaimed that they had access to "the Truth, the only Truth." On some days, the idea of the Church of the

Holy Unknown appealed to me, as I had come to suspect that most of us do not have enough maturity or humility to understand what true religion and God are all about. But I am grateful that my particular Mormon upbringing inadvertently gave me walking shoes with which I could leave my own footprints on the path into the invisible and approach the lip of the Great Perhaps.

In his foreword to the 2007 edition of *Best American Spiritual Writing*, editor Philip Zaleski describes our innate desire to stumble upon the magical text that contains "the elixir of transformation":

> We find it in the lucid nightmares of Borges, the theosophical visions of Balzac, the mythic voyages of Verne. . . . How often has a sinner made a volte-face toward sanctity after hearing a passage that conveyed . . . the elixir of transformation? . . . C. S. Lewis' life forked when on a whim he purchased from a railroad book rack a worn copy of George MacDonald's *Phantastes* and encountered for the first time that literary quality he later defined as "holiness." These Aladdin's lamps come in a rainbow of forms: a cheap paperback bought at Goodwill, a treasure map, a message in a bottle, an illuminated manuscript, a last will and testament, an inscription in a ring, a love letter found in the snow.[2]

I, too, like the idea of stumbling upon an illumination that catches one glimpse of the sublime, even if all I have is the insufficient vehicle of language trying to catch a star. Words being what they are, however, I have still known this joy during encounters with people and their spiritual practices. Someone's home turf (including that of my LDS tribe) is a powerful meeting ground where Spirit shows its face on occasion. When I see a flash of a person's humanity and she or he sees mine, we are not so separate beings. We are separate when we quarrel about my dad being bigger than your dad or about what exactly God said, thinking we are better, smarter, or more faithful because we follow a path *we* think divine providence has ordained.

PROLOGUE

Looking directly into someone's eyes, one faces a window to Spirit that inhabits everything from a vast sky covered with clouds resembling goldfish scales, to a rising moon at the top of a jagged peak, to the young Muslim mothers who tried not to smile at the jerry-rigged head scarf that kept slipping lopsidedly to the back of my head. When we open our eyes, we see Spirit—this grounding, this materialization of the light. When we open our lungs to breathe it in, it is there.

Chapter 1

DANCING WITH THE SACRED: PART ONE
1975

After my two oldest sons bolt out the side door, late for elementary school, scraping their backpacks against the already-scarred door frame, I look at the piles of breakfast dishes. Specks of cake mix, flipped from the wire arms of the electric beater yesterday, remain on the kitchen window above the sink. I open the refrigerator and notice an amoeba-shaped puddle of grape juice marring the shine of the glass shelf. I close the white enameled door covered with magnets, and I leave this messy kitchen, this reminder of my ineptitude, which will depress me even more if I think about it much longer. I need to talk to someone. But who wants to listen? Whom would I tell anyway? Maybe I should get on my knees and talk to God, but I need to move more than I need to stay still. I need to feel my body alive—my arms stretching up and out, my blood speeding through my veins. Midstep in the front hall, where family and visitors come and go, I am struck with an idea. Luckily, the baby is still asleep.

I turn the corner to the family room. It is filled with furniture, but because I feel compelled to dance, I am suddenly an Amazon. I push the wing chair to the wall, the sofa as well. Now there is space, enough space. It might be possible, instead of praying to God, that I could dance with him somehow, that maybe he could take me in his arms. Today. Right now.

CHAPTER 1

I thumb through my stack of albums. I find Prokofiev's *Concerto No. 1 for Piano & Orchestra, Op. 10*, lift the record out of the sleeve, and set it on the turntable. Aiming the needle, I find the groove and wait for the ebb and flow of the orchestra, the in and the out. The three beginning chords cause my arms to pimple with gooseflesh. I take two steps to the middle of the room and raise my arms above my head in a circle, fingertips touching.

I move, slowly at first, one foot pointed to the right—the most elegant ballerina in the most satin of toe shoes. At first, my right leg lifts poetically, delicately for such a long leg. The other knee bends in a *demi-plié*. The music swarms inside, splits into the tributaries of my veins and vessels, and becomes blood. Things become more primitive. I stamp the pressing beat into the floor. I bend to one side and then the other, my arms swimming through air. I am a willow, a genie escaping the bottle, the wind. I am the scars in the face of the earth opening to receive water that runs heedlessly in spring. I am light. I am air. The magic carpet of music carries me to places where I can escape—to the Masai Mara I have visited on television, where bare legs of tribal dancers reflect the light of a campfire and beaded hoops circle their necks, or maybe to the Greek islands I have seen on travel posters with their red-roofed white houses stark against the cobalt blue sky and water. The music lifts me out of this minute, this hour, this day. I am dancing to the opening and closing of the heart valves, to the beat of humanity, dancing, giving my all to the air, giving it up to the room. Whirling. Bending. Leaping. Twisting. Twirling and twirling to the beat. Yes! Dancing. Getting close to what God is.

After a dizzying finale in which the chords build until there is no more building possible, the climactic release comes. The final chord. The sound dies, as if it had never been. The room swirls, passing me by even as I stand still, panting, trying to return my breathing to normal. I am dizzy. I steady myself in the middle of the Persian rug and wonder why Prokofiev had to write an end to this concerto. I can hear the tick of the needle on the record in the black space left on the vinyl. I stand quietly until the room stops with me, until the sense of having traveled elsewhere fades away.

I look at this sky-blue family room in our home in Salt Lake City, where my husband and I are raising our children—the family pictures on the wall, including our first son, who was born with hemophilia and who died at the age of three from a cerebral hemorrhage. I look at his quizzical expression looking back from behind the picture glass. It is as if he is asking, "Why, Mama?" I pause, wanting to speak, wanting to answer him, but words have no meaning. Maybe they never did. My eyes shift to the framed copy of my husband's and my college diplomas; the Persian carpet with its blue stain where one son spilled a bucket of blue paint when he was two; the sandstone hearth where our youngest son fell not once, but twice, and split open his head, which had to be stitched together in the emergency room. Everything slipstreams in my peripheral vision: the bookcase with its many volumes of books, psychological tomes, scriptures, all of which are supposed to have answers; the leather wing chair peppered with the points of darts thrown when I, Mother, wasn't looking and before I, Mother, hid the darts in a secret place; the wooden floor I am supposed to polish once a week with a flat mop and its terry-cloth cover. I, the mother, stand here looking at the things that verify my place in the world and also at the evidence that I have not always been watchful at the helm—I, the mother who is supposed to make the world all right for her husband and children; I, the mother, the heart of the home, the protector, the nurturer. I think I should dance again, turn the music up loud before my mind chases me into that place where I feel bad about myself again.

I learned dancing from my father, who loved to polka when Lawrence Welk's orchestra played on television, and at dance festivals sponsored by my church when I was a teenager. We danced the cha-cha, the tango, and the Viennese waltz.

At age twenty-one, I danced myself into a Mormon temple marriage and made promises to help build the Kingdom of God here on earth. I gave birth to four sons, whom I dressed each Sunday for church meetings. I tried to be a good wife. I canned pears and ground wheat for bread, I taught Relief Society lessons and accompanied singers and violinists on the piano, I bore testimony to the truthfulness of the gospel countless times. Yet dancing to music seems to be my real home—the place where I can feel the ecstasy of the Divine.

Last night I twisted and turned in bed with my newfound knowledge that there is another woman in my husband's life and that my marriage may not always be there for me. I felt tempted to jump out of bed, open the blinds, and search the night sky for the letter of the law burnished among the stars—a big, pulsing neon sign that said, "Thou Shalt *Not* Endure to the End." Except that's all I know how to do: persist, endure, keep dancing. Things have to work out, don't they?

Mormons are taught not only to endure to the end, but also to persist in the process of perfecting themselves: "As man is now, God once was; as God is now, man may be." Lorenzo Snow, fifth president of the Church, penned the often-repeated couplet after he heard Joseph Smith's lecture on this doctrine. I have tried for perfection, but maybe I have not thought that word through to its logical conclusion. Maybe I have not wondered enough about who is the arbiter of perfection.

Perfection. Freedom from fault or defect. Is that possible? Perfection is a nice idea, but that definition makes the idea of becoming like God stifling. It is tied to shoulds, oughts, and knots that bind rather than release one to live a full life and to dance the dance. Even Brigham Young said, "Let us not narrow ourselves up."[1] Trying to be perfect when the world and my husband have no intention of complying with my notions of perfection is killing me.

I hear the telephone ringing. I do not want to leave this room just yet. I want to bring back the music, to keep God here with me, even if he has places to go, things to do, and I, too, have my responsibilities. But, I think, if God is my Father, then I am his daughter. I need to trust that he will always be with me somehow, that there will be a next dance.

Ignoring the phone, I think of something William James said in *The Varieties of Religious Experience* about how a prophet can seem a lonely madman:

If his doctrine proves contagious enough to spread to any others, it becomes a definite and labeled heresy. But if it then still prove contagious enough to triumph over persecution, it becomes itself an orthodoxy; and when a religion has become an orthodoxy, its day of inwardness is over: the spring is dry; the faithful live at second hand exclusively. . . . The new church, in spite of whatever goodness it may foster, can be henceforth counted on as a staunch ally in every attempt to stifle the spontaneous religious spirit, and to stop all later bubblings of the fountain from which in purer days it drew its own supply of inspiration.[2]

Why am I thinking about William James? Do I suspect that I am caught in the web of orthodoxy? Am I inflexible and is my spring dry? Am I living at second hand—unwilling to consider any options other than my parents' teachings and my Mormon upbringing? But I don't feel inflexible when I dance. I am the fountain that bubbles, even the source of this fountain— the water. I raise both arms to the ceiling as if to lift off, hoping I can stretch into the heavens. "Do not leave me," I want to call out, though I do not say that out loud. "I am with you," I hear God say, though he does not say that out loud either.

Daylight pours through the windows, exchanging the light in this room for that of the day. My hands press flat against each other in front of my heart. "Thanks for the dance," I whisper. "Thank you," I think I hear him whisper back. The telephone has stopped ringing. A floorboard creaks beneath my foot. I hear the refrigerator humming down the hall. Commerce and industry, motherhood and wifehood, calling again.

Chapter 2

THE KNIFE HANDLER

I am weighing my options as I check out Vernon with his straight, pencil-sketch lips that rarely curve. He is wearing his soft felt hat at right angles and moves with his head plumb-line straight with the rest of his spine. He is a man of some reputation—the basket-making teacher at the Ozark Folk Center and a master with the edge of a knife. I am his student, currently constructing a white oak basket for which I am suffering greatly. My wrists are burning after four days of whittling. I can barely lift the knife anymore.

At this moment, he and I are driving together in his ancient Dodge truck while my three boys are back at the motel in Mountain View, my fourteen-year-old playing watchdog over the television remote and his younger brothers. Vernon has narrow bones in his face, eyes like pale blue marbles, and hands mean with the knife. (*Mean* here means "good." I pick up local color like a chameleon.) I am not at Vernon's mercy or anything like that, but my breathing is shallow. My lungs are hurting. I am thinking I have gambled one too many times.

Last Monday after class, Vernon peeked in on me playing "Moonlight Sonata" on the piano in a small side room at the center. He stood in the doorway, listening. I saw him and lifted my hands off the keys. "I love piano playing," he said, coming closer. We talked about music, then drifted into the topic of old-time religion. "Why don't you come visit my church?" he said. "Just a ways off."

Now we are driving into twilight and the deep, dark woods to who knows what and who knows where, some place he calls New Nata, and

I am thinking for all the world that I am a fool who might get jumped or kidnapped or waylaid by crazy moonshiners or big bears. Or even Vernon.

But come on now. There is something about Vernon that is right-to-the-toe square. Being that curiosity is my deeply rutted habit, I had decided to take my chances and drove to his house, our prearranged meeting place, at the prearranged time. But why in heaven's name did I climb into this rumply Dodge truck with too many dents in one fender? Soda-pop stains shine off the dashboard. A scratchy radio plays local bluegrass. Keeping the beat, Vernon dips his stiff chin into the air in front of his poked-out Adam's apple.

It is the summer of 1981. My sons and I are spending a couple of weeks in Mountain View while my husband is a guest professor in the law school at the University of Arkansas/Fayetteville. I hoped to steep our three sons in Ozarkness—classes in fiddling (middle son, Jeremy, a wizard on the violin), bluegrass music (oldest son, Chris, hot on the guitar), whittling, broom making, whatever they might be interested in, though Brad is too young to be interested in much more than the fishing pond. Me, I am taking a basket-making class in which we chopped down a tree, shucked off the bark, and cut strips of wood for our baskets-to-be. Hours after class and its exertions, my wrist aches. Even while Vernon is turning onto another narrow road and we are cruising farther into the holler, I feel jabs of lightning in that delicate wrist that operates my right hand. I am a tall girl with small bones, except in the hips, of course. My hips were made for birthing—big basket of bones to hold a baby, cradle it until it decides it is time for open air, where there are people intent on music, God, and how to get back to the unmessy place peaceful enough to house angels.

About half an hour ago, I braked in front of Vernon's house, stretched my arms, and wondered what I would find inside this low-lying, cinder-block house with dark-brown curtains. I unlatched my car door and unfolded my tired pony legs. I stood tall on hard dirt, stretched, and then took cautious steps toward Vernon's. Some eyes might be watching, I thought as I side-stepped some puddles. Someone could be assessing this young mother from Salt Lake City, this big-city girl from the West. I sighed in relief when a dumpling of a woman answered the door. Greeting me with a tired gray smile, her blue-checked apron tied high around her waist, she said she was Ella, wouldn't I come in, she and her husband were expecting me.

Vernon appeared out of the misty-moisty kitchen, sleeves rolled up and an embroidered potato-sack dishtowel in his hands. It had seen some days—coffee stains, burnt grease, holes in the cloth. His wife excused herself, saying she had to look after water boiling around the lids of her Mason jars. "Snap beans," she said, smiling as if snap beans were the essence of life.

"Sit you down, girl," Vernon said, and I took a seat on a sofa that had seen a few too many bottoms in its time. The springs protested.

In class after my wrist gave out, I had watched Vernon, who could do more with wood than anyone I had ever met, treat my portion of tree trunk as if it were a cold slab of lard. Without rulers or measuring tapes, he stripped pieces for my basket, the same length, the same width, time after time. No rehearsing. No false starts or nicks in the damp insides of the trunk. Then he whittled my basket handle, all the time whistling, sometimes singing a few lines from songs I had never heard. And after class, when he overheard me playing those few bars of "Moonlight" on an old-timey piano I had asked permission to play—that was what got us started with all of this. "Music is my blood," I told him. "And I am curious about other people's music and their worship—how religious people think they are getting to the other side they talk about and what they do to hook up with Spirit, that something that keeps us all wondering."

Then he was walking to a cabinet where an old Victrola on top held its curvy head like a proud goose. "I've got something here," he said, shuffling through a neat stack of pamphlets, sheet music, and loose papers. "I've been thinking you need to know about this." He grabbed two thin, paper-covered books from the cabinet and sat next to me. The sofa sank even lower.

"Shape notes," he said. "You ever heard of shape notes?"

"Can't say I have," I answered, watching him open a small book called *Joy in Singing: 135 New and Favorite Gospel Songs for Group Singing,*

Singing Schools and Singing Conventions. At the bottom of the first page, I saw that it was published by the editorial staff of Stamps-Baxter Music of the Zondervan Corporation out of Dallas. Bible Belt stuff. First song: "Jesus Is Coming Again."

"Look at these shapes," he said. He was excited. He was taking me to the shores of a newly discovered land.

The notes were not round, the kind I was used to seeing on a staff. "How does this work?"

"Simple do, re, mi," he said. "You can use this system in any key. The do is always a triangle, re is a half moon, mi is a diamond."

I found fa, which looked like the upper half of a square box cut on the diagonal; sol, which was the kind of round note I was used to seeing; la, a pure square; and ti, a diamond with a rounded top, the diamond-ring variety.

"Wow," I said, leafing through the book, wanting to sight-read through such hymns as "I Want to Be More Like Him Every Day," "Keep the Prayer Line Open," and "Jesus Is the Friend of Sinners." The shape notes were arranged the way any round notes would be on the familiar musical staff, so it was not hard to read the melody line and hum softly to myself. I was in Southern Baptist Land, though I did not know the differences between First and Second and Calvary Baptist and whatever other names I had seen on signs in front of tall-skinny, small-chunky, and house-of-many-mansions churches labeled Baptist. I was still a Mormon at heart, rather innocent regarding other churches and their ways. "This book's for you," Vernon said, handing me a second one. "Both of 'em."

This was new territory, these shape notes, these black diamonds, triangles, and squares in these hills in the holler. They were something totally alien and unknown, even with all my training in music and my vaunted college degree.

"We best be getting on to church," Vernon said, springing from the sagging cushions. "I'll be happy to drive you there. We don't need two cars."

"Maybe I should drive my own car?"

"No, no. My truck knows the ruts on the road to New Nata."

"Well, is Ella coming with us?" I asked, using the sofa's arm to steady myself back onto my feet and peering into the kitchen at the woman lifting the lid of a deep-water cooker to release a cloud of steam.

"No. She has to wait out those beans and make sure they're sealed tight."

My hands limped out at the sides of my legs. It was not that I did not trust Vernon. He seemed straight, through and through. A man of his word. A man who knew how to rub strips of white oak silky smooth with the back of his knife. After all, he had salvaged the strips of my basket when my wrist gave out like a wounded puppy. He was a man who loved music. Yet I hesitated as I slid onto the cracked vinyl seat cover, closed the passenger door, and heard the truck's engine roar.

Now, the headlights are slashing branches and tree trunks in the dimming light. I have seen *Deliverance* and read *A Good Man is Hard to Find* by Flannery O'Connor, in which the family rides recklessly to their end. I am thinking of my three boys tucked back in the motel, husband David back in Fayetteville teaching classes, while I am out here on a bumpy road going deeper and deeper into the hills. The light is fading fast; in fact the light is gone except for a silver-gray lining on the horizon. The pinks and oranges have sunk away. The beam from Vernon's headlights bounces high and low and everywhere as the road twists and turns. The skeleton branches reach out across the road from time to time, close enough to scrape the top of the truck.

"Not far," Vernon says. His lips pressed tight, he holds his head up high to peer over the dashboard, past the smeared windshield, out into the darkness, where rabbits or coons might be making kamikaze runs across the road. Chuckholes. Washboard ripples occasionally. It is too late for me to run. My instincts are usually good, though I catch myself paying extra attention to the word *usually*. Just when we have rounded one too many curves and I think I should tell Vernon thanks but no thanks, let's go back, I don't have time for this and I'm not ready to be gone this long, a tiny church appears, white in the graying gloom, windows yellow with light. There is a high-ridged roof, dark shingles—a no-account setting for a church, so buried in the woods as it is, but maybe that is only because I do not understand back roads. Vernon seems to know exactly where he is going as he squeezes into the middle of assorted trucks, Fords and Chevys parked at cockeyed angles.

I slide out of the cab. Vernon and I walk side by side into white, through an open door, looking at the narrowness of the chapel, the pews on either side that hold no more than five bodies apiece. No crosses or statuary anywhere, just a pulpit, a few chairs on the dais, a spinet of a piano that looks to be out of tune, untrustworthy, and beaten into submission from years of hands hammering the keys, playing the black ones with tuck-and-roll fists.

Vernon introduces me to the first person we encounter, a sleepy-eyed woman in a comfortable jersey with white dots. She tilts her head low, though nothing is lost to her down-looking eyes.

"We'come," she says softly, pulling on the little finger of her left hand like one of those Chinese straw torture devices.

"She plays the piano good," Vernon says proudly, assuming that my gift is rare and automatically vaults me onto a pedestal. Then he turns to me in a slightly stiff way, almost as if made of wood himself. "You'll play the piano for the choir tonight, won't you?"

"I couldn't do that," I say before thinking about it, wishing I could bend over and pull up invisible socks that have fallen down in response to his invitation, wishing I could stop breathing in such a shallow way, trying to put this whole scenario together in my head. I am a woman who has studied classical masterpieces. I practice endlessly. I am precise. "I don't know your music," I say, remembering the songs in the shape-note singing books, nothing I have ever seen or heard before.

"But you can play, can't you?" Vernon insists, his pale blue eyes shocked that I would resist his request. "You know the notes."

"Sure," I say, "but not this kind of music. This style," I stutter.

"What do you mean, *this* kind of music?" he says, his whittling hands tight on his hips. "Music is music."

"But . . . " I say, realizing that nothing I say will make any sense here. "This is all new to me."

"God is in the music—when we sing, we shout. It's not about doing it right."

I swallow big time. Besides being a perfectionist, I can be shy.

"Well, then," he insists when I do not respond. "You'll lead the choir, won't you?"

The lights in the ceiling feel hot and steamy, as if they were glaring spotlights on a stage already well lit. My blouse is moist under the arms and at the neck. I think about the door. I am one of the deer people hunt in these hills. The hunter is pointing his arrow, and I cannot escape, whichever way I move.

Two wiry men in overalls walk through the door and touch their hats to greet Vernon. "Evenin'," one says. A couple come through the door arm in arm, patting each other's elbows, black broad-heeled shoes on the woman, summer-mudded boots on the man. Women arrive in paisleys, swirling stripes, white lace-necked blouses, speckled splotches of color on cotton and jersey dresses swishing through the door, finding a place in the pews, wriggling into comfort on broad and narrow buttocks. The congregation gathers and sits and murmurs, a few eyes in my direction assessing, analyzing.

Vernon sits in the first pew, pats the place next to him, and I sit while the minister greets everyone—black smooth hair, long white cheeks, eyebrows rising to a point at each end, all this above a well-worn and shiny dark-blue suit, dark-blue knit tie. "We'come," he says. "We're gathered here in worship to thank our Lord, Jesus Christ. I say Jesus, yes Jesus."

"Amen," a woman in the congregation answers back.

Yes, I say to myself, nodding my head yes too, yes to the brothers and sisters gathered here wanting that connection, that sense of Spirit charging through the air on a white horse and piercing every chest sitting in the pews of this pointy-roofed church in the middle of the Ozarks. "Yes, dear God," I pray to myself, remembering what I am about to do. "Help me with this choir. Fill the music with thee and thy spirit. Please and amen."

"Our choir will now sing for us," the minister says, and a group of ten or eleven people gathers at the far side of the platform.

"Come on," Vernon says, handing me a hymnal, then stands to make his way to join the choir. He stops briefly to make an announcement to the people in the pews. "This here is Ms. Phyllis from the Ozark Center class. She knows music." In an aside, he tells me to open the hymnbook to number 51: "Little Is Much When God Is in It."

It is like standing over deep water as I face this group of curious onlookers, each of us doing the measure-for-measure assessment, peering across the borders of imaginary countries to see what lies there. I open the little book in my hand—my security blanket, my salvation. I smile at the blur of people—blues, reds, yellows, the primary colors, one-two-three. A few noses and eyeglasses here and there. Dive, I tell myself. Jump. I imagine there is a piano playing, giving the choir an introduction, but then I get the strangest sensation, as if I had already jumped and were being held at the ankle by a rope tied to a rock at the bottom of a lake.

I raise both arms. This is what I have done at my ward in Salt Lake City when leading the congregation in hymn singing. I look into these new faces on this wide variety of bodies, then raise one arm higher to signal the upbeat: one-two-three-ahhhp. But the signal does not work here. There is no sound. They all look at me in expectation, believing and trusting because they've been told I know music. It is as if the water surrounding me is filling my ears and nose and fish are staring at me with large eyes that never blink in their watery wondering. The only way out . . . try again.

Where I get the courage I will never know, but I try the upbeat again and add my voice: "In the harvest field now ripened," I sing thinly. The diamonds and squares and triangles jump all over the page, but I still know where a G sits on the musical staff, and then an F and a B-flat. I hold steady, the familiar five parallel lines to guide me. I gain in volume and clarity.

Miraculously, the choir is singing. I can hear their voices. We are in this together. Hallelujah. "Labor not for wealth or fame. There's a crown and you can win it, / If you go in Jesus' name."

Four verses. Four choruses. "We'll be happy, glad, and free"—the last line of the fourth verse. Everyone has gotten into the singing. Their faces are uplifted; their voices sound out all the way from their toes. We have come together in that harmonious connection that sometimes happens with music, that moment when all the voices are more than all the singers, that rare, beautiful thing. And during that instant between the end of the song and the reemergence of real time, I feel the rope releasing my ankle. I am rising to the surface of the water into open air. I spread my arms out wide and wider and almost burst with the feeling of fresh air in my lungs.

A few of the choir rock their heads in approval, their eyes closed. They do not look at me or at each other. They are caught in something bigger. Some of them lumber back to their pews without any sign of response; others step lightly on the pine floor, happy to be alive. There is the sound of big and little shoes finding a comfortable place to rest, a few coughs, a few purses clicking shut.

I touch Vernon's arm as we return to our front-row pew, just lightly, and his ear lobes turn pink. I am not sure who lives inside Vernon or if I have crossed some boundary I should not have, but I appreciate it when he turns and grants me a stiff, satisfied smile. It is not just that his discovery at the Ozark Folk Center has not let him down, which is the gratitude I am feeling. It is as if he knew what would happen before it happened, as if he has no conception of anyone who loves music doing anything other than making music of whatever kind. God is in the bones of music. He gave it to us. To sing. To play. To let rise up however it will, though it must rise up.

I am moved by this simplicity. I live in a world where my mind twists and turns, paralysis by analysis, maybe. I have worked hard to figure it all out—this business of God and how we serve God and yet respect the mind he has given us. Dependence versus independence. Surrender versus fight. And then there is that thing about people being godly and yet stiff in their ways, their goodness turning sour when blind certainty enters. I want to know God, even if God is the Unknowable. I want to know what it means to surrender to God's will—whether or not that means lying flat on the hard-packed country road and letting a Dodge Ram roll over me. I have put in time thinking about all of this. I am trying to listen, but it seems there are too many voices calling out, "Come hither. This is the way, the truth, the light. Listen to me, listen to me. I have cornered the Truth. I have caged it. If you will only listen to me, to me, to me, to us, to us, to us." Music is the safest place I know.

I sit in the first row in the first pew in this chapel in New Nata, Arkansas, hands flat on my knees in an attempt to keep them from tensing into nervous claws, thinking about my boys again. The preacher is well spoken. He has worked the hellfire-and-damnation sermon to a fine art. His voice is rising. The air is filling with his pleading, with the urgency of his voice telling us sinners squirming on these hard pews, our sins flashing in our minds, to listen with both ears. Beneath a three-armed brass chandelier whose low-watt bulb is glowing, he is asking us to surrender, to say, "I give up. Save me. Save me, now."

"Is there anyone," he asks, looking slowly at each member of the congregation, "who is filling with the Spirit, that Spirit telling you to come to the front and be saved? I know there's someone out there. It could be you." He is working up a sweat. A strand of his smooth black hair has fallen into his eye. He loosens his tie. "Do you hear Jesus talking to you? Do you feel the Spirit welling up inside you, that fire telling you to be saved before it's too late?"

I am suggestible. I am not impervious to someone filled with the Holy Spirit, and this guy is on fire. I can be caught up in the moment and carried away on the river that flows toward God. I fight my hands to keep them in place, spreading the material of my skirt, smoothing it, undoing bulges. I fold my arms, unfold them again. It is as if something is trying to lift me off this pew. Something has come and is working its fingers underneath my backside and is trying to get me to stand up and rush to the front of this chapel, to declare myself before this congregation and this preacher, to ask to be saved. What is this something? And why am I even here?

The preacher is eyeballing the congregation. He is waiting. His eyes pass over me, then come back to check. I could swoon, though I won't. I am precise. I am in control of these base emotions, this gushing, this rushing, this falling down, this being overcome. I lower my head. I relax my hands over the ends of my knees. I breathe deeply. I will stay sensible. Reasonable.

My moment passes as so many other moments have passed when I have paused in front of a decision—when I have pulled back, used my head, remembered to be realistic. This is beneath me, this backcountry business of being saved and throwing one's self publicly into the arms of God. People do not just throw themselves. They are supposed to think about it and what it means. They should be rational and sure about such a big decision. The preacher waits.

Suddenly, maybe ashamed of the silence, a young boy in a yellow sweater vest tumbles from a pew and stumbles in his black-and-white oxfords that seem too big for him toward the front, the pulpit, the preacher. His mother leans out over the edge of her row to follow her mighty off-spring with her teary, proud eyes. The preacher holds out his arms. He has someone to save. He has done what he has been called to do. He puts his long-fingered hands on the shoulders of this young champion for God who has come forward, this young warrior for the Right. He gathers the boy's shoulders in his palms and squeezes them with pride.

"We'come, my son," he says, his voice trembling, his suit coat fanned to the side while he tugs his pants back to waist level. "Jesus is your Savior, boy. He will protect you, young John Baker. Do you feel the love of God pouring onto your head right now? Do you know you are saved from this moment on?"

John Baker may be caught up in what he thinks he is supposed to do and what might make his mother or God happy, yet his sprinkled-with-freckles face shines as he looks up at his minister. There is clapping as the preacher and the boy grip hands and raise them as a referee does with the winner in a boxing ring. There is noise all around as people stand to applaud this young warrior who has chosen well. With a slight turn of my head and strained peripheral vision, I witness shiny lines of moisture on some cheeks, though I do not dare turn full around to look in people's faces on the chance they might look back at mine. I am not sure what is written there at this moment, though my mind is certain I am in control.

I check on Vernon, the man with no apparent emotion on his face or in the set of his body. His arms are folded to the square—firm and resolute. His knees are bent at right angles and his feet rest parallel on the scuffed floor. Yet I have seen him with wood. He can talk to it, feel its give and take, and convince it to bend to the will of his knife. It becomes supple and cooperative in the hands of this master who sits next to me, working his lower jaw slightly. I sit back against the pew and wonder about appearances. I gather myself into the pose of a casual observer.

With one hand resting on the boy's head, the preacher says, "We'll have John's baptism this Saturday. Y'all come, and praise the Lord for this fine young man. Give it up out there for John Baker." Then he affectionately musses John's hair.

John smiles a crooked smile, bashful, then bows his head to the side as he walks back toward his mother, stumbling every third step on the shoelaces of his oxfords. The slicked-back do his mother must have styled for this meeting is now bent to one side, and yet he is still smiling, ready to take on the Lord.

"And I'm hoping you'll all follow young John's example," the preacher is saying when I tune back into the meeting. "There is a tent revival this coming weekend over at Desha. We should all make an effort to be there. Preacher White is visiting from Heber Springs and has a lot to tell us about. Maybe the rest of you laggards will take on the Lord Jesus for him if you won't for me. Don't wait, all of you. The time is drawing nigh."

For a fleeting moment, I wonder if I should consider this revival, showing up in a Levi skirt and a homespun blouse. Maybe I am unyielding and too tight for my own good. Maybe I am stuck in thinking I have all the answers. Maybe I do not understand the first thing about Jesus and how he saves.

I wonder if Vernon is considering taking Ella with him if she has finished with her canning. How does he feel about all of this? I notice his bright pink cheeks on his shock-white face, his eyes filled with slivers of sky, and his jaw set. I wonder if he has been saved on an evening such as this one. I wonder if he has walked up that aisle to bare his soul to the preacher and the congregation, if he has offered his heart to receive the arrow of the Lord, though maybe that image is closer to the Catholics than the Baptists. On the surface he is so tight, as if he lives inside the fortress of his well-ordered, rote mechanism. Does he ever let down his guard?

Except, the afternoon he had found me playing the piano in a side room at the center Vernon had brought in a flat, supple board about a yard long in the shape of a figure eight with a wide waist. He also brought a jointed doll with hinged arms and legs, a round gingerbread-man face and a hole in its back into which he screwed a long stick. Vernon sat on one end of the board while the other end hung out over the edge of his chair. Then he held the doll out over the board and tapped it in time to my music. The doll's arms and legs flailed and flapped and made me laugh. It had a flirtatious look in its eye.

"This here's a dancing doll," he said with pride.

"Can I try it out? My boys would love this." I sat on one end of the board and took the stick in hand, the doll full of personality dangling on the other end. As I tapped the board, it began to dance, one arm circling full around. "Where can I get one of these?" I asked, excited, the ready purchaser of goods, the eternal shopper.

"Right here in the gift shop," he said. "Packaged for sale."

But now, as we are listening to the preacher wrap up his sermon, it occurs to me that I did not think to inquire whether Vernon had made the doll. If he had, he had probably been bursting buttons to tell me it was something he had whittled.

Maybe because he thought I knew music and how creative people always want to show off their stuff, he hoped I would take an interest in his talent. But I did not think to ask. I accepted his wooden facade and stiff-lipped ways as I said good-bye to him and went off to the gift shop to buy one of those dolls. I wonder if my boys are playing with it right now in Mountain View. My boys. I miss my boys.

"I better get back," I tell Vernon after the preacher says his Amen. "My sons will be wondering. They're waiting for me."

"Nice of you to come," Vernon says as he stands, his chest tight as if he wants to make sure nothing falls out. He nods to a few people. I listen to the woman with sleepy eyes, "Thanking you, ma'am," and watch a small smile creep onto her lips. Then we breast the cool night air, trucks revving their motors, beefy coupes rolling carefully back toward their homes, a few voices floating across the place where cars were parked during those few moments out of time. Maybe that is what it is all about: being out of time, listening for voices we cannot quite hear, all of us suspecting there is something that explains this concoction called life.

We are quiet as we bump back to the highway, where my car waits and where, on down the road, my boys wait. I am no longer spooked by the tree branches that scrape the top of the truck's cab. We are both full of contemplation and not in the mood for small talk. Vernon lifts his chin, straining to see over the dashboard, watching for critters of the night or for ruts that could scrape his oil pan. Though I have been thinking that he doesn't seem at home in his wiry body, everything contained inside, locked on a dusty shelf, maybe I am only imagining who Vernon is and what his life is about. Maybe I am looking in a mirror.

As we bump and jar and jostle, I hang onto the dashboard to keep from crashing my hip bone into the door or crush-sliding into Vernon. The only thing I know for sure is that Vernon loves music and making things out of wood. I have seen his baskets. He put the finishing touches on mine, and I wouldn't sell it for a thousand dollars, not after all those hours of wearing out my wrist and cramping my fingers. I saw what happened to him when I played the piano at the Ozark Folk Center and how he loved making the doll dance and whirl its arms like a tap dancer at the

Bijou—the doll he had probably whittled to life. A whittler. A knife handler. That is what Vernon is. I think about the edge of a knife and how it can cut, slash, and wound, and yet, how it can coax a face from the insides of a stick—its single edge a double edge. In that way it reminds me of music running inside Vernon and me, filling each of us, transporting us, eroding our hard hearts and rigid minds, the things we think we are, the things we think others are.

We make a right turn onto the paved highway, back in real time again, and before I know it I have said good-bye and am behind the wheel of my car, hot-footing it to Mountain View while a fiddle tune plays from a tape I bought at the center, rising out the open windows into the night, impressing itself on the leaves of passing trees.

Chapter 3

WITH A STITCH IN MY SIDE
The Precarious Walk Away from Mormonism

A stitch in the side: a pain near one's rib from walking or running too fast. The same pain from laughing too hard. This stitch in the side hurts either way it happens.

A needle and thread pulling at disparate pieces of old pajamas, old coats, old blouses, silk ties, and nicking the edges of cut fabric. A large needle of God poking into people's sides, connecting us to the whole, trying to pull everyone together.

Janus, the Roman god identified with doors, gates, and all beginnings, is usually represented as having two faces looking in opposite directions: the female facing one direction, the male facing the other, neither beholding the other. Neither is able to leave the other's backside. Mother God sews on one side. Father God digs fields on the other side, wearing out his overalls until they need to be mended. Mother God pokes him with a needle every so often to remind him to take better care of his work clothes. She has enough mending to do.

The needles of responsibility prick one's side: Do this. Do that. Don't be lazy. An idle mind is the devil's workshop. You can't sit still. You can't be a sloth. So much to do. So much time that must not go to waste.

God sewing. God waking us from a walking slumber to assure us there is a God who will be there when our seams come undone, who will sew us back together if necessary. God needling us. Mother/Father. One. Are we marionettes of God, dangling from threads? Can we walk anywhere without the hand of God directing us?

Threads with needles: How they hold us. How they hold me. I feel those stitches in my side.

In April, 1995, before leaving for a monthlong trip to Slovenia, I spoke with Linda King Newell, author of *Mormon Enigma: Emma Hale Smith* and chairperson of the annual Pilgrimage Retreat for Mormon women at Alta, Utah. I had been asked to be the keynote speaker at their annual meeting. "The theme for our conference," she said, "is 'Our Stitch in Time.' Do you have a title for your speech, especially since you will be out of the country until two days before the conference?"

"What about 'A Stitch in My Side'?" I joked. At first.

"Why not?" she said, always gracious.

I was in a hurry. "How about 'The Precarious Walk Away from Mormonism, All the Time With a Stitch in My Side'?" I tossed that out, laughing, but then said, "That's as good as any other I will come up with." We both laughed. We said our goodbyes.

Three days later, while sitting on the edge of Lake Bled watching white swans glide in and out of opaque mist, I was unusually patient. I sat on the dew-covered bench until the mist lifted enough to reveal the shores of the only natural island in Slovenia and the outline of the fifteenth-century Pilgrimage Church of the Assumption of Mary. Someone had said it was good luck for the groom to carry the bride to the top of its ninety-nine stairs on the day of their wedding.

Religion on my mind again. Churches. Assumptions. That stitch in my side. I laughed to myself when I thought of how audacious it would be to speak about a walk away from Mormonism to a group of

Mormon women. But then, why *not* talk about my exit from church doors? Why not talk about my encounters with Taoism, Buddhism, humanism, existentialism, fundamentalism, Sufism, Southern Black Baptistism, where the gospel music made me tap my shoe and want to break out in wildly ecstatic dance? Why not talk about my search for a religion that did not insist upon being "the one and only true Church of God" and yet could still captivate me as Mormonism once had?

I reconsidered. That meant I would also have to talk about the subsequent postpartum-depression doubts about having no niche in which to curl and sleep and be cared for, about the loneliness of walking away from something I loved, and the fact that there might still be a painful stitch in my side. In China, a crazy person is "a person with only one story to tell." Is my struggle with Mormonism that one, worn-out story that maybe I should stop telling? What is extraordinary about this story other than the fact that it *is* mine? Other people wrangle with their religions. I am not alone. But then, I do not know anyone else's story so well. And because I am a person who cherishes safety, it is safer to write about something I know. People can choose not to read my writing or listen to what I say, but they cannot quarrel with my experience, my story. They cannot take it away. It is mine. They do, however, have a right to get angry if I speak for them, if I witness for them. Julia Kristeva, a French critical theorist, says that writers must be aware of "the indignity of speaking for others. . . . We risk the indignation of excluding those others, whether we side with them or oppose them."[1]

After many years of dedication and every-meeting, every-church-calling devotion to Mormonism, I had decided, through a strange, broken-and-knotted-and-broken-and-knotted-again thread of events, that it was compulsory to find the path to God by myself, that I could not really know unless I had a direct, rather than secondhand, personal knowledge of the One, the Divine, the All. I needed to take this journey alone, even though there was a chance I might get lost. Other, sturdier individuals had died or gone insane before they had found this answer, but I needed to look for God without turning my face.

I had grown suspicious of my innocent teenage conception of God, learned from knowledgeable and sometimes not-so-knowledgeable teachers in the LDS Sunday Schools in Boulder City and Las Vegas. I had grown disillusioned, even downhearted about this loss of innocence, but I wanted to explore the Divine without the rhetoric of exclusivity. I would cross the street and run away from home. I would brave the world myself.

As I walk to the east, so to speak, from Mormonism to the exploration of the Other, I wonder if it is possible to walk away from the roots that held and succored me. How long can one travel east before it becomes west again? Is my struggle such an individual, such a particularly Mormon one?

Two Stories

One: Yesterday, I met Melena at a Slovenian university in Ljubljana. She is a professor in the pedagogical school, the university being separated into pedagogical and philosophical divisions. Melena was gracious in every way, yet there was something automatic about her. Maybe she had been programmed to be nice, to say all the right words to guests from elsewhere. She was something like a marionette. She reminded me of the stereotypes of communism, the form of government that had ruled Slovenia (even if Tito had put his individual stamp on it) until as late as 1990. But people in the know said that only the labels in Eastern Europe had changed, not the realities. It was evident that Melena was raised with certain concepts, with a certain language. That she had been molded by phrases not unlike the ones I had known. "This is the ideal. This is the way life must be lived."

While many of the younger people in Slovenia did not wear the mark of the past in the same way she did, she seemed trapped by the language and propaganda she must have listened to for the thirty-five-plus years of her life: slightly stiff, eager to please, graciously abrupt, overly polite, and a product of a culture that had rigid ideas about how one must behave and think.

Déja vu. I knew this woman.

Two: Ariel was once an Israeli fighter pilot. He is movie-star handsome, intelligent, and the most intense man I have ever met. Two of his brothers were killed in the Six-Day War, and Ariel and his family live in constant fear when separated from their young children. No wonder. When he was our tour guide in Israel a few years ago, he pointed out laughing schoolchildren on school outings, accompanied by parents carrying semi-automatic weapons. Someone might harm the young. A Palestinian could attack. The whole atmosphere of Israel felt combustible. Palpable hysteria everywhere, such as in the Old City, where I saw a young Hasid walking through the Arab Quarter at breakneck speed, carrying an Uzi, looking at no one, acting as if he could be contaminated or killed if he slowed his pace.

One afternoon our tour bus took us to an overlook with a spectacular view of Jerusalem. While we were pointing out this dome and that arch, a Palestinian pulled a money-changing scam on one of the older men in our group. He showed a wad of bills and counted them out, all the time double ending the bills so they seemed twice their value. Ariel shouted at the man in Arabic. The man shouted back. Their voices got louder. Ariel put his hand on the gun in a holster at his side. The two men were suddenly nose to nose. The Palestinian was fumbling with his tunic, a weapon maybe. Everyone ran for the bus. My husband grabbed Ariel by the shoulders, pulled him back to the bus, even as he was still shouting and fingering the gun at his side.

In stark contrast, that evening at a quiet social in Ariel's home where we met his wife and children and where all seemed normal, I asked him why he stayed in Israel when the tension was so intolerable. He explained that he had lived in Switzerland for two years but had not liked the way the people seemed closed, hard to know. He had felt isolated.

I read between the lines, maybe overdoing it with fiction-writer tendencies, but it seemed that Ariel had a passionate cause in Israel. He had something greater than himself to fight for. Dying for a cause seemed to be of more value to him than dying in a nice, safe, possibly boring life. Then he spoke of his brothers' deaths and how he would never forget. His eyes, his face, his hands were alive with his cause. His blood. His breath.

Thus, the mirror of Ariel.

Two facts keep me tied to Mormonism: (1) people are caught by the powerful language and precepts learned at a young age; and (2) humans strive to find a cause worthy of the human spirit. Having grown up listening to fellow Mormons testify to the worth of their religion in testimony meeting, even to the supremacy of their church, I knew their commitment to the truth was and is their cause.

This understanding made me wonder to what extent we are shaped by the concepts with which we have been raised. Is it possible to change tribes (the notion of a daisy becoming a dahlia comes to mind), or are people forever shaped, as Melena in Slovenia seemed to be, by the rhetoric of their young lives and idealism? How flexible is the language that Catholics or Mormons learn as children in catechism or Sunday school? How deeply entrenched? At these religious cores, will people always speak a language internal to their culture, only truly understood by others of their same persuasion? Is it possible to expand beyond the perimeters of this language? And is it necessary to have a cause in one's life, a conflict that engages you, that engages me? Do our lives matter more if we care deeply about something?

Many have chosen to stand firm within a religious structure, to defend those principles that seem to have morphed into unrecognizable shapes in the modern-day world, to serve as "freedom fighters," not unlike the Slovenian partisans during World War II. But one pause for thought: If the people in the front lines accomplish their goal, win their war, they may be out of a job, as is the case in Eastern Europe. What then?

Aleš Debeljak, a contemporary Slovenian poet, feels he is writing in the shadow of literary giants who have truly suffered for their cause as he has not:

> In a communist regime, constantly eroding under the radical criticism spear-headed by prominent members of the Slovene Writers' Union, young literati were left with little ideological taboos to debunk, almost no political blacklists to challenge, and virtually no censors peeking over their shoulders. They had to design their own responses to a predicament that currently haunts so many Eastern European writers: "How to address broader moral and social dilemmas of the time when they seem to be better dealt with by anti-totalitarian activists?"[2]

Is there always need for a cause to give meaning to our lives, even if the war has been fought and won? I think perhaps there is, in one shape or another. My original cause, formed by my upbringing, was to be a noble, devoted wife and mother who would serve God and her family and remain loyal to the end. This cause still informs me even after a divorce, a remarriage, and grown children. Can one escape one's original cause? Is there room for a new cause, or will it resemble the first one?

As a writer continually searching for new ideas, I continue to encounter Mormon themes, in particular, and spiritual themes, in general. A children's book I wrote entitled *Legs: The Story of a Giraffe* was chosen by the Seventh-Day Adventists as one of the ten best books in Macmillan's spring 1993 catalogue, but it did not sell well to the larger public when the marketing staff claimed the book "too sad" to market to bookstores. If they had believed in an eternal life, the ethos of the book would not have seemed so tragic. But there it was: my assumption of eternal life, not always shared. Themes such as this are like lullabies heard in childhood. They float up out of nowhere. They are whispers that haunt us even while we sing other songs.

I have tried to present stories from Mormonism to a wider audience, to help the culture at large see the beauty, complexity, profundity, and engagement of Mormonism rather than the usual scandalous/clichéd misperceptions, but I wonder if maybe the prospects for carving out a niche in a larger cultural frame are unpromising. Standing with my arms stretched out toward both my old world of Mormonism and the other world of many isms, I wonder if I have a home anymore. Have I lost something in my precarious walk away? Should I have stayed and engaged in the fight closer to the ward house? Am I doing any good in my corner of the territory? (I so want to do some good.)

But as for the nostalgic idea of home, it may be only an illusion I cling to. Does one truly have a home in this world anyway? We are all travelers and students here, and I am happiest when I consider myself a traveler and do not worry about having to belong, to be right, to be safe. Maybe it is best to surrender and be still. To make peace with heaven and earth and be a Siddhartha, ferrying travelers and seekers across the river. To be content with not knowing all the answers. Regrettably, I am not quite ready to sit by the river in bliss. I am still engaged in the search for Milan Kundera's "unbearable lightness of being."

However, I have to wonder if I am being noble or foolish as I venture out into the world to test my paradigms. In "Why Poetry Today?" Richard Jackson describes how Kundera, the exiled Czech novelist, characterizes the modern writer in the Don Quixote gesture.

> What he finds, suddenly, is what modern man finds—a world that no longer fits his expectations, however learned, from religion, society, family, state, philosophy, science, etc. And worse, he finds a collective world actively or passively subverting his images and models for it. For Kundera, the contemporary writer and citizen is exiled; in order to assert his freedom and his will, he must question a world that tries to force its dogmatic answers on him. That questioning of everything, from external modes of authority to the very motives of the self . . . must be continuous.[3]

But there is a thin line to consider as one establishes oneself as a questioner of authority. By taking a walk away from Mormonism, I have found that

I cannot tout myself as a more valid authority on the subject simply because I have asked questions. So-called bravery may be a lot of puffery. I cannot negate the place, the roots, the ground whence I sprang. It is not my wish to establish an imperious throne on which I can sit and toss beads, strands, and crystals of wisdom to the masses. I admit that I have had some need to assert my will, a small thing perchance and an impetuous, immature thing maybe, but I have wanted to know what the word *freedom* means, freedom of choice, free will. But freedom can be a lonely place. When there are no walls to keep you in your niche, what do you have to tether you to the earth? What cause do you have? So the question I have asked myself is just how far can I walk away from Mormonism until I have walked into something I am not, until I lose myself, pull out the roots that have nurtured me? What is the other side of so-called freedom?

God plucks at me. Pricks my side. In the Ufizzi Museum in Florence, Italy, I glance at a painting by Gabrielle Moroni and think of the statue of the gold angel Moroni perched on top of the Salt Lake temple, blowing his horn eternally. I see a baptismal font in the Baptistery of the Duomo in Florence. It is not like the fonts found in today's Catholic churches, those used for baptism by sprinkling—a corrupt practice, according to Mormon belief. The font is obviously deep and large enough for a small body to be covered, and part of me thinks, "Aha, just as my teachers told me in Sunday school. Ah yes, Mormonism is the truth after all." In the middle of this thought, my traveling companion, not privy to my thinking, tells me that baptism by immersion fell into disuse because of plagues and concern about spreading disease, rather than because of some corruption of the church.

On the last day in Slovenia, when I am very late trying to catch a train from Ljubljana to Vienna, I stand in line until I finally reach the woman at the counter and ask for a ticket to Vienna. She tells me something in Slovene

I canot understand. I plead with her. "What are you saying?" She repeats the same words. She points her hand to another line. "What? I can't change lines. Please. The train is due any minute." And who should show up like Superman and Superman, but two Mormon missionaries from Utah, of course. They take me to the right ticket counter, wait while I buy my ticket, and carry my too-heavy bags to the train. Sitting across from them as the train pulls away from the station, I wonder why, of all people, I am being saved by Mormon missionaries. And do I *want* to be saved by Mormon missionaries—young boys like these, saviors in embryo? Earnest and good and honest and fine young men? But somehow, in the young-girl part of my heart, I admit that people can always count on a Mormon missionary, even though there are other guardian angels who do not wear plastic name tags on their suit coats.

Something in me wants to prove that the Mormon Church is the only true church, even if the thought disturbs me. Why is that question always at my back? Always on my tongue? Always there like a stitch in my side? Because there is always and forever a part of me who fell in love with Mormonism before she fell in love with anyone or anything else.

It is a story of true love. People were there to nurture me, to guide me, to encourage me. I learned to dance, to give speeches, to play the piano by accompanying almost everyone who ever sang or played an instrumental solo in our ward. I have been given much. I have been blessed by my country, which I call Mormon. I am a Mormon in my blood and in my bones. One ancestor was baptized by Hyrum Smith, the prophet Joseph Smith's brother, in Nauvoo, Illinois. Another drove the wagon for Joseph Smith's important occasions and then for the Heber C. Kimball Company crossing the plains to Zion. These men are in my blood. And yet, my paternal great-grandmother was one of the first suffragettes in Utah. A public speaker. A singer for Brigham City holidays and grand occasions who didn't spend enough time baking cookies and wiping noses. Another Danish grandmother—a convert straight from the Old Country said to have cradled a bundled-in-a-quilt menorah somewhere on her wagon when she rode west—used to brew beer in her basement, no teetotaler she. Thank God for the variety of ancestors, not all of whose stories would qualify for a Daughters of Utah Pioneers anthology. So what is this thing called Mormonism, so revered in certain places in my heart and mind?

I think again of Melena, who is still committed to the principles of communism even though the regime has changed to something other than it was. She is a good woman. She believes in good principles, things like all people being treated equally, like materialism being an insatiable monster of sorts. She is shaped much as I have been shaped by the communal character of Mormonism. But in order for me to grow, in order for me not to be static, I must question. That is the way of my being. If I am to continue on the unrelenting path to God, I must question in order to discover new values, to transcend old ways of comprehending. Mine is a path to God, not to Mormonism, and this path has been taken by thousands before me with no knowledge of my particular mindset. I need to be prepared for the face, possibly many faces, of God that I am ordinarily unable to see. What we see may surprise all of us. Dash our expectations.

According to Richard Jackson, my colleague from Vermont College of Fine Arts MFA in Writing Program who took a group of students and writers like me to Slovenia, the poet and the poem must always be at the frontiers of the heart and the imagination. Wallace Stevens, in his poem "Of Modern Poetry," says that the poem must question everything it confronts: "It has to construct a new stage." At the same time it must fight a simple nostalgia for a simpler past:

> It has not always had
> To find: the scene was set: it repeated what
> Was in the script.
> Then the theatre was changed
> To something else. Its past was a souvenir."[4]

The language I speak, even now, has been created by phrases such as *Sisters, Brothers, the priesthood, the laying on of hands, spirit, testimony, obedience to the Word of God, the building of the Kingdom.* I am who I am because of these words, yet I ultimately need to question them, if only to find their further reaches. Words are not cement. They are fluid. If humans are now as God once was, as early Mormon prophets have said, then all things are capable of change and transcendence, especially our habitual ways of seeing the world. Should I therefore not question the language I use and long-held assumptions that may have outworn their usefulness?

Maybe all of us are incapable of walking away from the truth. Maybe the truth surrounds us at this very moment. Maybe we are, indeed, in God's hands, or maybe we are a cell on the body of God, as the Hindus say. The truth is in front of me, to the sides of me, as it is behind me.

Maybe I need to revise my thinking about the stitch in my side and consider that it may be from laughter after all. Maybe it is God poking me to say that no one can walk away from the One because we are all part of the One. Maybe I have been in too much of a hurry, rushing to somewhere I already am, maybe panting too much, caught on the horns of a dilemma I have created to keep my forehead scrunched, my brow knitted, myself occupied with a cause. Maybe God has a larger sense of humor than anyone will ever comprehend. Maybe the stitch in my side is a gentle, though sometimes painful, reminder that we are on our way back to something that transcends this planet, this mortal life, these earthly and querulous ways, these confused times. Walking away. Walking toward. God is everywhere. We cannot walk away because we are inside God. East is West and West is East.

I can see each of us as pictures on cardboard, the kind I used to thread yarn through when I was a young girl, a needle in hand, learning the feel of the needle, the yarn, the ancient art of sewing. The Mother aspect of God is threading each card, still doing her mending, keeping us close together, keeping the pieces from falling apart. The yarn is filling in the outlines of these pictures of people holding smaller needles—mending, sewing, maintaining, caring, yes, but probing as well. Needle. Thread. Our stitch in time.

Chapter 4

OF SAINTS AND GODDESSES

In medieval paintings of Santa Lucia, she is often depicted holding a large metal plate with her all-seeing eyes resting on its surface. When she refused to marry the pagan she was betrothed to, her spurned fiancé, who despised her devotion to Christianity, informed on her to Roman officials. She was imprisoned. Her guards tried but could not burn her. They resorted to gouging out her eyes with a fork. After all, she had chosen Christ over Diocletian, the emperor. But they took only her eyes, not her opinions or her faith.

In the midst of aging hippies, I sat half lotus on a round cushion wondering what my New Age friend Leslie had concocted for Santa Lucia's Feast Day, December 13, 1976. My husband and I had been invited to celebrate this day with Leslie and her husband, Ray, at their home in Holladay, a suburb of Salt Lake City. Snow pelted the windows; logs cracked open in the river-stone fireplace; my cheeks felt poinsettia red in this overwarm room. Crunched between the shoulders of a curious group of dream-workshop participants (the group I had come with), sweat-lodge builders, folksingers, metaphysicians, and curious onlookers such as my husband, we waited.

Dressed in a flowing white gown and singing "Santa Lucia," Leslie appeared. Her long, white-blonde hair crowned with a circle of lighted white candles, she walked carefully, keeping the candles on an even keel. She touched each of our hands. Light from the fire and the candles in her crown cast glass-bead shadows across her face in this ceremony for the return of the light, the solstice, the turning of the wheel of the earth.

The second time around, Leslie lit one candle at a time, cupped it in her hands, and delivered it to each of us, a round of paper at the base of each candle to protect our hands from melting wax. Everyone's eyes reflected flames. Radiant souls on fire. Faces shape-shifting. Half Danish / part Welsh and thus a mystic Celt, I looked for messages from the flickering candlelight. The wax dripped down the sides of the candles in Leslie's crown. I held my breath hoping no flame or hot wax would touch her hair, all the time with the uncanny feeling that I was watching the face of the Goddess—catching glimpses of the Divine Feminine, the Great Mother, the Virgin Mary, the Lover of the Beloved, and Santa Lucia—all in the face of my friend. Firelight can do such things.

In the freewheeling decade of the eighties, Leslie, wearing a long purple cape and a tiara, called me to stand in the middle of another circle— a much smaller gathering of only five people. The season was spring; it was my fortieth birthday, and her living room had been transformed into a ceremonial space with jerry-rigged velvet curtains and a sideboard converted into an altar—candles, a bowl of floating gardenias, two vases of purple irises, and a statue of Isis. The men in the group wore loose white robes. The women wore long white gowns. Mine was a draping Roman-looking concoction covering only one shoulder—an item Wonder Woman might have worn to prom.

My youngest son was eight years old, causing me to wonder about who and what I was in addition to mother and wife. Leslie had followed her dream of helping women explore the goddess within. Tonight, she had offered to do this for me. Why not accept the goddess within—the one who knew how she wanted to express herself in the world and what she wanted to give back? It was time to move on from my bad habit of equivocation and the familial tendency toward self-effacement. I had nothing to lose by committing myself in a ceremonial ritual.

Leslie led us through a ritual acknowledging the four directions—a process compiled from Native American and Wiccan traditions and her fecund imagination. She instructed me to stand and receive a purple velvet cape, which she tied around my shoulders. Part of me took this occasion seriously. Part of me vacillated. Through ritual and ceremony one could mark the passages and phases of one's life, honor the good, the highest, the best in one's self. But was I indulging Leslie because she was my friend? Because I wanted her to live in her fairy tale and manifest her dream? Maybe it was make-believe to think I had a goddess within. A child of God or a god in embryo, maybe, but goddess? The word sounded slightly scandalous to my ears trained to think about God as he.

When I was young, I had loved listening to *Let's Pretend* on the radio on Saturday mornings. "Cream of Wheat is so good to eat that we have it every day. . . ." I loved playing dress-up with the luminous pink silk trousers and frog-fastened turquoise and yellow silk tops my father bought when his naval cruiser stopped in Shanghai at the end of World War II. Mother kept this extravagance of exotic fabric in the substantial Kirby vacuum box in a storage closet. My older sister, my brother, and I were forever dragging the Chinese clothes from that purple box with faded lettering and entering worlds where we could be anyone: Chinese, young, old, regal, demure, powerful. Dressed in those vibrant silks, I could hear nightingales. A houseboat could arrive any minute to take me down the Yellow River to palaces filled with jade and princesses with crystal chimes hanging from their puffed-up hair.

Why not be in my own myth now? A character in a fairy tale, tiptoeing onto the tangent of inevitability?

From a shadowed corner, Leslie lifted a forest-green velvet bag lined with satin, embellished with a strip of brocade, and tied with a coarsely woven ribbon in the pattern of a ladder. From the depths of that bag, she drew out an exquisite sword—its hilt knobbed with opposing heads of Gorgons, the design on its blade fashioned after a Celtic knot. Knights. Honor. Gallantry. It was not a let's-pretend cardboard fabrication, yet, when I ran my finger along its edge and found it too blunt to cut, I realized this sword had not been made to plunge into someone's heart. This ceremonial weapon had been made to defend the honor of one's self within one's self.

Leslie placed this symbol in my hands. The basket-weave metal handgrip weighed heavily in my left hand. The tip of the sword in my right hand felt light by comparison.

"Let this help you achieve clarity," she said.

I wanted to say, "Wow!" suddenly feeling duly impressed and open to a new story about myself. But then my contrarian tendencies infiltrated. Was this playacting?

"Remember the Lady of the Lake," she said, her pale blue eyes like picture-book illustrations of ice princesses. "The sword remains in the stillness of water until it is needed for the one who knows how best to use it. You are not in alignment with your true source of power if you see power as something outside yourself or as something for combating someone else. It emanates from your deepest, most authentic source. It comes from self-acceptance, integrity, and commitment to your evolution. With the gift of this sword, you are being asked to knight yourself, to empower yourself in the talents and gifts you carry in this lifetime. It is a call to take risks in sharing your gifts with others."

In a sudden departure from vacillation, I became still. I looked directly into Leslie's eyes, dropped my nervous equivocation, dropped all pretense. I accepted the gift she was offering. This focus on my higher self, the one often kept tucked away. This ceremony. This experience of finding the goddess within.

"Our Father, Who art in Heaven . . ." Our Mother, Who art in Earth? Hallowed be thy names. Many have ideas about who and what God, Yahweh, Allah, Shiva, the Unutterable Name of the Divine is, but does anyone really know? We can guess, conjecture, muse, study sacred writings, listen to testimonials and eyewitness accounts, but aren't we all hoping to know something infinite that may not be knowable to the small brains cramped inside of small craniums on the shoulders of our small bodies walking down narrow streets in large cities in big countries in a vast number of universes?

I have my cultural impressions of God, gleaned from the religion of my birth. The Mormons believe there is a God the Father with "body, parts, and passions." But there are rumblings about a Mother. The pragmatic words "In the heavens are parents single? / No, the thought makes reason stare. / Truth is reason, truth eternal, / tells me I've a mother there" were penned by Eliza Snow, a nineteenth-century Mormon poet with close ties to Joseph Smith, founder of the religion.[1] These words were then set to music to create "O My Father," a favorite hymn. "The Origin of Man" document issued by the First Presidency of the LDS Church in 1909 states: "All men and women are in the similitude of the universal Father and Mother and are literally the sons and daughters of Deity. . . . Man, as a spirit, was begotten and born of heavenly parents."[2]

Even with these mentions of the Mother, the Divine Feminine seems a rather quiet entity, mostly ignored by the religious masses, except, that is, for her appearance as the Virgin Mary, whom Mormons respect but do not revere the way some religions do. I sometimes feel envious of my "lapsed-Catholic" friend Mary and her devotion to and adoration of *La Virgen de Guadalupe* and the altar on which she lights candles daily. Myths abound in which the Goddess of All Things is the Earth Mother. The Peruvians call her Pachamama, "Mother Universe." Mystical matriarchal figures such as Shakti, Eurynome, Demeter, Gaia, Tiamat, and Corn Mother originate from folk wisdom and celebrate the realm of the feminine—the Earth.

As for the truth of the matter, all I know is that sometimes I like to whisper, "Dear Mother," to the embodiment of human life and its continuity, the nurturing side of Divinity.

I have tried something bolder, like addressing the Divine Mother in my morning prayer, but the words "O Goddess, the Eternal Mother" or "Our Mother in Heaven" don't trip so easily off the tongue of my mind as "Our Father, Who art in Heaven." The mere thought of those words makes me feel like a daredevil or a blasphemer. *Heavenly Father* is imprinted indelibly in the language center of my particular brain. But why has the pronoun for the ineffable become he, him, or his rather than she, her, or hers, or even it? Doesn't the ultimate God and Knower of All Things embody all aspects of humanity: the female and the male, the yin and the yang, the creator and the created, the lover and the beloved, and whatever can be imagined beyond duality?

Maybe the great mystery of Divinity has nothing to do with pronouns or gender, but rather with the enigma of the union of the feminine and masculine elements and the expansion that occurs when such a union occurs. Nature speaks through these symbols: the seeding by the wind that cross-pollinates, the nourishing by rain that splits open the seed, the coaxing to life from the warmth of the sun.

This insight leads my thinking (which, granted, was formulated by Christianity via Mormonism) to wonder about the Godhead or the Trinity. If there is a Father and a Son, might not the Holy Ghost be the Mother, the female aspect of God whispering words of comfort and wisdom from behind her veil? Something like Michelangelo's *Pieta*, where Mary holds the human body of Christ in her arms, strokes his lifeless cheek, gazes down at her beloved son. I have cradled four newborn sons in my arms and luxuriated in their smell, their newness, the pulse beating in their necks. I have also held a dying son and stroked his slack skin with the backs of my fingers, even with one knuckle. I have felt his human body glazing over as life departed. The weight of his enervated flesh on my lap. I mourned this son. I wept for him.

I can also feel my own mother's arms holding me when I came home crying after a bad fall from my bicycle. She picked pea gravel from the scraped skin on my thigh. She washed and bandaged and loved me, and scolded me, because she wanted her daughter to be safe. My mother could be exacting and harsh, but, still, I can relate to the caring aspect of God better than to an Old Testament God who is continually frustrated by his children (who rarely obey him), a God who demands total obedience and threatens extinction to those children who do not comply.

"Turn to the Motherhood of God, the Mother-aspect of God," writes Andrew Harvey in *The Return of the Mother*. "Allow its unconditional love to begin to penetrate your mind, heart, and being. Whatever religion you belong to, . . . whatever non-religion you don't practice, imagine the Motherhood of God and turn to it in fearless intimacy, and allow its love to reach you."**3**

In the fall of 1997, Leslie had changed her name to Ariel, recently published her book *The Mayan Oracle,* and was now living in Maui. I had moved to Denver after my divorce, and she telephoned me there because our friendship would never have an ending. "Why don't you join a group of thirteen women I'm taking on a mythic trip to the Yucatan?" she asked. "We'll be visiting Mayan temples from Tulum to Chichén Itzá to Palenque, to better understand the Mayan calendar and the harmonic language of light."

Ariel's adventures were not unlike leaping up into a starry sky and dancing with the flitting gasses in the cosmos. A flower was more than a flower in her world, a song more than a song. Everything brimmed and bristled with symbolism when someone kept company with Ariel. I decided to be one of the thirteen (thirteen being an alchemical number, Ariel told me, sacred to the Divine Feminine because it allows energy to flow optimally) and to reclaim a sense of possibility.

Gathering at the airport in the Mexican state of Quintana Roo with women mostly from Park City—some of them old acquaintances—we drove to Playa del Carmen to stay at a motel on a lonely beach of the Riviera Maya rather than deal with the *turista* hype of Cancun. As the sun set over the Caribbean, scattered groups of us walked barefoot on the wide beach. White sand squeezed between our toes. Our scarves blew like stiff flags in the serious breeze. We pulled sea air into our lungs. I walked farther than the others to contemplate something Ariel had said.

Squinting to see more distinctly, I watched the low-lying strings of clouds parallel to the sea and the light of the day fading into the night. I could see the outline of a pale star ready to pop as soon as darkness allowed. "Starseeds," she had said. "Each of us was seeded by the stars on the opposite side of the sun. We have forgotten that we are made of the same material as stars, literally. Remember," she told us, "you are torn by the illusion of separation from love. You are not separate. You are one with all things, and you need to hold the light high in remembrance of this."

Before bedtime, all of us gathered in a conference room to discuss the star beings that left information encoded in stone: their symbols, their star glyphs, their wisdom, which had been disregarded and disdained by those who captured the human receptors of this wisdom—the Mayan people.

"We all have the great opportunity to be living in a time of a new emerging myth on Earth," Ariel said. We sat against the drab-beige wall in the conference room of the motel. "In this myth, we have access to a broader perspective—a picture that celebrates all aspects of self and creation. It focuses on integrating polarities and, in so doing, contributes to individual and planetary evolution."

She drew the Lamat card from the Mayan Oracle deck of cards, a representation of one of the twenty Mayan archetypal star glyphs taken from the Mayan Tzolkin, and passed it around for all of us to see. It was a portrayal of four curtains being drawn back to show stars glittering against a night sky. "See the curtains parting in Lamat, the way they are opening to the cosmos? Lamat is the way-shower. It opens star gates and expands the seeds of your consciousness beyond previous boundaries. It represents the harmonious cycles of celestial bodies in sacred relationship. Meditate with Lamat to expand your consciousness. When you hold this card, allow yourself to be receptive to harmony and the remembrance that you are a starseed and also a way-shower. Allow yourself to empathize with this expanded love and clear perspective."

When it was my turn to hold Lamat, I studied the parted curtains painted on the card. I gazed through their portal into an aerated black hole inviting me to investigate these greater frequencies, these "liberating star harmonies with their unspeakably beautiful celestial sounds" that Ariel had spoken of earlier. The image entranced me, its vast infinity.

"A few housekeeping details," Ariel said, after we finished our meditation on Lamat. "In the morning, wear your bathing suits beneath your clothes. We can swim at Tulum if you'd like. And, I forgot to tell you," her voice filled with excitement, "after we have finished touring the Mayan temples, I have arranged for us to meet with a Mayan elder in Mérida." Excitement fluttered its wings through the room. "As you may or may not know, the Maya have not disappeared from the face of the earth as most people think, but live on quietly in out-of-the-way villages as well as interspersed among people of the cities. The Maya still live." With that thought, we said goodnight and soon said good morning.

After swimming in the robin-egg-blue waters near the pre-Columbian ruin of Tulum—"the wall"—and scouring the grounds to find my personal connection to this place, I lingered in one of the watchtowers, imagining what had been placed on the stone altar built into that room: a candle, a flower, an arrowhead, a turtle's speckled shell. Sea breezes darted through the openings, the once-windows (could there have been curtains?) carved out of stone. Birds nested in high corners. The sea rolled out endlessly beneath this watchtower. The scintillating color of turquoise water contrasted with white sand. The arc of a sporadic palm tree escaped the geometry of cliffs. I felt the grandeur of this once-walled city, the aspirations of its builders, a sense of commerce bustling through the now-empty plaza when Tulum had been a port for the Yucatan Peninsula. Except I was bothered by something I had just heard: the modern-day Maya had stopped coming to this temple, which they used to visit often to burn incense and to pray. The tourist industry. The invader. I and the other goddesses were contributing to the invasion in our attempt to find enlightenment. Was that right?

The following day we boarded our two minivans to drive to the jungle and to the crumbling Nohoch Mul pyramid in the ruins of Coba, which some of us crab-crawled to the top, scrambling across loose stones that could give way at any time. But this pyramid was only a warm-up for the temple of Kukulkan at Chichén Itzá. After crossing the border from Quintana Roo into the state of Yucatan, we all stood and stared slack-jawed at this sky-touching pyramid rising out of the earth. The Maya must have been trying to reconnect with the original star people when they built this place. Maybe they thought they could hear God better if they listened from greater heights. Climb, climb, and get back to the sky. Thousands of hand-cut stones were laid side by side, then stacked one by one. Stones hewn from the heart of Pachamama. Stones now crumbling after hundreds of years of rain, sun, and feet trying to reach the top.

The climb required stamina. Finding enough oxygen to breathe in this humidity severely tested my lungs. Reaching the halfway point, I looked back to measure distances, and suddenly the world turned vertical with a sickening déjà vu. The height was dizzying. The narrow steps had been measured for people five feet and under and were much too small for my long feet. I also heard faint echoes of cries from humans being sacrificed, severed heads rolling down these very stairs, maybe past the exact spot where I stood—bumping, bouncing, and being catapulted into the air streaming blood.

Maybe that was Hollywood talking, but even so, I held onto the chain for the first time and resorted to lip-synched prayers with each hazardous step: Listen, Father. I am trying to come to you while Mother is in the earth and in the soil and in the fiery bowels with the lava, magma, and underground fissures. I know I am an insect on the face of this pyramid who knows her smallness more than ever. And dear Mother, you have given birth over and over. Your rich soil feeds the inhabitants of the earth. Your plentiful soil offers gold and silver, mangoes and bananas, red and yellow parrots, and condors. But I am sensing that you, Mother, have to cooperate with the sky, as I have to cooperate with the sky. You need what the Sky Father has to give—his rain, his sun, his wind. This temple is your wedding place. Neither the Father nor the Mother can exist alone. You are one when you are two together and create the miracle of life.

Finally, at the top of the pyramid, covered with sweat, I breathed again and walked oh-so-carefully around the precisely laid-out rooms of the temple top with their astronomically aligned stone-carved windows meant for telling time and measuring seasons. I found my friend Joy in one of the rooms, and we watched the slant of the daylight sliding across the floor and across our feet and tried to imagine others who had stood here: the builders, the worshipers, the curious, those who paid quarterly homage to solstices and equinoxes, even those who were there to be sacrificed.

The next day, we explored Uxmal: the House of the Magician, the House of Turtles, which had some connection to the rain—the umbilical cord between the Earth and the Sky—the Ballcourt, the Governor's Palace with its sculptures of Cha'ac, the rain god. This visit was in preparation for the night Ariel had planned for us. She had made under-the-table arrangements with a guard sympathetic to Mayan beliefs for us to come back after closing hours. She convinced him to allow us to hold our final ceremony in the Nunnery (named so by the Spanish)—a building hypothesized to be the training site of healers, astrologers, shamans, and priests. In this place where Mayan wisdom had flourished, Ariel hoped we would find the key to our divine nature.

It was dark when we funneled into the Nunnery Quadrangle. No electricity, no lamp posts. Only darkness and the vast, gaping courtyard surrounded by stone steps leading to doorways chiseled in walls. Each of us had dressed in a flowing dress and cape we had brought for the occasion. Each found a separate doorway, each stood beneath a stone lintel that spanned the opening. Ancient ceremonies had been conducted here, maybe for instructions in the art of temple priestesses, though none of us were certain what a temple priestess might be asked to do. Eleven of us stood inside our stone archways and watched a drama being enacted between Ariel and Joy—Ariel calling out to the goddesses to come forth and claim the goddess within, Joy singing her extemporaneous response.

It did not happen all at once, but as we listened to their voices calling and answering across the courtyard, the sky opened up like a crystal chalice and spilled into the quadrangle of the Nunnery. Maybe it was a common phenomenon in these latitudes, but suddenly there was a light show from the sky—shooting stars, heat lightning, fireflies. A profusion of stars danced, charging the atmosphere with electricity that resembled sizzling wires and darting sparks.

Answering Ariel's call, each of us stepped out of her doorway, down three stone-cut stairs. When I walked into the middle of what seemed to be a living sky, I dropped my cloak. I listened to the sky, which I had never heard before. I stretched my arms overhead and felt the stars shooting into me, through me. I was light and pure energy, transformed into night sky and receptacle of stars.

When the stars on Orion's belt rose over the tip of the House of the Magician and my senses were wired even more than before, those three stars became my sons frolicking in the night sky. My grown sons now. My musicians made of stardust, playing their instruments among the wild music of the cosmos, their amplifiers the heavens themselves: lead guitarist Jonny with neon wings, Jeremy's bow igniting his fiddle strings, Brad's drumsticks turning into candlesticks burning at both ends. And I could hear their father and their departed brother, Geoffrey, singing in the voice of a comet swooshing through space. Energy. Matter. Light moving at its own speed surrounded us.

Ariel walked majestically through the courtyard. Her shoulders were covered in a cape of night stars. "In love," she whispered intensely when she stopped by my side. "Go in love. I give you the new name of Tall Deer, most graceful Felisa formerly known as Phyllis."

She moved to the next woman, leaving me standing there, repeating my new name. I pulled back my shoulders and stood quietly in the swirl of stars, full of a new knowledge that a hunter would be struck numb by a deer who could stand absolutely still and unafraid. "In love," I whispered, and the sound echoed through the canyon of stars.

When I wrote in my journal the next morning, I recorded the feeling of traveling through space with no wings or propellers. I had been embraced by the night until there was no time. I had been transported inside a huge red heart rising like a hot-air balloon. Flames poured out as the heart opened, though they were cool flames that bathed and purified. I felt myself rising. Spinning. Spiraling. One woman on the stairway to heaven.

And yet . . . I stopped writing, suddenly aware that there was always an "and yet" in everything to do with me, always a lead out of the present moment to consider the "real" nature of things. How much of this was imagination? How much was hyperbole?

And yet . . .

After the night at Uxmal, we traveled on to Mérida to meet with Humbatz Men, the Mayan elder. In an office building with stairways and doors and all things recognizable, we squeezed into a small square room to hear this well-educated man describe the history of his people. It seemed odd to be listening to an elder dressed in khakis and a plaid shirt, let alone in a very mundane office space in a conventional building in the middle of an industrial city.

Humbatz Men told us of the recent troubles in Chiapas and Oaxaca. Of disagreements between the Mexican government and the Maya, such as the Mayan's being denied the right to hold ceremony in their own temples. The native people were being crowded out even further, he told us, and their claims to property were not being recognized. He did not talk about star gates or Lamat or the galactic harmonic language of life. He did not chant. He did not speculate on the inner circle of Mayan wisdom or even act as though it existed. His was a pro forma, mildly militant speech, not the words of wisdom we had hoped to hear from a Mayan elder—we supposedly alchemically tuned friends and devotees of the woman who wrote *The Mayan Oracle*. Ariel had spent years decoding the Mayan calendar; we had embraced her interpretation. But who or what was her guide? Fact? Fiction? Yearning to create a new myth to be recorded in the annals of great mythology?

The evening struck me as sterile and anticlimactic. Though we were welcomed, behind the words we were actually being told: "You are white North Americans. Why are you really here, and do you have the first clue?" Appropriate questions, but for the Eager Thirteen, detaching from the illusion of the humble native / the primitive innocent / the meaning of the symbols from the Mayan calendar was not easy. All of us left the building unsure of what had happened. Ariel seemed subdued. Her cause. Our cause. The Mayan's cause. Whose was it really? What did she or we really know as time and culture rolled over the top of our imaginations, past each of us, nonstop?

I fly back to Denver, to Washington Park and Clarkson Street and my real life. Even though I have been truly and utterly amazed by the stars and the awe of something made manifest on such a grand scale, truth be told, when I kneel to say my morning prayer, I still cannot supplicate the Goddess. I feel like whispering and looking back over my shoulder when I say, "Goddess in Heaven Above." I feel the worn track in my brain. The habits. The patterns. I am not ready to transfer loyalties. I am the hesitation.

On my knees and resting my cheek on a log cabin quilt in need of a few mending stitches, I think of those mystical dancing stars and the sky crowding out the darkness of night at the Nunnery. I think of Humbatz Men working for the everyday welfare of his people. I think of how I have a habit of being equivocal, of always questioning proclamations and truisms, of always wondering if people are bored with life and in need of games to feel alive. But, on the other hand, can my act of envisioning the Goddess give birth to a new me?

I feel my own mother smiling from wherever she might be, reaching from the sky, from the heavens, the roots of her body an extension of the Mother. God has always been my Father, and yet, as I raise my head, she is with me. I hear myself humming the tune to "O My Father," the part in the second verse: "Truth is reason / Truth eternal / Tells me I've a Mother there," pointing to the Mother I believe in, a Mother who intertwines with the Father as they become One.

I know I need to rise and begin my day, but I hear the philosopher in me asking for one more minute of my time. Where does the male principle end and the female begin? Is it ultimately one continuum with no real separation? Why are there men and women anyway, except they can't replicate themselves without each other, unless they are worms or cells that can divide, and how interesting is that? What is the Goddess? feels like a different question than What is God? The Goddess feels more of this earth, more approachable. She is the mother holding out her arms to receive her child, and yet she seems more severe at times, telling it like it is, giving and taking, but definitely not always giving (though she herself might say that she is always giving as she sees fit). I am thinking it is impossible to have small answers to this question.

I rest my chin on tented hands. I raise my eyes to the ceiling and to the heavens beyond the ceiling. I want to praise you openly, Mother, to sing your praises as I have sung praises to God the Father. I do not wish to submerge my desire for you, to pretend that you are folded into and subsumed by the Father. I feel your energy, your spirit, your nurturing, and the way you have held me in the body of my earthly mother. Yet, I feel the Old Testament anxiety creeping into me from time to time when floods run high and hurricanes rage, when cracks open up in your body and people are swallowed and broken. I am afraid of the knowledge that you can erase all of us in one second, should you choose. You and Yahweh.

Should I get up and light a candle? Is that a sufficient act?

Or maybe I need to think in a way I have never thought before. Maybe it is time to get past the idea of Father or Mother, of God or Goddess. It takes two to tango, everyone knows. Is the tango what matters here, not the two? Maybe it is time to get past the "and yets," to stop focusing on whether things are real or imagined, and to question my tendency to speak for whatever side is opposed to the one being discussed.

I pull myself up, smooth the wrinkles in the quilt, rub my kneecaps, and stretch my arms out to the side, fingers splayed, head leaning back until I hear my neck crackling. Then I look in the mirror above my dresser. What a sight! This me, this busy little organism, noisy contraption, this ever-swinging pendulum. I smile at my reflection and at the way I can shift from being contrite, self-effacing, and humble to being sure, boastful, and dismissive. Maybe it is most important to forget the quibbling and praise all things. Maybe I can only know God/Goddess through unabashed adoration and by accepting the spark of light inside each of us—children of the Mother as well as the Father, a sliver of God and Goddess, children created by their union, Their Oneness.

Chapter 5

DANCING WITH THE SACRED: PART TWO
1991

One particular Bedouin caught my attention. He was carrying plates away from our feast, preparing for after-dinner entertainment. Omar Sharif, I could not help but think. What else does a first-time-in-Jordan, US citizen know—those molten eyes and their hint of "Take me to the Casbah"? Of course this association was my movie-acquired understanding of a man like this one. He could have been a thousand things, maybe a Muslim appearing for tourists to make ends meet, to feed his children, or he could be a wanderer or a gypsy. But it was useless to care about definitions that evening as we gathered in that tent in the desert, two small groups of tourists wanting a glimpse into the mysterious life of the Bedouin (for a slight fee, of course).

One week before that night, my husband, David, and I had sailed down the Nile hoping to understand a portion of the ancient wisdom of Egypt. But the Sphinx and the gargantuan pharaohs carved into stone were hugely silent. We could only guess with our clichéd bits of Egyptology—King Tutankhamun, Cleopatra, Rameses, Isis, Ra the Sun King—and our memories from our Sunday school Bible studies: Joseph with his coat of many colors, Pharaoh's dreams, Potiphar's wife, and Moses, of course Moses.

At nights on board our sailing vessel between visits to Luxor, Edfu, Aswan, we danced after sunset with the lively crew: ouds, doumbeks, throaty voices singing songs we had never heard before, lithe bodies swaying much like the leaves of the river reeds. There is something about dancing: a lightening of bones and a suspended sense of time and space. I felt lost in my body as we turned and swayed on the boat's deck, released from my neck, no brain to run the show, swept away by the flow of the unconscious in my flesh and in those other dancers. Nepenthe. A release of cares, such as the fact that my marriage was on its last legs.

At the end of our Nile run, we boarded a tour bus and headed toward the Sinai Peninsula. We were excited to see the place where Moses had parted the Red Sea with his staff, found his way through the impenetrable clouds covering Mount Sinai, and camped out at the top for forty days and nights, all the time waiting for inspiration. On a cold morning at four, we laced our hiking boots and set out for Mount Sinai's summit, hoping to climb back into antiquity, before the Bible was the Bible. Just as the sun slipped over the horizon, we reached the top. With a crowd of tourists speaking every conceivable language, we looked for signs of charred ruins of a bush or crumbled bits of stone tablet. But instead, the mystery seemed to be embodied in the purple fog-like clouds that bubbled out of the crevices and into the valleys between the multiple hills below us. The clouds shifted constantly—a cauldron of mist and fog. David and I agreed that this was a superb place for anyone to talk to God. Good call, Moses.

By midmorning, we were back to our own exodus from Egypt, heading toward Jordan, our tour bus crossing the Sinai Desert. An hour into this leg of our journey, one woman in the group who had fallen victim to the dreaded tourists' gambu shouted at the bus driver to stop, then bolted for the door, telling us she would be right back, don't interfere. While we waited for her return, someone caught sight of movement on the wind-shaped sandy horizon. It looked like the rising of three small ships from the sea. We all made guesses about what this was until we could definitely see three Bedouins riding camels, their heads wrapped in scarves, their feet covered in soft leather.

Bedouin—a word with mystical, romantic properties. My lips formed the word again, *Bedouin*, as several of us climbed off the bus, partly to distract the newcomers from our hapless tour mate, who had hidden on the other side of the bus, and partly from curiosity. I held a packet of pencils, something I had brought to give to children rather than money or sweets. In broken English, one of the Bedouins asked if we needed help. No, we would be fine, we answered. The wind teased the fringes of the man's black-and-white tribal scarf. I stood in the awkward gap after his offer and our no, then took a step forward and reached out to hand him the pencils. "For your children." He swooped low from his seat on the camel's hump, his hand touching mine.

I wanted to stop time at that touch: me in this frame of Bedouins, the desert gypsies with heads swathed in bold scarves, the camels with haughty faces and strong smells. But the bus driver said, "Time to go." Reluctantly, I said, "Shukran," and "Ma'assalama," and climbed back on the bus to drive off in a black belch of exhaust to the shores of the Red Sea, the Gulf of Aqaba our front door.

The next morning, with the gigantic sun rising red on the water, the women decided they needed to blend into this exotic setting somehow. Because I had studied Middle Eastern dance and had told them about the joy of moving like a woman rather than a reluctant maiden, they asked if I would give them a dancing lesson, these six women of all sizes. Of course. What else did we have to do in the hours stretching before us? After I passed out a paltry collection of scarves gathered from everyone's private stash, we all stood shoeless in the sand where I demonstrated how they could make a figure eight with their hips, snake their arms, and twirl the scarves in the stiff sea breeze.

"Let your scarf be your guide," I shouted into the wind. "Follow it. Over your head, behind you, to the side of you. Forget who you think you are. Forget about Me, Me, Me. Surrender to the exotic, to the beautiful, to the unconscious." And for a moment, everyone danced—children opening their arms to falling stars.

When we stopped to catch our breath, everyone agreed: we needed to perform for our partners that night. Yes and yes, those we all loved should see the sylphs of the Nile gliding through the sand by the Red Sea.

To prepare, we asked our guides to take us to the bazaar, where we could buy jingling coin belts, necklaces, finger cymbals, and, of course, more gauzy scarves. The anticipation of our performance that night was heightened when we noticed two of our Muslim guides peeking through the splits of palm fronds. But the appearance of the Touring Seductresses of the Sinai was short and sweet. We made a dramatic entrance to the accompaniment of a tinny tape on someone's boom box, clanking our cheap finger cymbals that weren't well enough made to ring clearly. We didn't care about perfection. We cared about something we suspected was possible. In unison, we began with the step/thrust-hip move we had practiced, which carried us across to "center stage." Then, each woman took her turn soloing with her scarf, turning on the sand and stretching her arms and herself toward the night. The scarves were magic—the way they made willows out of women who had been sitting on a tour bus for too long. The transformation continued. It was something worthy of diva status. But the fifth woman to take her solo—a woman who struggled with her considerable weight—lost confidence in both herself and the dance. She stopped. She dropped one end of her scarf into the sand. We coaxed her to continue. She wrapped her hand in one turn of the other end of the scarf; then she giggled. No other choice possible, all six of us dissolved into laughter with her. The spell of the dance evaporated. Poof. Though laughter has its magic, too.

Afterward, everyone was in a glorious party mood. We strolled the beach, where light from a crescent moon striped the water and a velvet breeze caressed our skin. The couples slowly returned to their cabanas in the settling darkness. As David and I walked through our open door, however, the interior space felt sterile after the silky night and the laughter. Silence opened its mouth. We had been trying too hard to solve our differences, both at home and here in Egypt. Trying to renegotiate the ground rules of marriage, neither side yielding, we had lost our way to each other. It seemed that we had worn each other out after thirty years of marriage and that there was nothing more to say. If only I could have revived the seductress in me and spun a thousand-and-one-nights story to leave him wanting more; if only he could have turned to me and said, "My beloved, you are the only one for me. There is no other." On that exotic night, we opted for the sound of the ocean lapping at the shore and the sight of slanted moonlight on the cement floor.

Where was the mystery of the dance now? The mystery of the dissolving self, that sacred place where petty arguments are nothing and one can forget one's obsession with other possibilities of how the world works? Why couldn't we reach across our differences and melt into our own dance? Instead, beneath our courteous surfaces, we both clung to our stubborn, recalcitrant, petulant my-way-or-the-highway–ness.

Now, as we sat on cushions in a circle in a Bedouin's tent in Jordan, I watched the man who had cleared plates tuning his bulbous-backed oud and another one warming the reed on his nay. I felt my blood rising in anticipation of music, sweet music, and maybe dancing.

And then there was music. It sounded much like the recordings my teacher had used in Middle Eastern dance classes. Out of the blue, it seemed, a thin, high-heeled woman wearing a pink linen pantsuit, a gauzy scarf wrapped around her hips, a dangling necklace of metal beads, and an exotic jingling bracelet to match, a woman not traveling with our group, stepped into the center of the temporary dance floor and began to move in the style of the belly dance. To my eye, she knew almost nothing about the dance, maybe one brief lesson in a bar one night, if that, but she was definitely making the most of her daring. Though she was flirtatious enough and the object of much attention, there was no roundness to the undulation of her hips and stomach, no soul to her dance. She did not understand about giving herself to the music. Seduction without the seduction.

It could be a competitive urge, but I think it was more about my need to say, "Wait, this isn't what dancing is all about." I stood up to join her. David watched me rise to my feet. "Go for it," he said. He clapped his hands in time to the music. "Oompah," our tour director Shirley said, too, clapping her hands. "Yes. Oompah!" She was the one who had arranged this evening in the Bedouin tent, where we had broken bread with these men in scarves and robes, our tour group sitting cross-legged, eating hummus, pita, and skewered lamb with another small tour group from England.

I borrowed the scarf hanging around David's neck—the black-and-white scarf we had bought at the market, the one usually worn with a black cord for keeping it snug to the head. Goddess in pink, move over. Twirling the scarf over my head and behind my hips, I commandeered a major portion of the space provided for dancing. Maybe I was pushy, rude, and self-obsessed, but I had heard the call of the dance. I lost awareness of the woman in the pink pantsuit and everything else; then suddenly I saw that "Omar" was swaying with me, his right hand clapping his left palm, his sinuous torso reminiscent of carved sand dunes changing shape. I tossed the scarf back to David, who watched with curiosity.

Omar and I circled each other: boy meets girl, boy circles girl, girl weaves the web as her arms snake through the air. Surprisingly, I felt shy as a country girl fresh from milking a cow—something rural in my ancestral memory carrying me to the condition of bashfulness. But his eyes did not leave my face. They instructed me to stay. To be here. Now. This dance was beginning to feel intimate, as though it should not be watched. But gradually I raised my eyes to his and met his gaze, which was not frightening or boorish but rather direct and unflinching. I could almost feel a fingernail brushing slowly across my cheek.

Maybe because of his unexpected tenderness, I stayed with his gaze. As we danced, our feet became unnecessary. I could hear the beat of the hand drum and the exotic melody on the oud—someone making love to the strings. This dance was not child's play. This dancer was not the awkward teenager with slumped shoulders hiding her new height, being pushed to the center of the living room floor at a family gathering to demonstrate the latest move from her ballet lesson. This dancer was not the one who laughed nervously, then rushed to sit back down on the sofa between the safe shoulders of her brother and sisters.

This dancing was a call to The Dance. It was a call to be still inside, to be calm, and to listen to every sound outside of the self. There was no room for the self here. My body was fluid, all parts working together, and our eyes became something other than eyes, something fluid, more like slow lava rolling over the lip of a volcano. The pounding of the drum inserted itself with a 7/8 beat that mesmerized in the way only a 7/8 beat can, something so foreign to our multiples-of-two or 3/4 rhythms in the West. The dancing, the drum, the plucked strings expanded the sides of the tent until the night came in to dance with us, its stars slipping beneath the flaps.

Maybe that was how it was in the beginning when atoms whirled to spark life into being: the creative magnet exerting its force, the female responding. And for a moment, God was not up in the sky. He was not sitting on a throne in a faraway heaven. He was here, looking into my eyes, assuring me of the glory of being a female, the one who brings form to God's ideas.

So many times I had hidden in that place where I could not show myself—a snail so bare and squashable outside its shell. But that night, that Bedouin, that man who was one sliver of God as I was one sliver of God, spoke silently that there was nothing beyond, outside, or above that moment. No you. No me. Only the now. Maybe we were making powerful love with each other, even though our fingers did not intertwine, our hands touching only air, the space between us remaining open and yet filled at the same time.

Chapter 6

LOOKING FOR THE DALAI LAMA

Reincarnation was not a topic discussed in my Mormon Sunday school classes. Nevertheless, somewhere in my Nevada childhood I had heard about Buddhist monks who believed in such a thing. There were times, especially when my father closed his eyes in the La-Z-Boy armchair in his home office and did not know I was watching from the hall, that I suspected he might be a reincarnated monk from ancient China. He had a hint of Asia Major and a faraway look in his Caucasian eyes. He belonged in a mountain forest among singing pines and few people. In long robes at the edge of long gorges full of scree and boulders that water tumbled over, singing its song.

Tibet, hidden in its high, secretive mountains. China with its Yangtze River, sampans, cormorants, from one of my favorite library books, that wore human-made rings secured around their necks so they would not swallow the fisherman's fish. I had been fascinated with the Far East since my father returned from service on a naval escort carrier in World War II. Since he brought home a small ceramic Chinese face in hand, complete with a laughing smile and what looked like a real-hair moustache. Since he unrolled the Chinese brush painting of two koi swimming beneath a tree branch and hung it above his typewriter. Maybe that had something to do with why, in 2002, I ended up saying yes to my friend Shirley Smith, a member of the Chinese People's Friendship Association in Park City, Utah, who invited me to go with her to Tibet as a guest of the Beijing People's Friendship Association. With the Chinese.

"Overland to Lhasa," she told me. "To Tibet through eastern China—a route forbidden to foreigners until 2000. This trip is a big deal for the Chinese," she chatted on. "They want the world to see how they are improving things for the Tibetans." Then she paused. "I know this proposal is ironic, given how we both love the Dalai Lama."

I did not know what to say, but my mind did. *With the aggressors? Into Tibet? Not a chance.* What about the Free Tibet bumper stickers I had seen everywhere in Salt Lake City? The Tibetan monks who had been burned out of their monasteries during the Cultural Revolution? The exiled Dalai Lama with his fathoms-deep smile and infinite wisdom?

"All you need to pay is your airfare," she said, answering my nonresponse. "The Association will provide food, lodging, and travel expenses. You know you could use something like this." She was privy to the facts: my parents had recently died within three weeks of each other, my father first. My second marriage had just ended abruptly. My mind was in a prolapsed condition.

"Tibet," she continued. "You might never have a second chance."

"How can we, in good conscience, do that?" I finally said out loud, my elbow planted on my desk, the fist that held the phone scrunched against my cheek. But then, what did it matter that we would be in the company of Han Chinese, who would of course try to convince us of the validity of Chinese claims to Tibet? Chinese culture was over four thousand years old. Maybe I should listen to their side of the matter, as my father would have done. I could peek into the real Tibet when the Chinese were not looking—take in those high, barren mountains, the people who lived there, and in Lhasa visit the Potala Palace, where most of the Dalai Lamas once lived. That must have been my rationale when I said, "Yes. Okay." That, my admiration for Lao-tzu and Li Po, and the chance to dynamite my personal losses into tiny specks.

Thus, I found myself (1) riding in a caravan of two minivans and five SUVs with a host of Chinese NASCAR-type drivers, a news crew from Beijing TV, and reporters from China's big-city dailies; (2) listening to speeches about the validity of China's claim to Tibet in the company of other adventurers from the Netherlands, Belgium, New Zealand, Japan, England, and the United States; and (3) pursuing my hidden agenda of searching for Buddhist monks and signs of the Dalai Lama, even when I knew he was in Dharamsala in northern India.

Gentle and exceptionally kindhearted, my father was a man set down in the wrong place and time: the southern tip of Nevada, surrounded by leggy creosote bushes, horned toads, never-ending wind, and dry lake beds with Paleozoic trilobites. During the Great Depression, he, his father, and his brothers needed jobs. They had driven from Utah to the site where Hoover Dam was being built. At first my father found work as secretary to the city manager of Boulder City (the town built to build the dam). Post–Hoover Dam and a few children later, he shined his shoes brighter, bought self-help books, and turned to life-insurance sales.

Our family moved to Las Vegas when I was eleven. Because Dad wanted to teach his children the value of work, he asked me to help him once a week in the New York Life office he shared with another agent. I cut out news clippings, sent out form letters to new parents and newlyweds, licked postage stamps and squared them with the top right-hand corners of the envelopes I had addressed. On breaks I watched him joshing with the other agents around the watercooler. He seemed nervous—putting on a game face, hiding the sheep in wolf's clothing. My conclusion: this mild, monk-like man whom I could imagine in long robes was stuck in a profession where corporate and customer respect was awarded to the slicksters with brassy self-confidence.

When I noticed him at home poring over the pages of Napoleon Hill's *Think and Grow Rich*, I decided he could use my help. Being an all-knowing youngster, sure of how the world worked, I understood how he could cope better with everyday life. *You're just as good as the other guys,* I told him. *Don't let anyone make you feel second-class.* But the words, which he would rather not hear spoken from the mouths of babes, only roused his ire and the "you-better-watch-your-mouth-you-young-upstart" look in his eyes.

Not born an aggressor or an alpha dog, he was more suited to life in a Buddhist monastery, chanting prayers and gleaning wisdom from sutras and suttas—something he might have done once upon a time. In lieu of that option, he thumbtacked words of advice to his bulletin board in his home office, typing them on half sheets of paper rolled onto the platen of his Remington typewriter, complete with carbon copies. These he distributed to my two sisters, my brother, and me. "Above all, be kind. . . . Your smile can make someone's day. . . . My strength is as the strength of ten because my heart is pure." He read us Aesop's fable about the contest between the wind and the sun to remove a man's overcoat on a cold day, the moral being that persuasion is better than force. And yet, though he always had a smile for everyone, he often seemed one step removed—puzzling through life's challenges behind his eyes: a lover of daydreams, preoccupied with imagination and spiritual conjecture.

As all of us flew the nest to college and marriage, this man we loved began to disappear, to fade, almost as if he had been pushed too hard into a wall where the barrier of his skin turned gelatinous and uncertain. I found it strange to watch this transformation into dementia. My father was gradually exchanging his place on earth for something none of us could see. I wanted to catch his shirttail, tug him back inside the realm we had once inhabited together, watch his eyes fill with light—none of this "Where are you now, Papa?" *Papa, my papa, pieces of your mind floating away, uncatchable. Daddy, my dearest daddy. My father.*

I had seen the Dalai Lama in person twice, the first time in Salt Lake City, late 1980s. Standing almost elbow-to-elbow with him at a small reception, I saw a strong hint of the father I had known as a child, the one who had just suffered a nervous breakdown at age sixty-five, the one who now became feisty when anyone told him what to do and interrupted people with his favorite song, "Blow the Man Down." The Dalai Lama's oval, open face and receding hairline reminded me of my father's. Like Dad, he wore big eyeglasses and furrowed his brow into a little dip of bird wings. A smile seemed permanently imprinted in the laugh lines of both of their faces, and a mischievous laugh seemed ready to break out at any minute.

An hour later, sitting in the midst of an overflow crowd at the Huntsman Center, I listened to the Dalai Lama say that all sentient beings want to be free from suffering. He advised the audience to look outward, away from the self and one's trials, and to pray for the universal body. With those words, I developed a subtle attachment to His Holiness the Fourteenth Dalai Lama—this wise, fair-minded spiritual model who stood strong in the face of adversity and aggression, this man who understood compassion as Jesus did. I subliminally adopted him, this model of my untarnished father.

Ten years later in Denver, I stood in a long line under a hot May sun waiting to hear the Dalai Lama speak again. Hundreds of miles away in Arizona, my father lay flat on his back around the clock in the home of a full-time caregiver. While he waited out the time left to him, I waited for the doors of the auditorium to open. I wished that time could reverse itself and that he were standing in line next to me. He would have liked the Dalai Lama. They could have been friends.

A frantic young Tibetan woman dressed in a long silk, wraparound dress and long-sleeved blouse was working her way down the line, two young boys wrapped around her thighs like vines. She reached where I stood and repeated bits of what I had been overhearing: "We take the bus from Wyoming. My children must see the Dalai Lama. No tickets." Perspiration beaded her hairline. Hair in the shape of a farmer's sickle stuck to her damp cheek.

Impulsively, my father's generous spirit most likely directing my hand to my pocket, I dug out the extra ticket I had been saving for a friend who had been iffy about coming. I handed it to the woman, "With one ticket, maybe they can find a place for your boys, too," I said, then asked the man behind us to save my place in line. She followed me to the box office and waited while I explained the situation to the woman behind the glass. "No tickets," she said, but then held up her hand. "Wait. I'll figure something out. Tell her to be patient. This will take a few minutes."

When I turned back to her, the Tibetan woman removed the white silk scarf wrapped around her neck and placed it around mine. "For you," she said, catching hold of my hand to hold it against her cheek. The moment was brief. Her cheek was soft and damp with perspiration. Our eyes said everything we could have said out loud. I thought of my father, how he would have nodded his head in approval, how his blood would always be mixed into the blood pumping through my heart.

A half hour later, inside the vast shell of the auditorium, I searched the audience to see if I could find the woman and her two boys. When all attention focused on the Dalai Lama approaching the podium, I suddenly noticed her sitting in the front row in the VIP section, her boys on the floor, still intertwined with her legs. The ticket seller had definitely figured something out! I watched her watching the man she had ridden on a bus from Wyoming to see: His Holiness the Fourteenth Dalai Lama. Wrapped in his deep red robes, an ochre stripe visible over his shoulder, he laughed before he spoke, full of mirth at being alive and in that setting. I watched the devotion on the woman's face and in her posture.

The Dalai Lama was unassumingly brilliant as he discussed dependent arising and how humans exaggerate their own status and that of others when they view each other as independent and separate. He sighed. He laughed often. He charmed, then talked of how a child trusts its nurturer, how that is the model for kindling kindness. "Cultivate a boundless heart toward all beings," he said. "Let your thoughts of boundless love pervade the whole world."

Driving home that day, I contemplated his words and their similarity to what Christ had taught. Consider others as yourself, Buddha said. Love one another, Jesus said. Dependent arising, the Dalai Lama said. The Buddha said to overcome anger by love, evil by good, and the miser by giving. Jesus said to love your enemies; do good to those who hate you; if you have not charity, you are as sounding brass or a tinkling cymbal. These teachings had more similarities than differences.

When I reached home, I placed the *kata* the woman had given me around my shoulders. I sat in the lotus position in front of my home-made altar topped with a miniature Buddha and a forged brass ball. *Om mane padme hum*, I chanted in the quiet of my bedroom, the mantra that could help me achieve the six perfections of generosity, tolerance, patience, perseverance, concentration, and wisdom. Above all, I wanted to be a better person, a more loving human being. I considered the words I had just heard: "Look outward, away from the self and one's trials."

How could I not have seen my father's trials, his struggles to make ends meet? How could I have been so arrogant as to think I knew anything? And now I was forsaking him by looking to the Dalai Lama as his vital embodiment—my father at his best. Both cared about people and their struggles. Both taught compassion. If only Dad had had a stronger sense of his own value and been more compassionate with himself. If only I could make amends for pushing him too far with my punk advice and need for attention.

The Chinese-Tibet Culture Expedition by Vehicles, September/October 2002, was the dream child of the Beijing People's Association for Friendship with Foreign Countries. Under the direction of Wang Jian, they launched this overland adventure through Kunming, Dali, Lijiang, and Shangri-La in Yunnan Province and then across the formerly closed eastern border of Tibet, or to be politically correct, the T.A.R, the Tibetan Autonomous Region. Their intention: splash large in the news.

"In one-half hour, there is an official ceremony at the China National Museum," Wang told us when we gathered in the dim lobby of the Dong Fang Hotel on a Beijing morning. "Bands, folk dancers, speakers, gifts for you," he said, handing us each a yellow windbreaker and plastic raincoat, a dark blue baseball cap with yellow lettering, a yellow backpack, a first-aid kit in a yellow zip bag, and a utility knife personalized with company logos and Chinese calligraphy. "Please wear your jackets and caps to the reception. Important dignitaries will be there."

We tried on our rustling nylon jackets in the lobby amid a good deal of chatter. *What have I gotten myself into?* I wondered as I donned the cap emblazoned with the English words "GT Radials" and "Grand Tour of China / Great Fortune Forever," dressing myself as a member of a team I was not sure I had joined. Wang handed us each a cardboard stick topped by a yellow pennant with the slogan "GT Tires / Chinese Tibetan Culture Tour."

"March across the stage at the appropriate time," he said. "This tour will show to the world the new look of Tibetan-populated areas and how this region is flourishing after Chinese reform. It will enable you, our foreign friends, to have a complete and objective understanding of Tibetan culture as well as our policies toward religion and ethnic minorities." Wang raised his arms parallel to the floor. "Follow me."

Carrying our flags, wearing our caps and noisy jackets, we drove in a van to the front of the museum, which was directly across the street from Tiananmen Square. I imagined the hundred thousand people gathered at the Gate of Heavenly Peace and wondered if there were any dead spirits hovering, frantic at the appearance of these puppets for a party line. But I was distracted by clarinet squawks—a teenage marching band in white uniforms assembling into loose formation—and a large group of elementary-school-age children tossing bright bouquets every which way until reprimanded by their leaders to stand quietly.

After introductory speeches, Wang spoke while someone translated. "The Tibetan Autonomous Region is opening to the world," he announced. "We will now have greater access to the Rooftop of the World, to the possibility of tourism and hydroelectric power."

At the end of his speech, he motioned to our group. Time to parade across the stage and wave our yellow flags, hooray. I was in a different dimension, parading across a platform in front of a crowd of cheering Chinese, a string attached to my wrist so my flag would look happy to be waved, a string attached to the corners of a smile making me look happy for China's presence in Tibet. Did I have any morals, marionette me?

The waiting press waved microphones in our faces. Why had we decided to undertake this arduous, dangerous trip into the mountains? Aware that I stood across the street from the place where protesting voices had been silenced, yet feeling bold and careless, I told the interviewer that I had been influenced by the teachings of the Dalai Lama. "I want to see the birthplace of Tibetan Buddhism, but," I added, always the diplomat, "I also want to understand Chinese reasoning." There were two sides to every story, my father had always said.

We flew to Kunming that afternoon, where we attended a sumptuous banquet. Our table host, a local party official, convinced us that fried dragonfly was a delicacy. "Full of protein. Good for you." I took a bite and chewed calmly until the antennae curled around my lip. Trying to keep my stomach under control, I forced my attention to the task of manipulating the highly polished, pointed chopsticks once again. All evening I had been trying to pluck delicacies from the lazy Susan, but having been trained on chunky wooden chopsticks in Chinese-American restaurants, I had no skill with slender points. I was starving by the time Shirley and I unlocked the door to our hotel room. The phone rang. One of her Chinese friends was calling to say that our interviews would be on television first thing in the morning. We should set our alarms.

Hair uncombed and teeth unbrushed, we waited in the early morning light to watch the newscast from Beijing. There we were on a nationwide broadcast, standing in the throng across from Tiananmen Square in our yellow jackets, holding cardboard sticks with pennant flags. After the cameras zoomed in on Shirley speaking about the need for friendship between our countries, it was my turn to speak about my admiration for the Dalai Lama, but my televised vocal cords had nothing to say about the Dalai Lama, only a few words about wanting to understand Chinese reasoning. His name was absent, unspoken, evanescent as a bubble blown with a plastic hoop that pops after a three-foot rise. The news station had borrowed my voice and edited liberally.

"What do you think of that?" I asked Shirley when the segment was over. "They edited out my comments about the Dalai Lama."

"We're in China," she said, her words born of a fifteen-year travel relationship with the country. "They see things differently. We both know how we feel about the Dalai Lama. We will have our chance somewhere to make that known. At least we were on national TV," she said, laughing. "Not bad. And we both looked good, I thought."

"It's better to look mahvelous, dahling," I did my best Zsa Zsa accent, "than to feel mahvelous."

Shirley unzipped her travel bag, held up her toothbrush as if it were a conductor's baton, then marched into the bathroom singing "Hello, Dalai."

I joined in with the song, then stopped, miffed. "I hope nobody I know was watching. We've been had." But, I caught myself, was a two-fisted response necessary? Or was it best to watch, listen, learn, and remember about dependent arising?

For three days we traveled the relatively developed roads in western China through Kunming, then to the prefecture of Dali—an exquisite gem of a city with fortified walls, keyhole gates, red wooden footbridges, and picturesque streams bordered with lush grass. We watched a traditional dance performance by women resembling edges of leaves. We hiked Cang Sham Mountain with a local party official who wore shiny leather shoes and carried an umbrella to protect himself from falling snow. As we crossed the border between China and Tibet, which the Chinese insisted was no border at all, each settlement seemed shabbier than the last. Chinese citizens were moving here daily, we were told, to bring progress to this new frontier. Manifest Destiny.

The landscape of eastern Tibet was stark—range after range of mountains rising out of blue-gray mist in landscape similar to the high-range country of Utah. Bleak stretches of emptiness. Immense snow-covered mountains. We climbed higher on half-paved roads, sometimes in snow, sometimes in pouring rain, but almost always under the scrim of gray clouds. We waited in long lines for tinny trucks with no traction to best a steep hill or for a bus to be towed out of a quagmire. And, from the moment we crossed the nonborder, landslides and avalanches intermittently blocked the road. While we waited for front loaders to dig through the rubble, we joked that this reclaimed China was sliding away from itself.

We traversed one mountain after another—a slow rollercoaster full of switchbacks and long, lonely miles, often at an altitude of sixteen thousand feet. Above our caravan, Tibetan families walked along age-old, pencil-thin trails. Yaks, children, and adults carried bundles of food and goods on these tenuous paths from which it seemed they could tumble at any moment. At the edges of the road, clumps of huddled workers wearing knit caps, white protective masks, and heavy sweaters pushed wheelbarrows and chipped at boulders with small hammers. Some pushed wheelbarrows to rickety cement mixers where frayed belts whirred noisily. Despite this hive of activity, the much-touted road into Tibet was not really a road. It was a winding track established by nomads being turned into a highway made of illusion and territorial dreams. These indomitable mountains we were traveling over would always win out.

When I was a child, my reincarnated dad was a bishop for the Boulder City Ward of The Church of Jesus Christ of Latter-day Saints. Lay members were called by higher authority to serve in this leadership capacity for several years at a time, and my father been chosen. I remember him standing at the pulpit on summer days, wiping sweat from his forehead with a folded handkerchief while overhead fans made more noise than his voice did. I remember his pale blue eyes and frameless eyeglasses glowing with wisdom in the sunlight pouring through tall lattice windows. I was proud of him for being a respected leader. I relished being the bishop's daughter.

People in the ward loved him, shook his hand after meetings, and called him Bishop or Herm instead of Herman. He loved them back, often taking his concerns for them to bed at night. Ward members with problems walked across his dreams. He wanted to carry the weak ones, to help them find their strength. People like Brother Ralph, who could not stop drinking even though he said he wanted to. Dad encouraged the uncertain ones who hovered at the edge of church meetings to come back to the light of Christ's teachings. He taught through his endless kindness. I looked up to this father when he operated out of this, his highest self.

But there were less elevated moments when he added up the number of insurance commissions he had earned for the month and the total fell short of the sum owed for bills. This shortfall happened more frequently after we moved from Boulder City and he was no longer a bishop with the accompanying stardust. In my estimation, he felt irritated by his small-fish presence among barracuda at the office. His anger began to show.

"You know how to get his goat," said my mother, the person most suited to be the family organizer, confident of her opinions about how to actualize a good life. She said this to me one day after I, age thirteen, was the stunned-though-not-innocent recipient of an explosive spanking from my father. Being the middle child, I knew how to bait him when my attempts to get his attention failed. I knew how to point my sassy barbs—"You think you know everything"—that would stop him in his tracks and make him turn around and glare. It was war at times, when I tried to get my busy, distracted, daydreamer father to take notice. Maybe I was the adversary's assistant, working my father over, just as China tested the Dalai Lama's compassion for all sentient beings.

He could be mercurial, but nonetheless, I adored my father, who loved to dance when Lawrence Welk's accordionist played a polka on television, uninhibited, clowning around, out of breath, a man who made up goofy songs and animated the characters in our bedtime stories. I was his defender and ally. I also wanted him to be a mover and a shaker, to make ends meet, to be strong, which would make my mother happy and keep her from worrying about the next dollar. I wanted him to stand up for himself when he did not get the respect he deserved. When I told him so, I spoke the words I suspected my mother thought but muzzled herself from saying.

We motored for long days up and down the uncommonly steep mountains, toiling from switchback to switchback, altitude higher, then lower. At the side of the road, constant lines of bent laborers pulverized solid rock to pea gravel with their minuscule hammers. Only one more rock to disintegrate, these Sisyphi of the Stone were resigned to their daily task for daily bread. Or maybe they were frightened of being anything but diligent, all too aware of the Chinese vehicles speeding past with their official occupants. We passed hundreds of them as we traveled from one county prefecture to the next. At each dusty stop, we received the traditional white *kata* from local officials and listened to speeches recounting the merits of China's contributions to the economy of the T. A. R.

The expedition provided a grand opportunity for the drivers to show their skills. They not only negotiated landslides, but also built bridges from wooden planks when raging streams had taken out the road, then drove across the unpredictable planks while we waited ahead holding our breaths. The drivers were in love with driving distances, changing tires, and beating the unbeatable odds—an impressive group of men working in concert in ways I had rarely seen in the United States. Our trip should have been promoted as a road rally rather than a culture expedition. But the gung-ho drivers of our seven vehicles carrying foreigners, officials of the Friendship Association, and journalists and photographers from the *Beijing Daily*, Beijing TV, *Beijing Youth Daily*, China Central TV, Beijing Radio, and Chinese National Radio—Chen Lin, Li Li, Han Hao, Zhou Yuanzhao, and

Yang Tao, among others—were also capable of gunning their roaring-lion engines recklessly through the mountains of eastern Tibet.

One rainy day, the road became impassable, again, thanks to a dump truck stuck in a mud sink. Impatient, our drivers, with big flags flying on the fronts of their vehicles to announce VIPs coming through, blasted their engines, shifted into Low-4, cut across virgin land in the high mountain meadow, and thrashed the wet ground with their GT tires. The Tibetan herders, their wives, their children—cheeks chafed a high red, noses running—stood on and off the road, stoic in their fur-lined *chubas* protecting them from the autumn wind turned bitter cold. With Sphinx-like faces, they watched our minivans and the invincible SUVs come to an abrupt halt as each sank up to its axles in the wetland mire. The wheels on our van could not even spin in the here's-laughing-at-you mud. Stuck. Big time.

Stranded in a mucky swamp, the passengers in our vehicle rolled down the windows and listened to the drivers shouting into their walkie-talkies. They tried planks; they tried winching; they pushed, rocked, and tilted. Finally, after many phone calls and a long wait, a front loader arrived, boldly bouncing across the meadow into the brackish, black water, its big CAT tracks crushing grasses and cattails.

Watching this devastation from the backseat, something in me cringed. I had suddenly become an Imperialist Pig without asking for the privilege. I was the trespasser: a colonialist collecting colonies to add to my list of where I had traveled. It was easy for me to call the Chinese aggressors, but maybe I harbored a sense of entitlement inherited from my British ancestors in their dealings not only with the Hindus in India, the Australian Aborigines, the Maoris of New Zealand, the Royal Hawaiians, and the Native Americans, but with the settlers in the first thirteen colonies. This was a repeat of what had been done before—these layers and layers of idiosyncrasies and flaws that swam through the gene pool. But me, an aggressor?

I wanted to roll down the window and shout, *I love you Tibetan people. I am a spiritual seeker who loves your spiritual leader. Wait a minute, you drivers. Stay on the road. Be patient.* I climbed out of the minivan, sloshed through black mud, and stood with my arms folded on a less muddy clump in the saturated fields. I watched the front loader rescuing the VIPs. I wrapped my jacket tighter as the sun sank to the horizon, and I suddenly knew that I was part of the reason the Chinese could lay claim to Tibet: an agent of this grabbing for territory tourists will pay to see.

The main purpose of the trip—no surprise—was to convince our group that the Chinese had every right to occupy Tibet. Taken to museums in several new towns that the Chinese had built, such as Bayi Town (Linzhé), established in 1995, and Nyingchi, we viewed weathered scrolls with boldly brushed Chinese characters—treaties signed between the Chinese and the Tibetans "proving" the Chinese had a right to this territory. In extraordinary reception halls, we sat at desks decorated with gold filigree and painted with snow cranes and dragons. We met with religious leaders—Catholics and Tibetan Buddhist monks. "The Chinese have proven gracious on our behalf," they said, bowing graciously. But as the monks sat back down in intricately carved chairs in the chambers recently built for the local government, they said little. Their answers seemed vague. They deferred direct questions. The Communist officials spoke for them and announced that monks had every right to practice their religion.

The night before we drove into Lhasa, Shirley had a dream: When we arrived at the city, we were asked to pay $200 apiece if we wanted to see the real Lhasa. We were taken out to an empty, dusty plateau, and in the distance two Tibetans walked toward us, holding out their hands, as if to ask why.

In Lhasa, the city considered the Holy Grail of Tibetan Buddhism, we stood in the public square at the foot of Red Mountain with a marching band and dancers rippling ribbons from the ends of skinny sticks while singing cheerful Chinese lyrics. We, the honored guests, looked up at the massive Potala Palace. It clung to a steep incline—a medieval castle, a fortress, a statement of authority. At the top of the hill, the thirteen stories of the Red Palace, which housed the remains of past Dalai Lamas, grew up out of the center of the White Palace as if it were a flower emerging from a bud. While a local dignitary, speaking with a scratchy microphone, proclaimed China's friendship and good intentions, I was pained by the tiers of white walls covering the hillside, the wall hangings, the switchback stairs, the slit windows, and colorful awnings that inhabitants had been forced to leave behind. The vibrations of all the vocal cords and all the instruments faded to nothing at that altitude (the average altitude in Tibet being fourteen thousand feet). The words of the speeches floated up and away as if filled with helium. The palace's ghost-like magnificence was like a human body on life support. The Dalai Lama was not there. Real Buddhism was not there. Potala Palace was a museum with a few caretakers.

Not until we drove to Jokhang Temple, a practicing, working temple, did I feel any spirit of the people and their connection to Buddhism. It had first been built during the Tang Dynasty in the seventh century when Princess Wen Cheng, the second wife of Songsten Gampo, thirty-third king of Tibet, carried a statue of Sakyamuni in a cart to her beloved. It suddenly sank into the mud by Wotang Lake. Divination informed the princess that the lake was a witch's heart and that she must fill it to demolish the hag. With the help of one thousand goats, she accomplished this task and built the first "House of the Lord" in Lhasa—then known as Ramoche Temple.[1]

Crowds of Tibetans jammed Barkhor Square, then pushed into a sunken room in the eastern section of the square filled with votive candles and smoky incense. Emerging from that room, they crowded into the courtyard of the temple and waited for their chance to enter the place where monks sat on cushions, candle flames stood straight, and Buddhas smiled their carved smiles at those trying to hold on to something so precarious. Pilgrims who had come from hundreds of miles away to earn better karma for the next life approached the temple. They bowed. They fell to their hands and knees, which were covered with protective blocks of wood that sounded hollow when scraped across rectangles of cut stone. They prostrated themselves body length by body length, pulled themselves toward the temple—up and down. Each a jointed jackknife opening, closing, opening, scraping across stones, yearning, looking for Spirit, for an opening into the realm of transcendence, an end to the karmic wheel. Each praying that his or her ignorance would be uprooted to allow rebirth to cease, to be freed from suffering.

A few months after the trip, I received a DVD in the mail from my acquaintances at Beijing TV. Curious, I put it in my DVD player and sat down to rerun my time in China. And there I was, as I had been in the Chinese newscast, standing in front of the China National Museum after the flag-waving ceremony. This time I was saying the words I actually said—that I had been influenced by the teachings of the Dalai Lama, that I was looking for traces of his origins in Lhasa. "Because of him," I said, "I look forward to seeing Tibet. But," I added in my diplomatic voice, "I also want to understand the Chinese reasoning."

Someone had unedited the television broadcast that Shirley and I had seen in our hotel room in China. History had been revised. I felt an anger rising. We had been used to promote China's point of view. Why was there always this business of territory? A one-upmanship/one-downmanship, the haves/the have-nots, the "this is mine"/"this is not yours" sensibility?

But the Dalai Lama had not played his cards in the same way. "True compassion," he wrote in *Becoming Enlightened*, "comes from appreciating that the aspiration of others to enjoy happiness and avoid suffering is the same as your own, giving rise to a sympathetic wish that they, too, be free from suffering. . . . Real compassion does not depend on whether the other person is nice to you."[2]

So why had I wanted my father to be more aggressive when I found it so distasteful in others? Why had I thought that I knew more than he did, and what gave me the sense that I was somehow the all-knowing one? What is this "I know better than you do" burr in the saddle of humankind?

In his midsixties, Dad had his big blow and spoke his truth, basically telling everyone where to stuff it. His words came out in one giant tidal-wave sweep-away of those who had taken his niceness for granted. Though I was not home at the time, this is the story I heard.

Someone from the church had called and asked my parents to help a transient couple needing a place to stay for two days. For some unknown reason, these visitors felt entitled to the amenities of our home, lounged around the house, and did not seem in a hurry to be on their way. Something about them stretched my father's kindness beyond its limits. He snapped. He blew. He delivered the riot act, the bald truth according to Herman, no one spared: these people were bums; my mother was bossy and condescending; no one appreciated him and never had. My aunt, who came with my uncle, who had been called to help, was boring and obnoxious. The doctor and the paramedics were called. Dad was subdued, restrained on a stretcher, and taken to the hospital for observation. Afterward, my cousin, who had also been called in to help that day, said that Dad was not talking crazy talk about Martians. He had just been telling everyone the truth of how he saw things behind his pleasant appearance.

After he opened his safety valve too wide to ever close it again, people said he had gone over the edge. *Crazy.* This embarrassed Mother, who kept him close to home after that. Even he could not deal with the fact that he had been a volcano incarnate, blowing his top. He never recovered after this explosion, though I often suspected he had gone into hiding to protect himself from the marauders who stomped on his generous nature. Better off as Flat Stanley. One-dimensional. Hushed. Safe in a brown envelope tucked away in a desk drawer.

And now he is gone. My Papa. Eyeglasses. Round face / receding hairline. Water-blue eyes. Three dark moles on his tanned face. Papa dead. Papa buried. And yet the flame of his candle had lit other flames—guiding my hand to my pocket to give the Tibetan woman my extra ticket, sending me after that invisible netting that holds all of us together. Most of the time, Dad smiled at those who failed to respect his good, even divine nature, myself included.

I often wished him to be someone other than he was—visibly stronger, less off-the-wall, more of a man's man. I mocked the crazy hats he wore when he mowed the lawn, the way he started conversations with strangers, not all of whom were happy to be interrupted while looking for the right head of lettuce at the grocery store, and the way he made up tuneful ditties for every occasion. I with my immature ideas of real men. But what about my father's particular self, not my father as an abstraction called "man"? What about the oak birthing the acorn that becomes the oak again and again? How much like him was, am I?

I misjudged him at the watercooler in the New York Life office. I thought that he was afraid, that he did not have the moxie to stand up for himself. But he was onto something I did not understand, just as the Dalai Lama was with regard to China, just as Gandhi had been with Great Britain. Dad pursued the path to something larger even as he understood his inability to order up another combination of atoms, neurons, and neutrinos for himself. And in the process, this reincarnated Buddhist monk born into Mormonism in Utah in the early 1900s taught his children of both Buddha and Christ—that one should love one's enemies and have a kind heart.

But while my father reclined in his chair in his home office trying to escape the crush of earning an income every day and dreaming of sitting on a high mountain ledge, looking down at clouds, and composing haiku, he should have trusted me more than he did. He should have known that my dependent/independent self wanted him to be free from suffering. The Tibetans and the Dalai Lama, too. Even the Chinese.

Chapter 7

IN THE BODY OF THE SERPENT

The first snake I saw not in the pages of the encyclopedias my mother bought from a door-to-door salesman was a rattlesnake hit by a speeding car on the curve by the Railroad Pass Casino, the driver probably unaware of having extinguished a life. It was definitely dead, even though its rattle twitched in the air as my father slowed the car for us to see what had happened. For days, my six-year-old self saw ghost images of that twitching tail, almost like a message from the other side, saying we should have stopped and laid that creature to rest (or at least paid our respects).

During the summers, my brother and I spent a lot of time roaming the Mojave Desert south of our red-shuttered, whitewashed house in Boulder City, searching for hideouts of who-knew-what creatures. We were valiant explorers, Steve and I, mostly picking on red ants, whose relatives had bitten our bare toes one too many times. We burned a few of their back ends with a hit of direct sunlight through our magnifying glass. Mostly, we hoped we might see a snake's eyes inside a dark hole, just enough to scare us but not enough to be dangerous. We never saw one, though there must have been a few watching us, biding their time until we messed with them.

Then there was the day when the July heat blazed like a campfire, the never-fail blue sky turned yellow, and the sun pulsed against its own circumference. The ground beneath me was hard clay—the way desert soil gets when rain dries and sun sucks the moisture out. That day, I was out playing on one of two T-shaped, six-foot-tall iron stands my father had cemented into the ground to hold our clothesline in place. The wash baked in the morning sun; the diapers and towels had stiffened into thin boards. I hung upside down, holding on with my knees, swinging back and forth. Observing my backyard through the tangles of my gravity-pulled hair, I watched my stretched-out hands swaying limply under my head—hula hands portraying trees swaying in an ocean breeze. And there it was, stark as stark could be, crawling across our backyard. *SSSSS.* I could see the diamonds on its back, even the scales rippling as it moved. It had no feet to make tracks, only the S movement of its body for propulsion.

I pulled my long, thick bangs to one side to check out its upward-pointing rattles, the ones that increase in number every time the snake sheds its skin, my daddy had told me. I saw something I had been warned about, something deadly with writhing scales on its back, diamonds connected to each other like the chain-mail curtain over a knight's face, a triangle head, eyes resembling shiny black beads, always open, seeing everything, especially me.

Using every muscle I could, I flipped myself up to catch hold of the crossbar and scrambled to a sitting position on top, as far away from the snake as I could. I needed distance from the tail that sounded as if small drops of noisy water swirled inside.

"Daddy, watch out. There's a snake."

Not far from me, my father dug with a hoe, making a deep hole around the base of the apricot tree so we could give it bigger drinks of water during the hostile months. He wore a white safari hat his brother had bought for him at the five-and-dime. His eyeglasses refracted sunlight when he looked up. I hoped he saw the snake crawling across the hardscrabble earth.

He took a few dead-on steps, raised the hoe over his head quick as quick, then bared his teeth as I had seen him do a few times before—a menacing expression that meant whoever was in his way should move aside and fast. With one stroke, he severed its head. I could see its back end still wriggling, still raising its rattle of a tail and shaking it like a maraca player in a mariachi band.

When I saw the head separated from the body, the back portion still trying to get traction, I felt something for the creature. It had been a living thing. It had a mother somewhere. Who were we to chop off its head, just like that, just because it might hurt us? Why couldn't I have stayed on top of the clothesline and my daddy just have backed out of its way? But maybe the snake could have raised itself up high and shot its venom into my dangling foot. So my daddy may have saved us that day. Saved us from something awful and menacing and dangerous and evil and bad. Maybe.

SSSSS: the hiss of a snake, the sound of danger. *Achtung! Peligroso!* The thought of a snake winding its way up one's leg or across a body part has always been a mortal terror. And nobody likes to be called a snake: a low-down, sleazy, and slimy creature. Though mere mention of snakes causes most people to be nervous, even terrified, the serpent played a highly respected role in Mesopotamian, Sumerian, Egyptian, Greek, Roman, Chinese, Hindu, and Norse (among other) mythologies. Eight letters of the alphabet were created by ancient linguists observing a snake moving through sand—S, W, M, N, Z, V, O, and Q—making snakes the source of much of our written language and all my beloved books.

Mrs. Thomas, my fourth-grade teacher in Boulder City, read Norse myths to us every day after recess while we curled up on braided rugs brought from home. I pressed my hands together between my cheek and the rug, rested my chin on my flattened knuckles, and listened dreamily to the story of Odin setting out to find the cauldron filled with a magic potion concocted by dwarves. The potion was said to impart hidden knowledge and ancient wisdom. To reach its secret, guarded place, Odin disguised himself as a serpent and slipped past the vigilant dwarves. Then he drank every drop from the cauldron, which, Mrs. Thomas said, gave him an even greater thirst for wisdom. *Not a bad thing to want wisdom, even though I wonder why Odin chose the body of a snake.*

Then there was the complicated story of the serpent creeping through the Garden of Eden to tempt Eve with ripe red apples and also the cultural banter about how Eve and the serpent were the beginning of the problems and ills of the world. On Sundays, when I was not in school waiting to listen to the daily adventures of Loki, Heimdall, Freya, and Odin from Mrs. Thomas, I attended the LDS Ward where my father was bishop.

One Sunday before I knew how babies were conceived, my teacher stood at the front of our class in a coral and brown plaid dress and a primly parted hairstyle, opened her Bible to Genesis, and read how "the Lord God planted a garden eastward in Eden; and there he put the man whom he had formed. . . . And the Lord God commanded the man, saying, Of every tree of the garden thou mayest freely eat: But of the tree of the knowledge of good and evil, thou shalt not eat of it: for in the day that thou eatest thereof thou shalt surely die."

"It was necessary for Eve to partake of this tree," the Sunday school teacher told us, even though I privately questioned why anyone would disobey God. "Otherwise, none of us would be here. We could not multiply and replenish and have families."

Not sure what she was talking about, I still heard the word *families*, so I remember being curious about why Eve paid more attention to the serpent's words than to God's. In retrospect, I must have intuited the value of the advice that it was time to leave her idyllic life and open her eyes to mortality. I think Eve had the same thirst for wisdom that Odin did. Even Jesus said, in Matthew 10:16, "Be ye therefore wise as serpents, and harmless as doves." Maybe the truth of the snake has been twisted out of shape as cultures have been assimilated or obliterated by new ones, all in the name of progress.

We are exposed to a good many things that fascinate us while holding a meaning not yet revealed. If we are fortunate, opportunities to explore more deeply come to us.

In the spring of 2000, I found myself traveling with a group of nine women from Park City. My friend Joy, owner of the Expanding Heart, a metaphysical book and gift store where I worked part-time, had invited me along to help with my recovery from a disastrous live-in relationship in which I had become entangled after the end of a long marriage. Convinced by one of the women in the group that our lives could be changed by spending time with a shaman named Theo in El Valle Sagrado de los Incas in the heart of the Andes, we flew to Peru—to Lima, then Cusco. We had read books about shamans—how they came into their power and how they interacted with spirits of the Otherworld and the intelligence of plants and animals. We also read about the talking vine from the jungle, something we might experience if the shaman deemed us worthy. A curious group of cultural rather than practicing Jews, Catholics, Lutherans, and one Mormon not immune to guidance from the irrational, we wanted to know more about the parallel worlds we felt around us but could not see.

Theo's lavish compound had been built by his Castilian father, who started the first medical clinic in Cusco and trained his only daughter in Western medicine and his only son in shamanic traditions. Our home for five days while we acclimated to the thin air at twelve thousand feet, it had faded rose-colored adobe walls that surrounded us when we strolled through gardens of hibiscus, roses, and opulent red, white, pink, and poisonous oleander bushes. Theo and his assistant, Robyn, cautioned us to move slowly and to rest whenever possible to avoid *soroche*, an altitude sickness common to tourists.

Between naps on our second day, all of us sitting in a circle on cushions, Robyn outlined our upcoming schedule. Theo then stood to tell us that, after centuries of maintaining silence, the Land of the Condor was now ready to speak to the Land of the Eagle. "It is time," he said, "for the Condor to speak out and inform the Eagle about the wisdom of the Earth, which is being disregarded by humans, their machines, their progress."

I assessed this man standing before us in a plaid flannel shirt tucked into khakis secured with a fine leather belt, who was nothing close to my pre-Peru expectation of an occult medicine man—no loincloth or bird feathers. He was a courtly, refined gentleman with a receding hairline, the best of the European, Hispanic, and Mesoamerican cultures he inhabited. Though different from most men I had known in the bustling *norteamericano* scene, he was not someone I would have assumed to be a shaman, even as he waxed philosophical about Pachamama (Mother Earth).

"Pachamama will speak if you will pay attention," he told us. "The plants have gifts they want to share with humans, but they have no tongues with which to speak. They have a message from the world beneath your feet made of the same ingredients as humans are made."

At our community table three times a day we ate light meals of vegetables and fruits. We were given cups of tea made from coca leaves to sip as often as possible to help us adjust to the altitude. One day at noontime, the hottest part of the day (the average temperature being fifty-two degrees Fahrenheit), Robyn invited us to smear red mud on our bare bodies, find a warm place on the stone patio, lie in the sun until the mud on our faces, torsos, arms, and legs cracked into a thousand pieces, and then stand for a bath that she poured over our shoulders—a bucket of fragrant water scented with floating rose petals from the garden.

On the fourth day, Theo and Robyn drove us by van to a trailhead, and we hiked to the Pisac ruins in the Urubamba Valley. The path was steep. We hiked slowly to maintain a good working relationship with the thin oxygen. Clusters of giggling Quechua children dressed in brightly colored vests and blankets draped around their shoulders—colorful dots above us—traversed the mountainside with their mothers and one or two young llamas frolicking behind. They wore flat narrow-brimmed hats that covered their blue-black hair except for the long braids that decorated their backs, either in a single queue or in a swooping loop of two connected braids.

As we hiked higher into the thin atmosphere, Theo pointed out ancient irrigation systems that were still functional. "Notice the green, *verde*, the ever-green," he said, and how could anyone not notice the abundance of the green land everywhere? "It is the color of hope," he said, "*Esperanza*." After we finally reached the ruins, rested our backpacks against the crumbling walls, then peeked through the rough-hewn windows for views of the valley below, Theo told us how the Incas kept track of time and the seasons by watching the slant of sunlight through one particular window, to which he pointed. We jockeyed for positions at this window and oohed and aahed over the expanse of green terracing both sides of the valley below. Every piece of fertile ground appeared to be cultivated, though this green would luxuriate no matter what anyone planted.

When everyone had seen enough, I found myself standing alone next to Theo and the long rectangular window filled with sunlight. We made small talk about the number of hectares an individual can cultivate, and suddenly I felt transfixed by his dark brown eyes beneath the straight brim of his green felt hat, similar to the ones the Quechua children wore. They were *über*-intelligent eyes, expressing something much deeper than I ordinarily saw in human eyes, that thing for which I am always looking and which I will always call Spirit. It inhabited him and every movement he made. I had watched him walk through his gardens at the compound, dipping his nose into the cup of a flower and inhaling its perfume, no hint of Latin American *machismo*. I had never seen him hurry, even though anyone could see he was a busy man often paged to his office and library, which occupied one full side of the compound.

Without warning, as I looked at Theo's eyes covered with a liquid sheen, my recent sorrow returned in an unbidden rush. Suddenly, it was as if Theo and I had entered the circuitry of water that fell from the sky and traveled the earth before evaporating into clouds to fall again. That was when his features shifted to a question. He checked for a safe distance around us, no one listening, and his words came at the very moment we were looking at the essence of the words *verde, verdant, verdure*.

"Why are you so sad?" he asked quietly.

I hesitated because I had been locked inside my sadness for several months and had grown weary of this state of mind and wary of intruding on others. But maybe truth can be touched when there are no barriers between the raw and the real. The rawness I had been feeling suddenly opened like a tearing piece of cloth, exposing a jagged clarity. I felt exposed—a finger touching an overly tender raw place, locating the hurt, pressing. I took a deep breath to preserve equanimity. "The thing I call home. I don't know where it is anymore."

The liquid of his eyes seemed to be a pool catching my sorrow. I heard the word *esperanza* rising to his lips even as he said nothing. He reached out to touch the back of my hand with a featherlight touch. "You are beginning to understand," he said, then slowly, without breaking the slender thread of our attachment, rejoined the group to speak further about the Pisac ruins. I could still feel the trace of his finger on my hand. I stood back from the rest of the group and remembered something I had read, that one has a choice whether to laugh or cry, whether to live or die, even if the dying is only on the inside. *Esperanza.*

That night back at the compound, as we gathered for a short bedtime speech from Theo—a recap of the day and a preview of the next—he made passing mention of the fact that, if we so desired on the next and last night with him, we could receive a teaching through the talking vine, but only if that was something we felt certain about doing. Listening to his calm words, I felt the desire to know more of what he and the plants knew. I trusted his spirit.

I had read about the vine called *Banisteriopsis caapi*—the plant that grows deep in the heart of the Amazon rainforest and is used to make the psychotropic potion known as ayahuasca. Joy and I and our other roommate, Susan, had discussed the idea that shamans believe each plant has a spirit that is conscious, that it has a soul, and that it has a message to pass to humans. We had discussed whether or not taking the ayahuasca potion was something we felt comfortable doing. We had each been debating—to do or not to do—from day one of our arrival.

After we turned out the lights in our room, we whispered across the distances between our beds. "I hate not to try this when we've come such a long way to see Theo," Susan said in our drifting-off-to-sleep state of mind, "but it scares me."

"I feel as though we can trust him," Joy said, "but it frightens me, too."

"Theo is a good man," I said. "And we don't have to decide until tomorrow."

I'm not sure this is wise, however, my mind began its contrarian debate after the others drifted off to dreams. *After all, you didn't have a sip of tea, coffee, or alcohol, not one drop for the first thirty-eight years of your life. The Word of Wisdom. The law of health, remember. Even if you're not an active Mormon and don't follow those rules exactly, your body is still a temple. It must not be defiled. But why can't you open yourself to the possibility of leaving your perimeter? Of taking a chance? Maybe you can learn something important here. What does "defiled" mean anyway?*

Semantics aside, when I actually considered ingesting the psychotropic potion, my lungs constricted. My throat tightened. Yet the S curve of curiosity worked its way beneath my surface as my breathing relaxed into sleep.

On a visit to the Greek islands a few years earlier, I had purchased a statue of the bare-breasted Knossos serpent goddess stretching her arms upward and holding a snake firmly in each hand. Her breasts poked out boldly, like nippled headlights, over the top of her apron decorated with the familiar diamond motif, the one found on the backs of rattlesnakes. I liked the bare, unashamed breasts. I was drawn to her empowered stance: "This is me. This is my strength. I am informed by these serpents I hold in my hands. They are my wisdom. Together we are powerful and uncompromising." Yet this boldness I admired was not part of my heritage—neither societal nor religious. A woman did not allow her breasts or that kind of strength to show in public. Strength was to be hidden behind a mask of equanimity in my culture.

My mother was the strongest one in our family, though she tried to acquiesce to my father's patriarchy, even if he frustrated her at times, even if she was the one who would have been the better breadwinner. Self-effacement was the essence of what I had learned as a female child: Don't be a show-off; you are not the owner of your God-given gifts. A woman's visible strength seemed to be equated with pride and manliness and was thus discounted in our religious culture as well as in the wider culture of the fifties. A woman could be soft and tender, always the good mother, and always the model of good breeding and discretion. So maybe it was the bold, no-nonsense breasts almost shining from the serpent goddess's chest as if they were lights (nothing to do with Barbie doll boobs or a seductive come-on physique, but something much more magnificent) that caused me to pay handsomely for this statue, to have it packaged carefully to protect its outstretched hands holding snakes, and to keep it on my desk since that time.

We were not in a jungle listening to mysterious night noises. We were safely gathered together in Theo's library in a compound surrounded by adobe walls in a small city near Cusco. It was dark outside. Mats had been arranged on the floor, and we were each told to find a place and to get comfortable. Folded shawls lay on the mats for covering ourselves if we felt cold. As I sat cross-legged awaiting further instruction, I noticed a centuries-old painting of Christ and the Virgin Mary hanging on one of the walls and was struck by the contrasts in this room.

Should I bolt now? Get up and wash my hands of all this mumbo-jumbo about talking plants? Was I only a tourist of the exotic? Trying to find a not-so-cheap thrill to make myself a more interesting person? Did I really believe in this kind of healing, or was this sheer voyeurism? Pictures of my mother's cautionary face flashed through my mind, her eyes in their sternest, most reprimanding expression: "You have your free agency," she was saying in Mormonspeak, "but you know which choices are the right ones to make. Hold on to the rod, the iron rod."

As I watched Theo and Robyn pour clear liquid into smaller containers set on a long table, I remembered that I had already crossed the do-not-cross line. I wanted to heed my own intuition for a change, though one last mental telegram from my protector/mother inserted itself and stood in the middle of the road of my thoughts: *God and the angels are displeased with you, my daughter, for straying so far off course.*

Theo called us individually to the altar where he had unrolled his *despacho*—his offering to the spirits of the land. "What is your name?" he whispered to me. I told him, understanding this was more a ceremonial ritual than a reminder. "And what do you want from the plant, Phyllis? Remember to ask for the best and most convenient thing for yourself."

His choice of the word *convenient* stopped me for a second, but then I knew I wanted to find a much larger, less constricted vision of myself. He handed me a small cup of the ayahuasca potion, which I sipped before returning to my mat to wait for my message. Trouble is, I felt the pesky urge to pee. Struggling to my feet, I stepped cautiously between the other women lying on the floor. I found the restroom, thinking I had a few minutes until the potion took effect.

After relieving myself, I stood to wash my hands at the basin. Staring back at me from the mirror was the head of a huge, lizard-like snake with eyes on either side of its head and lumpy, ridged skin where my neck usually sat. "Where's my head?" I kept saying as I stared at the frightening reflection in the mirror and put my hands up to the sides of my reptilian face, which felt scaly and all the things you never wanted your complexion to be. I was a snake. A big one. I, Phyllis, who still had enough consciousness to be aware of this change in herself, was definitely disappointing God, who had told me (and Adam and Eve) not to partake of the fruit of this Tree of Knowledge. I had given in. My time for right choice, however, had passed. I needed to get back to my mat, to a prone position, to not look at this head any longer.

The room was darker than before, and from somewhere, a hand reached out and helped me back to my mat. Lying flat, I felt as though my body had instantly become serpentine, propelling itself through a jungle, experiencing a micro-microscopic world through unblinking eyes and veil-like scales. I felt the jungle terrain against my belly, the rises and falls in the ground, up, over. I was being propelled across the ground by the movement of twisting muscles, a movement very different from walking by moving long bones connected to many small, even tiny, bones that carry the burden of human weight, those two flesh-covered sticks finding places to plant themselves with every step.

It was like being inside a fast-moving stream of neon, a fluid mesh of quilted diamonds puffed up parade-balloon size, the leaves and grasses magnified to the tenth power, the legs of ants and spiders gigantic jeweled chains. I was the inside of electricity, inside the circuitry of light, inside chlorophyll, inside the exchange of oxygen and nitrogen, maneuvering across damp soil crowded with vines and pithy stems. Brilliantly colored cells swirled both inside and outside my serpent body as it glided across the jungle's fragrant breast. I was swimming inside a spiraling double helix and hearing a message that nothing was solid, not even in real life, and that there were no boundaries, no sharp divisions between ants, beetles, moths, snakes, and humans, no boundaries, but rather an exchange of energy. We were each other, and the long rope of the body I shared with the serpent was twisting through this Eden more dazzling than anything I could ever have imagined.

I don't know how long this molecular floorshow lasted. I am not sure how long we lay there, stretched out, covered with Peruvian shawls woven on backstrap looms. We had begun early in the evening, Theo and Robyn making sure that we were comfortable, that we each had a bottle of water before we departed to talk to the vine. But when I woke and become aware of my body lying flat in a room washed with a crepuscular light, no more neon flashing, I had no idea whether it was day or night, only that I had been somewhere I had never been. I felt spent and limbless, yet aware, somewhere in my chest cavity, of a subliminal knowledge that something had affected me to the core. Something powerful. I knew of my connectedness to all things in a way that was not cerebral. The plant had spoken fluidly, brilliantly, into the nucleus of each of my cells, imprinting them forever.

Robyn bent over me, her chestnut hair hanging low on her shoulders, her head backlit by the indeterminate light, asking in a whisper how I felt. I squinted at the room, this spacious library with antique leather- and paperbound books lining the walls. Dimly at first, as if waking from a long sleep, I saw the others sitting up, rubbing their eyes, returning from their separate journeys as well. In the indistinct light, I heard someone calling out, "Help me. My stomach keeps having these spasms." I saw the blurred flurry of Robyn rushing to her side, a small bucket and towel in hand. Theo followed to help, and it was then that I noticed my friend Joy curled into herself near a corner. On my bottom, I scooted across the floor, negotiating the space between mats, to her side. In whispers, I asked how she was doing.

"I saw a snake, and each scale of its body was filled with light that could heal people. In fact," she said dreamily, not back to reality yet, "I'm being comforted by two serpents right now." She rested her back against the adobe wall, and she and I sat shoulder to shoulder, sharing each other's shawls for warmth, molecules swirling around us, alive. When Theo finally came across the room to ask how we were faring, we told him how we had each been inside the body of a serpent. He smiled broadly. "You are lucky," he said. "Very lucky. Not everyone has this chance. The serpent is the most powerful of all animals."

Several years after I returned home to Park City, Theo and the ayahuasca experience were still very much a part of me, coming to mind at strange times. By coincidence one day, my eyes, which always scanned book titles in friends' libraries, found a copy of *The Serpent Grail*, by Philip Gardiner and Gary Osborn. I pored over the pages written about the serpent, snake, Leviathan, or dragon—each interchangeable with the guardians of some cryptic treasure and/or representatives of the life force of the universe.

The snake shedding its skin was a central symbol of ancient myths. Egypt's Osiris was encased in the body of a snake before he overcame death and emerged through the snake's mouth, symbolizing resurrection and the skin-sloughing, reemergent process of the lowly snake. The Greek god of healing, Aesculapius, who carried a caduceus and was associated with the Egyptian Imhotep, "he who comes in peace," was said to have revived the dying or recently dead using the blood or venom of a snake.[1] The caduceus, the two-snake staff—the symbol used by historical and modern-day physicians—was said to illustrate how humans should strive to stay centered and not be pulled out of balance by duality. According to Gardiner and Osborn, the original Elixir of Life may have been made from a potion of snake's venom and snake's blood—the red and the white, the wine and the bread, the blood diluting the venom and creating a substance for prolonging life.

A search for snake oil on the Internet told how it originally came from China, where it was called *shéyóu*. It is still sold in traditional Chinese pharmacies as a remedy for inflammation and pain from rheumatoid arthritis and bursitis. Apparently, the fat of the Chinese water snake contains a higher level of the polyunsaturated fatty acid EPA than is found in American snake fats and therefore does not have the same dubious reputation.[2] A pharmacology student told me that the saliva of the reptilian Gila monster was the basis of a drug for diabetes. The U.S. Food and Drug Administration has approved the drug Integrilin, derived from a protein found in the venom of the southeastern pygmy rattlesnake, for treatment of people suffering from chest pains, unstable angina, and small heart attacks.[3]

Out of the blue, I received from a friend an Internet clip that featured Jill Bolte Taylor, a neuroanatomist. She had suffered a major stroke and undergone surgery for the removal of a blood clot the size of a golf ball, which had been pushing against the language centers of her brain. It took her eight years to recover. As a student of the brain, she had the unique experience of truly realizing what was happening to her and of being able to pay close attention from the inside of the experience. Speaking through cyberspace in the clip, she picked up a plastic model of the brain and demonstrated how it is divided into two very distinct hemispheres. She talked about how the left brain thinks linearly about the past and the future and how its propensity is to separate its owner from others. Taylor lost that portion of her brain during her stroke, and, when the chatter of her left hemisphere went totally silent, she said she was "shocked to be inside a silent mind, but immediately captivated by the magnificence of the energy around me." She said she had found Nirvana in the purity of her right brain alone, a witness to the life-force power of "the fifty trillion beautiful molecular geniuses that make up my form":

> I look down at my arm and I realize I can no longer define the boundaries of my body. I can't define where I begin and where I end. Because the atoms and the molecules of my arm blended with the atoms and molecules of the wall. And all I could detect was this energy. . . . I could no longer identify the boundaries of my body, I felt enormous and expansive. I felt at one with all the energy that was, and it was beautiful there. . . . I was no longer the choreographer of my life. . . . My spirit soared free like a great whale gliding through the sea of silent euphoria.[4]

When she spoke about "gliding through the silent euphoria" and not being able to know where she began and ended, it was déjà vu with Peru, Theo, and my time in the body of the serpent. Having been told most of my life that snakes were loathsome creatures designed to serve the cause of evil, I knew that being in the body of a serpent that night in Cusco had affected my respect for the interconnectedness of the infinitesimal and the large, as well as for the wisdom of the snake. It had changed my relationship with all things.

Jackie Bibby, a daredevil Texan who holds the Guinness records for sacking ten rattlesnakes the fastest (17.11 seconds), sitting in a bathtub with the most rattlesnakes (81), lying in a sleeping bag with the most rattlesnakes (109), and holding the most rattlesnakes in his mouth (9), and who also lost half a thumb to a rattlesnake after he suffered a "wet bite," would not dream of crushing the serpent with his heel as Adam and Eve had been instructed. He said he had never been cruel to any animal. "Don't crush the herp," Jackie pleaded in one interview. "He didn't do anything to you."[5]

The day after reading about Jill Taylor, while I was at work in the Expanding Heart, I noticed an unwrapped box of *Medicine Cards* left open for customers to peruse. Business was slow, so I leafed through the booklet that came with the set. I turned to the page captioned "Snake" and read that "snake medicine people," who claim power and guidance from snakes, are a rare breed. "Their initiation involves experiencing and living through multiple snake bites, which allows them to transmute all poisons, be they mental, physical, spiritual, or emotional."[6]

The illustrator had rendered the snake to resemble the figure-eight infinity symbol, the tail portion of its body twined around a clutch of eggs. It was drawn inside the hoop of a Native American dreamcatcher. I read a poem on the adjacent page:

> The poison transmuted
> Brings eternal flame.
> Open me to heaven
> To heal me again.[7]

I thought about what Theo had said about the wisdom of Pachamama and the things the Land of the Condor had to teach the Land of the Eagle. I thought what it must be like to be a snake living inside the earth, gliding through tunnels created by gophers, moles, and other tunnelers, slithering in the silence around the roots of trees and bushes. The snake, being cold-blooded, needs less oxygen underground and can stay there for a long time. It is at home in the body of Mother Earth. It travels in secrets I cannot see with my eyes, adjusted as they are to sunlight, my nostrils unable to breathe where soil is involved.

People in simpler times looked to all creatures for their innate wisdom, including the snake. The message from the ayahuasca, which substance, in my opinion, should be taken only under the guidance of a shaman in the shaman's native surroundings, may be to reconsider the misaligned creature known as the serpent and to allow it to teach the incomprehensible to a modern-day Western mind. Cobras graced the crowns of pharaohs; serpent-headed columns were found at the Pantheon; Vishnu slept on Shesha Naga, the Cosmic Serpent; *obelisk* meant "light of the serpent." The twining tendrils of vines wrap around other stems and lattices and through the cracks of fences. The rose is a beautiful, fragrant flower with thorns that prick fingers and draw blood. Whenever we feel a sting or a bite or a thorn prick, we most often also seem to find fragrance or beauty or wisdom.

As I stood at the counter with the Snake card singled out from the pile of *Medicine Cards*, I was once again lying on a mat in Theo's library, entering the circuitry of swirling color, swallowing my tail until I had no beginning and no end, no separation between myself and Other. I once more felt Robyn letting go of my hand. I felt her covering my shoulders with the shawl, making sure I had no wants as I left one shore for another, swimming through molecules and magnified atoms into the realm of the All and Everything. I heard Theo telling Joy and me, "It is a gift to be with the most powerful of animals. You have been honored."

Chapter 8

Dancing with the Sacred: Part Three
Spring 2000

Early in my study of tai chi, the ancient Chinese discipline of meditative movement, I watched and imitated the form as demonstrated by the teacher a thousand times at least. Having learned a lifetime of dance routines, after all, I imitated what I thought was being shown: another dance. But one afternoon, after seeing these moves again and again, I suddenly understood I had never seen them at all. I had been watching the external movement of the teacher's arms—the positions, the choreography, the curl of the palm of her hand and fingers. What I had not seen was how she worked from the center of her body, her chi, her life force, her particular vitality.

After the breakup of both my first marriage and a rebound romance, I made yeoman efforts to get on track again. But vestiges of sadness still clung to me like glue on paper. When my friend Joy invited me to travel with some Park City women to Peru for a visit with a shaman, she also invited me to join her and husband, Miles, afterward in Ecuador with another group called Eco-Trek. Thus began my six-week journey in Peru, Bolivia, and Ecuador, undertaken not only for the purpose of meeting with shamans from the indigenous tribes of the Andes and being taught by their five-thousand-year-old wisdom, but with the subliminal hope of healing.

After I spent a week with Theo in Cusco, everything seemed anticlimactic when I joined up with the Eco-Trek group in Quito. As our eight-person group drove up and down dusty roads between the capital city and Otavalo to meet with various shamans, I felt lukewarm about the *perfumeros*, *paleros*, and *tabaqueros*. In their dark rooms, I did not feel connected to much about them. They presided over tables (looking suspiciously like borrowed school desks) covered with sacred implements and lighted candles, their timeworn faces capped by headdresses of upright parrot feathers. Feeling more like a curious tourist adding notches to her exotic-travel belt, I eventually participated in a group healing one night at which all eight of us stood naked in yet another dark room, this one exceptionally cold, on the bottom level of the shaman's house (next to a room where cattle were kept for the night). When the *perfumeros* sprayed each of us with flower water after they had swished it around in their mouths, the experience felt more like a dankest-dungeon dream.

In the name of being open to experience, we were crazy—freezing in our bare skin, sniffing cattle dung, and being sprayed with scented water that had been in someone's mouth. We were submitting ourselves to strange healers who did not know any of us from Adam and whose bankroll would be substantially fatter when we left. Did any of us have a boundary across which we would not travel?

Things changed, however, when we drove to Quilajalo the next morning. In broad daylight, we all shook hands with Alberto Taxo, a shaman living with his wife, Elba, at a retreat nestled in a valley surrounded by the Imbabura, Mojanda, and Cotacachi mountains. In my first sight of him, I saw a man dressed in an open-collared, pale blue, long-sleeved shirt and a turquoise pair of cloth pants, no shoes. His long, graying hair was fastened back in a ponytail with a handwoven tie. He had a six-inch, predominantly white beard, clear blue eyes, and a smile indicating an openness of heart. Something about him appealed to my aesthetic. A Sunday-school painting of Jesus, perhaps. A beautiful man, no doubt. Sunlight flitted through the overhead leaves casting moving pictures on our faces. Light radiated directly from his. I knew I wanted a blessing from him.

"If you wish to have a healing," he announced, "please wait in the communal room." He pointed to a large building—a tall, round, thatched-roof lodge built of thin branches and trunks of trees bound together with hemp. While the others waited outside—having had their fill of healings for the time being—five of us filed into a round room, removed our shoes, and found a seat on the poured concrete rim circumscribing the hard-earth floor with a fire pit in the middle. While we waited for Alberto, I prayed to whatever god would listen that my sadness would lift from me. In my mind, I gathered it into an imaginary burlap bag with a Spanish *frijoles* label and tossed it into the fire with the hope that it would be purified. I had spent enough time with painful teachers. *Bastante.*

Alberto appeared near the fire burning in the pit, three large feathers in hand. I shifted uncomfortably on the hard concrete. Maybe there was a soft spot. Through the haze of drifting smoke, I witnessed the individual healings of the other four members of our group. I watched the long feathers in Alberto's right hand tracing patterns in the air and the trance-like state of his face.

When it was my turn to stand by the fire, Alberto looked at the whole of and the extension of me. We did not speak. Using his large condor feathers and carefully chosen herbs and incense, he began a ritualized healing, the same as he had done with the others, circling and humming. Then, he stopped. He looked at me more carefully. He squinted his eyes.

Setting the large feathers on a table made from the sawed-off stump of a tree, he moved directly in front of me. Out of nowhere, it seemed, he gathered a handful of barely there downy feathers similar to fluff from cottonwood trees in early summer. He closed his eyes. He raised his head, chin up. I stood there in hiking pants, yellow T-shirt, and bare feet. He circled one hand in front of my heart. I felt exposed in a way I had not been when I had stood naked in the dimly lit room the night before.

111

My toes dug into the hard-packed dirt to help preserve my posture, my dignity, the mask hiding my frailty.

A cloud moved from the sun's face above the spacious room, floated past it, away from it. My eyes lifted to catch pieces of light piercing the high ceiling of woven grasses, then squeezed shut as, suddenly, I felt an intense pressure against my chest. The bottled-up sadness trapped inside pushed against my skin and toward the open air, where it could run free in every direction. I felt scared. This pressure could swamp my heart. But then, suddenly, it evaporated, poof—a bubble on the surface of a mud pond. I felt boneless. A rag doll.

Keeping my head down, I peeked at the bronze face of Alberto Taxo through the shimmer of water in my eyes, his gray hair released from the woven band and expanded into lucid whiteness, his face and skin transparent. His eyes still closed, he bent toward me and blew slowly, carefully, and continuously across the line of my breasts. Slowly, slowly, my insides filled with fresh chi in place of the stagnant water that had been standing too long. Alberto tossed the baby feathers into the fire, nodded to me, and walked toward the open door of the lodge and into the broad light of day. Except I could not remember him passing through—this man of breath and Spirit. It was as if he evaporated into thin air.

The noisy single-engine plane nosed through a barricade of clouds. Bold slashes of blue attempted a takeover of the thick gauzy skies, but the grayness was winning.

"*Mira,*" the pilot said suddenly, excitedly pointing toward the tip of the right wing. "*Un volcán.*" Christine, our group leader, who sat in the copilot's seat, translated. All eight members of the Eco-Trek tour group strained forward to catch sight of something we never thought we would see: massive, roily, dust-filled clouds of darkest gray belching out of the earth's interior, molten magma embellished with lines of fire oozing over the volcano's lip. But then, too quickly, it faded in the distance behind us, and the pilot pointed the plane's nose downward toward the Miazal jungle in Ecuador's Oriente. We sank into a sea of even darker gray clouds, dropped into a clearing, skidded onto an underwater field of grass, and plowed through mud. Christine opened a battered rubber sack filled with a disheveled assortment of black knee-high, rubber boots.

"Always wear these," she instructed, sorting them into pairs, handing them out.

Most of our feet slipped around in boots one size too big, but who was going to complain when we were about to cross a terrain with who-knows-what creatures we might surprise? "Members of the tribe are waiting outside to take you to the village," she said. "The Shuar were a head-hunting tribe until about thirty years ago, but there is nothing to worry about. I have been coming here for a few years now, and I still have mine." She smiled a mischievous smile. "But remember. They are a proud people. It is an honor for each of you to be here. Show your utmost respect. I can bring you here because they trust me."

A head-hunting tribe. Maybe this visit was a conspiracy to bring in more meat for the children. My memory sifted through horrific images from old movies—long black hair dangling from shrunken heads hanging on tree branches next to a tribal village. Fires. Smoke. Frenzied drums.

"Things have changed," she said, as if overhearing my thoughts. I laughed nervously to myself, wondering if the medical student next to me was taking silent measure of his neck.

"One more thing," Christine added. "Women, do not look directly into the eyes of the men of this tribe. They will mistake that for an invitation to take you into the jungle for big passion."

"Big passion!" The five women in the group looked at each other with arched eyebrows. The men covered their smiles. Big passion might sound inviting on the right occasion, but not on the floor of the jungle in the company of ants and spiders.

When we climbed down the airplane stairs, eight Shuar tribesmen, who were approximately two-thirds to half our size, crowded around us—thin, small-boned, waving their hands, shouting in a language I could not understand. Tropical foliage seemed to be creeping toward the airstrip while we spoke. *Tarzan. Swinging vines. Question-mark snakes wrapped around tree branches.* Nevertheless, we followed them at a quick clip on grass-covered paths, across a line of cutter ants, into dugout canoes, across two swollen rivers, and back onto paths stamped out of tall grasses, until we reached a clearing with a compound—a lodge built of thin branches with a precisely woven palm-leaf roof. The natives showed us to our rooms with cement floors, well-brushed corners, and the smell of fumigants keeping insects at bay.

The healing I had received from Alberto Taxo was alive in me still. Some stuck, unyielding place in myself—some useless fortress wall—had crumbled. And so that afternoon, after we unpacked in our rooms, four of us hiked on a well-worn path through the sauna of the jungle until we arrived at a clear, shallow, broad river. It was at that moment that I broke out.

"Are there any piranha in here?" I asked Christine on a sudden whim.

"No." She eyed me suspiciously. "Why do you want to know?"

I flopped back into the clear water to let the slow current carry me. I had always felt at home in this element after taking Red Cross swimming lessons in Lake Mead as a child. A tadpole. A frog. A creature of water. Maybe I wanted to be rebaptized, to immerse myself from head to toe, to be cleansed by water and celebrate the way I had been feeling since Quilajalo.

Through the drops of splashing water, however, Christine looked at me with ill-masked horror. She dove in beside me. Suddenly, remembering she was responsible for each of us and our safety, I thought of stopping time and reversing the action. But we were both in the flow, floating next to each other, the sound of water in our ears, until we arrived at a widening of the river, the sandy bank, and the shores of the compound.

After searching the bottom of the river with one foot to find a secure place to stand, I shook the water off and pushed wet hair out of my eyes. Christine did the same. Gratefully for me, she was kind enough not to berate me in front of the two Shuar looking at us curiously from the edge of the river. *Anything could have happened*, her effort at silence said. *You need to respect where we are.* I cringed at the thought of my foolish impulsiveness and hoped I had not broken my bond with Christine or violated Shuar etiquette.

That night, the gaffe behind me, the eight of us were treated to a traditional dinner (nothing too surprising, mostly greens and legumes) at rough-hewn picnic tables set on a cement slab. After dinner, more members of the tribe joined our dinner staff to demonstrate the old ways of the Shuar. "Some of these practices are still continued today," Christine explained, "though mainly by the ones who want to preserve tradition."

Dressed in wraparound cloth rather than the bare-breasted jungle wear often seen in *National Geographic*, the natives portrayed two rituals: how they once greeted each other with a complex choreography of spears and how they entered each other's homes to drink a brew called *chicha*. "This is made by the Shuar women from manioc root and saliva, which they spit into the mixture and allow to ferment," Christine continued with a flat-line expression. "*Chicha* was carried with them whenever they went for a visit. And still is."

Before we were sufficiently prepared to think up a gracious way to decline, two of the women approached our table with a half coconut shell of this sour delicacy. *Saliva. Fermented saliva. Save me, somebody.* Their faces said they were fully expecting our pleasure at being able to share a drop of their strange brew. All thoughts of travel sickness aside, each member of our tour group passed the shell around and sipped the smallest possible sip of tradition with a straight face and subtly pinched nostrils.

After the *chicha*, gratefully, two musicians appeared out of the shadows with a guitar and a reed flute to play music from the Andes. ("The jungle is an extension of the Andes," Christine explained.) Several of the Shuar men approached timidly, held out their hands, and asked the women in our group to dance. When a rather minuscule, seemingly older gentleman with bones more appropriate for a bird approached me, I remembered the caution about eye contact. In the light of four inadequate floodlights shining from each corner of the dance floor, I followed his moves and concentrated on his feet. I spent much of our dance laughing internally about this protective measure and how it defeated the purpose of dancing and getting to know your partner.

When he asked me to dance a second time, I thought, *okay, what can I lose*. But I could not deal with counting his toes any longer. A few bars into the music, I impulsively reached across the space between us, my palm held high. This was a game I used to play with my sons: 4/4 rhythm, clap your knees, clap your own hands, then trade claps with your partner. At first he was confused, but after another awkward demonstration of me clapping my own outstretched hand, he finally clapped my hand back. Then the other. Both of us laughed and hopped around in a circle as if we were children. Except, I wondered, maybe I was being disrespectful by playing loose with one of the Shuar, though I definitely remembered not to look into his eyes.

When the party had been cleared away and the Shuar disappeared into the dark, Christine stopped me with an amused expression on her face. "Do you know who you were dancing with?"

"No," I said, raising innocent eyebrows.

"That was Whonk. He is the most powerful shaman in the Shuar tribe."

"Oh," I said, suddenly panicked. "Really?"

"Really." She smiled and turned to go to bed, leaving me there to stew in my mental juices. *The most powerful shaman? Had I done something irreparably wrong by touching the hands of the shaman?* If only I had known who he was. Maybe I would have been more careful. But maybe, intimidated by his title, position, and power, I would have kowtowed or bowed or, worse yet, avoided him. What did it mean to be a shaman here in the jungle? Was he sacred? Untouchable?

In my room, while I pulled down the sheets of my bed and searched for insect invaders with my flashlight, I thought about the word *sacred*. What did that mean to me? Respect? Awe? Veneration inspired by authority? Was the sacred always something external to lowly individuals who must remember their place—a more venerable being out there somewhere, a holier place than the one where each of us stood, an intermediary between ourselves and God? Or could the sacred be joyful, a direct and innocent connection to all that was good?

It was good to be with these shamans. Good to drink *chicha*, even if it was fermented saliva. It was good to dance with the most powerful shaman. Yet it was also good I had not known Whonk's status. I would have worried about the Sacred Code of the Other even if I sometimes had a push-pull response to rules that seemed arbitrary—a bar across the railroad track long after the train had passed, warning everyone to keep their distance when what was most needed was a close-up. Is it not a holy act to make meaningful contact with strangers?

The next morning, I saw Whonk speaking to our translator. In the daylight, I viewed him with greater clarity. He seemed younger, more agile, his skin more honey-chestnut brown. I could see strength in this man with small bones, a different kind of strength, a vitality I had not been able to discern in the dim light on the dance floor. He was no longer a tiny man, delicate as a bird, but powerful in his serenity, with his chi intact, with his at-homeness in the world.

"Please tell him he is a good dancer," I spoke up, feeling shyer than before but emboldened by the beauty of the day. "I enjoyed dancing with him, but tell him I apologize if I seemed disrespectful."

The translator laughed a belly laugh at what seemed to be a mammoth joke. "He was just telling me what a good dancer you are. He had a great time."

I looked at Whonk, even at his eyes that wrinkled into a smile on his sun-worn face, two missing teeth suddenly evident. I smiled my orthodontically corrected American materialist smile, but at this point, I was okay with the way my culture had mandated straight teeth. I was okay with me and my place in the cosmic order. He and I clapped our hands together one last time and laughed. That was the language we could speak. At that moment, I sensed that this was my final and most important healing: to have connected to a holy man, not as an acolyte on bended knee in the presence of a sacred totem, but as human to human, heart to heart.

When I attended Whonk's ayahuasca ceremony that night, I decided for the first time during my six-week trip of visiting shamans, not to participate directly in another ceremony. I was not an ayahuasca tourist—that was not my intention. Nor was I a woman trying to right herself with the world anymore. I was part of this tribal world, and my tribe was as sacred as Whonk's tribe was sacred. My love of dancing was sacred, too.

In the flickering candlelight in the dark of the Miazal jungle watching other members of my group participate in the ritual—first sitting at crude picnic tables to receive instruction and then, some of them moaning, one of them writhing with stomach pain, on woven mats, and I wondering what they were experiencing in their ayahuasca journey and whether or not they were encountering a totem animal—I knew that I would never fully understand sacredness. Except I believed that no one had a corner on sacredness or holiness. The whole earth was a holy place—its people, animals, plant life, and geography. I had been told this before, maybe a thousand times. I had read it before. But this night I knew that healing begins at one's center. With the charity of Spirit in my veins, bones, and cavities even, I was the one who knew how best to walk through the days and nights of my time here on earth.

Chapter 9

SWEETGRASS

"Could we could stop in Mount Pleasant?" I ask Bill, my second husband of twenty months. He is steering our car along the edge of the Atlantic Ocean while I watch the eternal flirtation between tide and shore. "I'd like to check out those baskets."

"Haven't we seen enough today?"

"But a sweetgrass basket. They're famous." I have been reading the pamphlet. "They're almost identical to coil baskets made by the Wolof people in Senegal."

"But do you need another basket?"

Admittedly, I am known for my zealous shopping habits and my penchant to get sucked into a new place and try to take it all home with me. A desk clerk at our hotel had told me about the baskets. "Their long, narrow leaf blades, called treads," she explained as she handed me a pamphlet, "are woven into rows of coils, then sewn together with strips of palm leaf."

"So?" Bill is waiting for an answer.

"So," I give him one. "Let's go back."

Thus there is nothing more to do than sit on the passenger side of the car, smell the ocean breeze, and run on like an encyclopedia. I may be boring, but I need to avoid the topic of our crumbling, about-to-end marriage. "The enslaved Africans in this area," I read out loud from the unfolded pamphlet on my lap, "were credited for the success of the American Rice Kingdom. They turned rice into the main cash crop of South Carolina.

"They used fanner baskets," I continue, "to toss rice into the air, thus separating grains from chaff—an art form from West Africa. They were called Gullah and Geechees. Both men and women were more valuable to their owners if they knew how to make strong baskets."

In a last-ditch effort at honoring the state of matrimony, Bill and I had planned a trip to Charleston, with its gracious architecture, rich history, and Southern hospitality. At the moment we are driving on the old Ocean Highway toward Mount Pleasant, four miles north of Charleston—eighteenth-century America's largest slave-marketing center, a fact easy to forget in the charm of the city, though easy to remember when we see Confederate flags on the bumpers and rear windows of passing cars.

Sweetgrass Basket Highway, a sign reads. We have arrived.

I crane my neck to check out a deserted basket stand we are passing but see no sign of sweetgrass art hanging from its nails and rickety wooden arms. No wares in sight. "The basket ladies must have gone to a late lunch," I say.

"Good," Bill says, turning on the blinker for a left-hand turnaround.

These people knew rice. I want to make a little song with those words as my father used to do, sing it to Bill to enchant him into wanting to look at sweetgrass baskets. But he has already decided my little songs are weird. I have already decided he does not understand my or my father's need for little songs. "Sea island people," I could sing. "Listening to the waves." That had a nice sound to it. Thousands of years of basketmaking. Sea island people taking charge when plantation owners, afraid of yellow fever and malaria bred in the low-lying swamps, hightailed it back to Charleston. Africa in those islands—more and more unwilling slaves brought to ensure the success of rice, and yet more and more African tradition brought to the Americas.

"Maybe . . ." I try to disguise a last-chance plea to change his mind. "Maybe we can find just one stand that's open?"

Beneath the bill of his baseball cap, he keeps his eyes on the road.

I feel the need for a basket blessed by sweetness, something like the smell of the ocean when the breeze is stiff, the smell of morning before the sun rises and the dampness from high tide evaporates. *Why is sweetgrass sweet?* We drive past the dunes and lapping waves of the Atlantic, the windows open, the salty aroma of sea wind filling the rented car, almost erasing the scent of stale air freshener and other difficulties.

Half an hour from our resort, we stop for an early dinner. Bill wants soft-shell crab. After being seated at a small square table in a run-of-the-mill roadside place with a run-of-the-mill crowd of tourists, I notice a group of thirteen or fourteen black women sitting at a long table. It is not hard to overhear their excited talk about singing somewhere, sometime soon.

I try not to eavesdrop, but the sound of their rich voices pulls on me like a magnet, musician in every pore that I am, lover of anything with a good melody and an interesting beat. There are women of all sizes, some of them filling more than their chairs, their ample bosoms resting on the edge of the table. Their voices waft like snatches of melody across the room.

Unable to concentrate on the menu, I rise and almost float to where the ladies chatter like songbirds. I cannot help myself.

At the table, the conversation is running so thick that no one looks up, but finally, after I stand there for a while, a thin woman dressed in a light tan, loose-fitting jacket, her graying hair framing her timeworn face, looks up and smiles a pleasant-enough smile. The ones on either side of her still have their mouths open, holding that next word, somewhat irritated that their conversation has been interrupted so rudely.

"Excuse me," I begin. The rest of the ladies stop talking for a few seconds to peer over their glasses or out of the sides of their eyes and look down at our end of the table. "I couldn't help but overhear you talking about choirs. Are you ladies in a choir?"

"Are we in a choir?" the woman in tan echoes my question. "Does a dog bark?"

"Right on, Sister," a bevy of voices chime in. Then everyone laughs. Mutual agreement. A chorus of pleasure.

"We're the best," one woman says, already wearing the crown of victory. "We're going to show those Georgia people this weekend. Battle of the Choirs, and we'll rise victorious."

"Is it possible to hear you sing?" I ask with great hope, even while suspecting that I could be viewed as a bossy white woman thinking black folk need to stop everything and pay attention. "I love gospel choirs. You're gospel, aren't you?"

"That's right, honey. We're making a bus trip over to Georgia in two days for the spring competition. Gone like a bird. Won't be around for you to hear us. Sorry."

"I wish you luck," I say, wanting to stay longer, join up with this choir, and go to Georgia with these women made up of 60 percent water just as I am. I can feel their liquid parts swimming with music, trembling just inside their skins.

Just then, "The Devil Went Down to Georgia" flits through my mind, the Charlie Daniels fiddle version. I think maybe this country-western tune is telling me I have no business intruding upon these women, somehow hoping to get on the insides of their skin with absolutely no invitation being issued. But, even so, I would love to be a speck on a shoulder of their bus driver. I turn to leave, and yet the word *bus* stays on my mind. A picture of Rosa Parks comes into my head, on the front seat of a bus beneath the sign that reads, "We reserve the right to refuse service . . ."— that historical wall of segregation that anyone over forty years of age carries in memory, that movie that plays vividly in my mind when I have any exchange with people who used to be called colored. How could anyone forget? I have read about Rosa and given serious thought to Emmett Till's unnecessary death. I have heard the sermon about having a dream. But still I know I am the Other, the Outsider here. I thank them for their time and wish them luck.

"What were you doing over there?" Bill asks. I sit back down at our table and replace the napkin on my lap. "Was that a good idea to interrupt them like that?"

"I didn't mean to be rude. I knew those ladies were in a choir the moment I saw them sitting there. I knew it."

I can't help but think that Bill definitely does not understand me if he does not know why I got up to talk to the women, if he does not understand the thing that happens when music slips into a room and performs its magic wiles on open ears that cannot resist any kind of melody, spoken or sung. I cannot help myself.

A storyteller named Mary Ritchie once said that sweetgrass is the hair of our Mother: each strand alone not as strong as when it is braided with other strands. Sweetgrass has a vanilla fragrance. It grows wild in wet meadows and at the edges of sloughs and marshes and bogs, on shaded stream banks and lakeshores in Europe, Asia, and North America. It also grows in bands not far from the high-tide line, usually out of sight of the vast ocean and behind the first dune. It flourishes in company rather than solitude.

Holy grass. Mary's grass. Vanilla grass. Manna grass. Bison grass. Sweet, sweet aroma that is pungent after harvesting, even more pungent when dried and moistened. It is pleasing to people and to good spirits, this sweetgrass. When it is burned, prayers, thoughts, and wishes rise with the smoke, spiral into the air in a translucent column of white, and ascend to the Creator, who will listen when the sweetgrass speaks.

Native American medicine men kept it in their pouches with roots and herbs, sweetgrass being one of a group of four healing plants, along with tobacco, cedar, and sage. Believed to have great power, it was often woven into ceremonial baskets. Sweetgrass kept the basket strong. In those times, when a gatherer pulled the grass out of its roots, like knives from their sheaths, she understood its power and made a tobacco offering to give something back in exchange.

It is now Sunday morning, and we are driving around Port Royal. Bill is helping me look for an unassuming church where I can join with the locals to worship. Since I heard about the Gullah descendants a few months before, I have wanted to be with them. I intuit a sense of their purity. My soul longs for purity. It also longs for a *tabula rasa* between me and Bill—a clean slate, a new beginning—but that happens only when a life is newly created. We have chosen not to see how we are the same, and that makes me think about religion, race, education, politics, and the differences that engender comparisons. The main thing Bill and I see is our differences. We are slaves to maintaining these differences, I think.

I once read something about the Mandinko, warriors from Mali who settled the Gambia River in West Africa and created a new kingdom with vestiges of the old one. As I recall, their new society was organized in a caste system—the highest being freeborn farmers who worked the land, the middle being artisans, praise-singers, and *griots* who were the keepers of oral history, the lowest being slaves, usually those who had committed murder, adultery, or witchcraft. Though the subject of whether or not slavery existed in sub-Saharan African societies before the arrival of the Europeans is hotly contested by Afrocentric and Eurocentric academics, slavery did exist in some of Africa's earliest organized societies, namely in ancient Egypt thirty-five hundred years ago, where buying and selling of slaves were regular activities in cities along the Nile. However, the early African tradition of slavery appears to be more benign when compared to the institutionalized systems of slave trading that would develop later.

Their slaves were not ordinarily considered to be subhuman like a pig or a cow, or three-fifths of a human being, or any of that lunacy perpetrated by European slave traders and whoever picked up on the trend. Though their children were subject to the sins of their fathers, they "could, over time, become identified as members of their owners' extended families. . . . After three or four generations, descendants of slaves could often shed their slave status. Thus slavery, on one hand, cut people off from their kin but, on the other hand, provided them with the possibility of becoming attached to other families and, after several generations, reintegrated into the web of kinship."[1] No lingering stigma. A way to eliminate differences, perhaps.

Bill is Jewish, and I was raised Mormon, two different cultures, though Mormons feel a kinship with Jews—their own Dead Sea in the state of Utah, their Zion, their own gentiles. Even if I have a great-grandmother who tucked a menorah in her wooden steamer trunk when migrating to Utah from Denmark in the 1800s, a line has been drawn between us—my way, your way.

But why does this behavior keep reappearing? Why do people repeat things like "My dad's better than your dad," or "My God is the only God, and you are thus an infidel?" Even black people compare themselves to each other—high yellow, chocolate, caramel, olive brown, ebony, coal black. We are all made of the same chemistry, yet somewhere buried in the human psyche there seems to be a tendency to make hierarchical distinctions, to see ourselves as purer, closer to holiness, more valuable.

There must be a way to transcend this insanity of differences, of pointing fingers, calling names, partitioning, comparing, and ridiculing. Music is one way—the universal beauty in operatic arias, violin concertos, zydeco rhythmic ecstasy, straight-ahead jazz riffs, and definitely in those blues and spirituals. Gospel singers know how to channel Spirit like a lightning rod, those same people who have built separate lives after their clash with sheer ignorance. If gospel music is born out of suffering and burned into pure essence by the fires of persecution, then that sounds like salvation to me. Maybe forgiveness is possible here. Please let it be possible.

CHAPTER 9

This twenty-month marriage has been coming apart stitch by stitch. Too much baggage, too much prehistory. As a stopgap measure, we have been staying at Kiawah Island in the confines of our plush hotel room, complete with acres and acres of a golf course, sand dunes, gigantic sprawling oaks, and palm trees. When my first marriage of thirty-three years ended, feeling earthless and unmoored I wandered into an on-again/off-again relationship with a much younger man with a drug problem—a setup for failure. When the inevitable fulfilled itself, I thought a quick fix and a second marriage would help me find balance. It has not. But the truth is that I am not built for the end of relationships—good, bad, or indifferent. I am dissolving into a 100 percent body of water.

As we flew into Charleston, in a break between covert tears while reading an in-flight magazine, I told Bill that the two things I most wanted to do on our trip were, first, to find a good blues club in Charleston and, second, to find a small, out-of-the-way African-American church where I could find some descendants of the Gullah people—the ones I had heard had dreams about catching the moon with a fishnet, the people who could convince flowers to sing and trees to fly, the men who could carve birds that lift out of their hands and flap their wings up, up, and away.

That is what we are doing this morning—driving up and down gravelly, uncurbed roads in Port Royal, the island where Union troops established a base in 1861 and where many escaped slaves, known as contrabands, joined the Union Army as laborers, cooks, teamsters, and servants. From a long-ago history book, I remember that President Lincoln had opposed the idea of blacks being accepted into the army, fearing this move would push border states like Missouri over to the Confederacy. Many assumed that a black man could not be trained to fight as well as a white soldier, even though Frederick Douglass, the abolitionist leader escaped from slavery, had said, "We are ready and would go." The Harriet Beecher Stowe in me hates this blindness, this disenfranchisement, and the fact that these unfair distinctions were and still are made.

So much history on these wide, looping roads on a Sunday morning where so many feet trampled over this ground before we ever arrived. Major General David Hunter took command of Port Royal in March 1862. Short on regular troops, he recruited contrabands into a segregated black combat unit. President Lincoln stood by his decision not to authorize funding to pay these troops. In January of 1863, however, he made a dramatic shift in policy with the Emancipation Proclamation, liberating slaves in those areas still in rebellion and saying that free black men would be received into the armed services of the United States. The black regiment at Port Royal celebrated by singing "My country, 'tis of thee, sweet land of liberty . . ." on that, the first day they had a country of their own, some for the first time. Sweet liberty. Sweetgrass. Though when the war ended, the "sweet land of liberty" closed its doors again.

I have a passion for black gospel music that carries the spirit of people who worship up and out of their churches: Second Baptist, Calvary Baptist, charismatic Christian, wherever I can find simple, innocent pleading to and celebrating of God. I want to experience worship different from what I have known in Mormon services, which, while loving, caring, and imbued with gentle spirit, seems anemic when hymns are being sung. I want to burst out and shout "Hallelujah!" and feel the music rise up from my toes. I want to tell black people that I am sorry for the arrogance, impudence, rudeness, cruelty, and hatred of some people with white skin who have called a dark skin cursed, who have been terrorists burning houses and hanging boys like Emmett Till, whose only crime was being black and who thus was not allowed the privilege of experiencing the rites of passage from boyhood to manhood because he naively whistled at a white woman.

But then I have struggled with a racist inside me. I am not immune to thinking that my white skin makes me superior, even though no one overtly taught me to think that way. I have observed this sick mentality in others, even in those who were my teachers. I am deep-to-the-bone ashamed of the time in high school in 1957 when I told my English teacher—a man raised in the South—that I needed to be allowed to move away from the African-American girl sitting next to me in class because it seemed she had not had a bath in a long time. He shook his head vigorously in the affirmative, much more than casually. "I understand," he said. We became partners in righteous calumny in our mutual act to continue to sully the reputation of someone darker than ourselves, no mention of individual personal hygiene. He assigned me a new seat.

And I wish that I had never accepted a dance in 1959 with a genteel black-skinned boy I will call Ned, when I did not have the confidence of my Christian convictions that all of us are equal under the sun and in God's eyes. I did not have confidence, period, at that point in time, viewing my physical self as a most awkward amphibian. I lived at the margins of popularity already and did not want to call further attention to that fact. Being smooth and swift with lip service regarding my unbiased beliefs, I said yes when Ned asked me to dance—"I'm bigger than prejudice," I told myself. After a minute of dancing a slow dance with him, however, I realized that there was a foreign-to-me hand in mine, that my skin was touching what seemed to be his much-different skin. Having grown up in the desert in Boulder City, a strictly Caucasian community, and then in Las Vegas, where the few African-Americans I had seen had been at a distance until I enrolled in high school, I felt that his black skin against my olive skin, forget white, was a transgression. I was failing the code of acceptability, the code of the norm. I was setting myself apart, God forbid.

I avoided the soulful eyes of Ned—this nice, sensitive, handsome boy who had asked me to dance. Too impressed, even encoded, with not-so-subterranean high school and societal opinion, I caved. Miscegenation laws were still on the books in some states, after all. A breach of these laws was a felony that carried a prison sentence. Even if Nevada had no such laws, these ideas had been carried like pollen through the air. I told him I was not feeling well, that I had to go home, which I did.

It was a lonely ride home in my parents' 1950 green boat of a Plymouth. Ned was nicer than most of the boys I knew, smarter, more courteous. He was someone I would have liked to know, but I was not strong enough to buck the huge weight of public opinion that I felt on my shoulders, though no one had said a word. This "public opinion" was probably more the perception of a young girl with insufficient respect for herself, someone capable of attributing all sorts of things to those bestowed with the term *popular*. What had they been saying, anyway? I perspired profusely. What did they think? I felt empty inside. My hand that had touched his guided the steering wheel and drove me home to the edge of the desert. The world had revealed itself as an unfair place. I was a party to the unfairness. I had arrived at a diminished place in myself.

But this morning, as Bill and I drive the streets of Port Royal, I am thinking that African-Americans are my spiritual fathers and mothers, maybe because, more strongly than ever, I have a ripening sense of what the word *downtrodden* means: down at the heels, downfallen, underfoot. I am thinking of a portion of my bloodline that worked the land in England with its class system, no change of caste allowed, though few would have said that out loud. I am wondering about the illusion of the so-called classless society in which we are now supposed to be living, this society in which being black has been to occupy a lower caste because of not-so-subtle institutionalized racism—something else people do not say out loud. I am feeling hapless in my own effort to bridge differences. I am feeling contrite, low in spirit, and think maybe someone who has been there too can help me see my way back. Down and out. Reaching out my hand. *Somebody catch my hand.*

We have been driving around mostly in silence for about fifteen minutes, looking for a church to fit my specifications, when Bill spots a tiny white clapboard building. He brakes. A dark-blue van is parked in front of a simply constructed church needing a paint job. A man sits in the driver's seat behind a steering wheel. Another on the passenger side.

And there are others in the shadows of the backseat behind the tinted window glass.

"Is this what you are looking for?" Bill asks, the motor of our rental car idling.

"Sure," I say hesitantly.

"You don't sound too sure."

"No. This looks good." I swallow, the swallow sounding in my ears, and I am glad he is here with me.

"If you would like me to, I'll talk to the people in that van and see what's going on."

"That would be nice." I am touched by his willingness to help.

When he turns off the motor and gets out of the car, I wonder why I am so obsessed with religion, spirituality, and the way people worship—God, Goddess, Father and Mother in Heaven, Yahweh, Allah, Jesus Christ, Buddha, Mohammed, Krishna, the Sun, the Moon, the Pope, Confucius, Lao-tzu, St. Francis and his birds, Mother Teresa, the Virgin of Guadalupe, Mary Baker Eddy, Joseph Smith, the Sufis, the mystics. Maybe life itself is the only true church, the only true religion. It teaches us everything we need to know sooner or later. Maybe I do not need to keep looking.

But, bidden or not, I feel God on the heels of every footstep, even though he does not seem to be listening right now, not helping me right a wrong situation, or maybe he is and I just do not want to hear the answer. I believe in the Divine; I know I do, though when I get on my knees to pray for guidance, I am not always sure what I am praying to. Maybe there is no he or she to be found. God may be a name I have used for reassurance. Yet I cannot take myself to the lip of that void. Maybe it is more that I cannot see the true face of God in my finite state. Maybe there is no choice to be made for something I cannot understand. But I can still feel Spirit when it is in the room—the What in all of us that is alive—though I am not sure how to open up arms and receive it. It is so big.

In my passenger-side rearview mirror, I catch sight of a bent dark-gray woman walking toward the church, leaning on a cane that stabs the dust with each step. A draping shawl over her shoulders, she looks like Mother Time getting an eight-month start on the new year. She makes her way slowly to the steps of the church with its bare-spotted siding, puffs of dust rising with each dragging step.

Bill is back. He smiles as he slides under the steering wheel. "Surprise. The driver of the van is the pastor. He says you are welcome to join them. The service starts in fifteen minutes." He puts the transmission in Drive. "We'll drive around before it starts. Okay with you?"

"What do you mean?" I say suddenly, the impact of his words sinking in. "*I'm* welcome to join them? I thought you wanted to do this with me."

"I've been thinking about it. You have respect for this kind of thing and at least you're a Christian. I would only be an observer. Some kind of sociologist. That's not fair."

"But . . ."

"Think about it."

I consider his words. I decide he is right. I can do this.

One basket a day. Six days a week.

A fanner basket was a winnowing tray, something like a hubcap—a circular, barely curved bowl of a basket. A thresher tossed the threshed and pounded rice into the air. Up. Back down. Caught. Thrown up again until the wind heard the invitation from the sound of the rice rising and falling. It carried chaff in an upward spiral, up and away from the falling rice. Rice and more rice until the bags were filled, until the wagons were filled, until the horses strained to pull the wagons to the docks.

One basket a day. Six days a week. Traditional weavers spent the Great Depression weaving sweetgrass, pine needles, and bulrush in Mount Pleasant. "My [mother and sister] didn't have a clock," Jeannette Lee recalled for Charleston's *Post and Courier*, according to the tourist pamphlet. "But the Greyhound bus would come through at midnight. That's when they'd stop and go to bed."

Early basket makers were men who made large baskets from bulrushes for storage and for carrying a row's worth of vegetables. Between growing seasons, they made baskets for plantation use and for sale by the owners— a good basket maker was a valuable asset. Bulrushes being harder on the hands, the women who wove, and who were asked to weave more and more, found that sweetgrass was more pliable, softer, sweeter. They turned to delicate baskets for small uses such as holding sewing, bread, fruit, socks, and rings. The ripping of the blade of the saw palmetto, the material used to tie the sweetgrass in coils, was and is their musical instrument, these daughters and granddaughters and great-granddaughters who carry on the tradition brought to seventeenth-century America.

One basket a day. Six days a week. What will be placed in this basket? What will be brought and what will be taken away? There is hope in the use of their hands and in the smell and feel of sweetgrass.

We navigate a few more dusty roads, Bill and I. I think of how I have been haunting African-American churches since back in the 1980s when I broke from the Mormon Church, starting at Calvary Baptist in Salt Lake City with my son Chris. I had always had a yen for the energy inside the music and the sermons that made me feel alive and surging with that ineffable thing known as Spirit. Somehow, when I was in the presence of African-Americans, the Blacks—whatever name describes a people with so many shades of brown and black—especially in their churches, I felt my own soul rising inside me, wanting expression, thinking it was safe to come out and show itself. I wanted to wear a purple choir robe and sway down the aisle in procession. I wanted to give everything I had to the notes of the songs, belt them out with no shame, nothing careful or prescribed, giving everything over to the Jesus Fire I heard them talk about. I did not want smoke from burned-out fires. I did not want secondhand worship.

At Calvary Baptist, we had sat next to an elderly woman in a purple net-covered hat and a green cloth coat. When Chris gave her a big hug after France Davis, the pastor, asked us to greet our neighbors in the pews, she said to him, "We're not so different, you and me. We just gots to get together." She held both of his hands in her small ones, her fingers as delicate as crocheted lace, and looked up in adoration at my tall, handsome son.

Bill circles the car back to the church and wishes me well. After I climb the dusty stairs to the front porch, I think that the inside of this church seems even smaller than the outside. Two slightly dusty windows allow a share of morning light. A congregation of eighteen people, including five children, sits in sparsely populated rows. I sit by an older woman with a green pillbox hat and greet her with my customary handshake. "I am happy to be with you today," I say. Her hand shrinks back from mine. She does not seem eager for more conversation nor does she invite me to move any closer.

A young boy sits across the aisle staring at me—this tall, long-nosed, long-boned white woman with graying hair. I smile at him. He smiles back, then ducks his head. I get the impression that I am an alien sitting on the pew of his Sunday experience.

I hope a choir will appear soon, dressed in their long robes, swaying from side to side as they rock down the aisle, but nothing seems likely to appear from behind the speaker's stand. The more I assess these surroundings, this church does not seem to have more than one room, with maybe a small cloakroom attached at the only side door I can see.

Just then, the minister appears from that door in his blue robes, the man who had been in the driver's seat of the van, a blue-black man who reminds me of the backdrop of the starry heavens. As I sit in a small sea of dark blue, the sun's slanted rays rest on the backs of the mostly empty pews.

"Good morning, everybody," he says, glancing my way. He seems somewhat timid or maybe uncomfortable, and I sense I might be an intrusion on the regular doings of his Sunday mornings. "We welcome our visitor. Let's all make her feel part of our worship today."

All heads turn in my direction. There are small recognitions and unspoken greetings, some distrust, disinterest, and mild curiosity.

"We are low in numbers today, which means we won't have a choir, sorry to say. Next week, Easter vacation being over, we'll be back in full swing. But, quiet now. Mama will now pray over us," he says, then stands back and folds his arms.

The same aging woman I saw working her way toward church rises slowly, her hand resting on the back of the pew, her eyes closed and her head bent back to beseech the heavens. The room is absolutely quiet. The April sun is warming the panes of glass and thus the room. I see a spot of sunlight across my knees and those of the woman next to me. I see a flash of reflected sunlight on Mama's eyeglasses. Refracted light playing on surfaces of pew backs and bent knees.

"I thank you for the lying down at night," she says, ever so slowly in a soft, low moan of a voice. Her hands are clasped in front of her. I can see the long muscles extended at the sides of her neck, the tired ones that have been with her for a long time. Her voice sounds like the sea that carried her ancestors here. It has a slow, mournful echo of a language I do not know, a language with its own music, possibly something from West Africa, possibly a deep melody from the Ancient Mother, the old whisper of wisdom rising up from the earth, saying, "Here I am, my children. Been through hard times. I'm weary. But, children of my loins, I'm standing solid." The solemn, grateful sound works its way through the layers of my skin, through my ears and mind. She is a lullaby I could listen to all day. The Mother caresses each of us with her voice, and in her arms we are beyond time.

"I thank you for the rising up in the morning," she continues. The word *rising* sounds like an actual rising up, a word stretched up into flight, and I feel myself rising with the upward thrust of her voice before it falls again, slow, steady, like the mellow waves that feather a shallow beach.

Tears slip through my closed eyes as she says, "I thank you for the blood that runs through my veins and gives me life." She sounds like a preacher herself, each word of her prayer an invocation and a blessing at the same time. I have never thought to be thankful for the blood that runs through my veins or for the rising up and the lying down—those too-simple things. Her powerful gratitude is woven into every syllable of every spoken word, even every space between the words.

My hand is all I have for a handkerchief. I cannot hear the rest of what she says, her voice being as soft as the way we used to sing "Swing Low, Sweet Chariot" when I was a child, and yet the hauntingly beautiful words touch me even without the full hearing.

Slaves. We are all slaves. Slaves to our fears, hurts, anger, jealousy, and greed, I think. Slaves to a small conception of our lives. Slaves to the chains that keep us silent, small, insignificant, and unable to speak because we do not believe in our worth. Except, I stop my musing, these people are no metaphor. They are the embodiment. Their grandparents wore the visible chains. They felt the scorn of words and hearts much darker than their skin. And here they are, giving thanks while I am crying—a spoiled, ungrateful child among those who have been rejected and spurned and who know the inside-out of crying until their tears have calcified.

At the end of the sermon, the minister calls the congregation to gather in a circle. He tells us to hold hands. I stand next to Mama and feel the flesh of her wiry hand, which reminds me of the strands of sweetgrass tied together like a cord with strips of palmetto leaf, a hand that has done much, that has been witness to much. Delicate, yet firm. Strong. Resolute. This is the hand of a redeemer, a healer, one who has seen it all and can still forgive, one who can open her arms and receive the least of her sisters. I feel her power through my fingertips, an electricity coursing through my hands and arms to the woman on my right. A circle. An unbroken circle.

"God bless this sister who has visited with us today," the minister says in his closing prayer. "Bless her to know that God lives, that Jesus will comfort her, that there is no way he brought us this far to leave us."

When the circle finally breaks, I cannot do more than say "Thank you" to Mama, my throat thick as it is, though I want to put my arm around her weathered neck and kiss her cheek. She is like the Earth to me, something old and yet timeless, something solid and something liquid. Mama. Mother. She looks at me from behind her thick glasses and I can see eyes that reflect deeper eyes and then deeper eyes and then a place of rest. Mama is the essence of this room, of this church, the protector, the One who watches over it all as she strokes the back of my hand. "Lead in the light," she says.

When I shake hands with the minister, I cannot pretend my face is dry. "Thank you for your sermon," I tell him, collecting my tears with my fingers. "And thank you for allowing me to be with you today." He smiles kindly, wondering at all the tears.

I walk out onto the small porch. Bill waits by the car. My face is a mess.

"I knew you would be crying," he says, patting my shoulder, trying to be a friend, yet not sure how to be. "These things really get to you, don't they?"

"Thanks for finding this place," I tell him. "It was perfect. Just what I had hoped for, if I could just stop crying."

And yet, as we drive back to our hotel past gigantic oaks draped with hanging silvery moss and tall pines that seem to be leaning slightly as we pass beneath them, my tears dry with the wind from the open window. I suspect that real suffering is cheapened by tears, that it is deeper than tears. They are an element of the initiatory, the cleansing agent to clarify and purify, as sweetgrass is a purifier and a reminder that the earth provides. But these tears are not suffering in the deepest sense. It is time to stop crying and surrender—a lily of the field, toiling not, spinning not. As I look up at one of those leaning pines with a halo of sunlight behind its top branches, I know that I am caught by a strong, fresh sense of knowing I have come too far for Spirit or for Mama to leave me.

It is night, and I am walking outside our hotel room, walking across well-groomed grass on this barrier island with its tennis courts, golf courses, nature tours, and bicycle paths to the beach, where sweetgrass had once grown wild and uninhibited. I walk just far enough not to worry Bill but far enough away from the buildings to feel the sky up there with its flickering points of light. I think about catching the moon with a fishnet, even catching a few stars in the same net, except if I reeled in the moon there would be no reflection from the sun, no light during the night for this planet where we live, and I must not be selfish and want this soft moonlight all for myself.

I sniff the air. I think maybe there is some sweetgrass nearby at the edge of the golf course though people say most of it has disappeared with the development. It is said to smell like newly mown hay. It is said to be useful for entering a blissful, meditative state. Sweetgrass: the first plant to cover Mother Earth, according to natives of the Great Plains; the sweetness of knowing we are growing in the midst of other grasses; the sweetness of feeling our roots crossed under this marsh where we walk.

Chapter 10

THREE MONKS OVER
KANCHENJUNGA

*Man's mind, once stretched by a new idea,
never regains its original dimensions.*

—Oliver Wendell Holmes, Jr.

I. Yuksom, Western Sikkim, Northeast India

Accompanied by his miniature daughter, who wraps herself around his leg as if it were a tree trunk, Vhichunz leads me through the wet meadow. His flip-flops snap against his boney heels while my gray-suede hiking boots turn black and soggy, soles increasingly slippery.

The footpath ends at a road that is barely a road. We wait for a Tata Jeep stuffed with Indian tourists to pass. Stray ends of golden and puce silk *saris* float from open windows; foreheads are smeared with a magenta pink paste made from flour; laughter explodes every time the Jeep bounces over a deep rut. It is Dhasara (remover of bad luck), one of the most important holidays in India, and all the passengers are rubbernecking to catch first sight of the Coronation Throne.

When we step into the tracks left by the Jeep, Vhichunz instructs his daughter to hold his hand. Then, in a delivery as matter of fact as a weather report, he says, "The name Yuksom means 'Three Monks.' They flew here from Tibet in 1641." I think maybe I am hallucinating. *Flying? 1641? Over Kanchenjunga, the third-highest mountain in the world?* The perimeters of real time must be playing tricks with me. I am still dizzy from a battle with high fever and dysentery. I stop to catch a breath.

"They bring Buddhism," he says while we climb to the top of a steep hill where a gigantic pine tree makes it seem even steeper. "Guru Padmasambhava said they would come."

The shaggy pine reminds me of an ancient California redwood my father once steered our family car through on a summer vacation. It looks as old as 1641. Vhichunz points to the Coronation Throne beneath the tree. Its four graduated seats are carved from dark granite. Time has erased the definitive strokes of the stonecutters' tools.

"The top seats are for the three monks and the fourth for the first chogyal," Vhichunz says. "The king."

He points to a small wood cover on the ground, situated between two golden-tipped stupas. He bends to lift the hinged lid and uncovers a small slab of what looks like plaster of Paris—the kind I once used to make handprints in elementary school. "This is where one monk landed. His footprint." The print seems a blurred smudge, maybe a footprint, maybe not, but I am willing to suspend judgment. After all, this is Sikkim, which the guidebook refers to as "the land where stars are thought to be the laughter of Gods frozen for eternity on the face of heaven." I had read that the Buddhism in Sikkim is a combination of Tibetan Buddhism and the animistic Bon religion of the aboriginal Lepcha people. Vhichunz must be this kind of Buddhist, the way he speaks so casually of flying monks.

In the autumn of 2004, on the fourteen-hour night flight from Chicago to Delhi, I read *Time Change*, an account of an American-born debutante's marriage to the last chogyal of Sikkim just before the three-hundred-year-old institution of king was abolished.[1] ("*Sik*kim? Sik*kim*?" None of our group of ten women on the plane was sure which syllable to stress.) In 1975, this small country, tucked between Nepal and Bhutan, became the twenty-second state of India, not all citizens willing. With China to the north, India most likely appropriated this land for strategic reasons. But even though Sikkim had been promised that integration with India would not threaten its cultural identity, the natives remained sensitive about each new incursion into their beautiful piece of the Himalayas.

When my world-traveler friend Shirley had called six months earlier and asked if I would join her for an eight-day trek in Sikkim, even she was unsure of its pronunciation. I told her I would call her back, then unearthed the Oxford *World Atlas* and traced two fingers across a grid to discover the country's whereabouts. It was so tiny—a pinprick on the map south of the Tibetan Autonomous Region, the atlas pronounced, using those three words that irritate me. Sikkim's proximity to Tibet, however, piqued my interest. Shirley and I had visited Tibet in 2002, together with the Chinese People's Friendship Association, but missed our chance to explore our mutual interest in Buddhism. We had no real interchange with Tibetans except with one carpet dealer, a *thangka* painter (the prize student of the Dalai Lama's official thangka painter, no less), and the officials at staged ceremonies—all in the presence of the Chinese. I still wanted to feel Tibetan Buddhism on a close, intuitive level, with no one looking over my shoulder, to get a sense of what had created such a marvel as the Dalai Lama.

I dialed her number and got her straightaway. "I want to go, but my knee. You know, the one with the cadaver ligament. It's acting up."

"Why don't you talk to your doctor?" she suggested. "See what he says."

The following weeks were filled with rooster comb shots and strengthening exercises at the gym. I studied a guidebook special-ordered from another planet, it seemed, because it took so long to arrive at my local bookstore. I learned that Sikkim was a home for exiled Tibetan Buddhists and that Rumtek was the site of one of its most important monasteries.[2]

In the early morning quiet of my bedroom, I restarted my defunct practice of meditation. I recited the mantra I had seen painted on rocks, prayer wheels, and yak skulls in Tibet. *Om Mani Padme Hum*: A lotus grows out of mud, but is not stained by mud. An impure body can be transformed into the pure one of a Buddha.

Admittedly, on these mornings I longed to fill the emptiness I still felt after giving up on two marriages and my religion. I wanted a place in myself where I was not obsessed with the "avoidance of the appearance of evil," whatever that meant in a Christian world where you are not supposed to judge a book by its cover, or to judge, period. I wanted a pure connection with Spirit, one-on-one, no intermediaries, just as Joseph Smith had wanted when he knelt in the woods to ask which church was the right one to join. "Ask and ye shall receive," he read in the Bible, and then found his truth. As much as my mother would consider me a heretic, I wanted to find mine too. There seems to be truth in many places, and maybe we need all of it to repair the world.

In the end, Shirley and I worked out a compromise. Instead of trekking for eight days, I would trek for two and spare my knee. While the others hiked on, I would return to Yuksom, hire a driver, and visit monasteries, Rumtek first on my list. It was a great plan except for a last-minute disaster.

A mere five days before the trip, I was hiking across a streambed in the Uintas in Utah and slipped on a wet rock. The fall literally turned me upside down. I landed face first on another rock and broke my nose. Blood covered the ground like water. The emergency-room doctor used a medieval torture device to stop the internal bleeding. I screamed like a banshee. But, even though my better judgment insisted otherwise, something in me was still determined to make the trip. For some reason, I believed in Sikkim. When I asked the ear, nose, and throat specialist if I could travel, he smiled whimsically, shrugged his shoulders, and said he guessed that as long as I could breathe I would survive the trip. With a bruised face, black eyes, and an appointment for surgery when I returned, I boarded my flight.

The bruises caught stares from people on the airplane, who likely assumed I was a victim of domestic abuse, but that was nothing compared to what happened after six days in Delhi.

Our group had been shopping, shopping, and shopping in between visits to tourist attractions—the Red Fort, the Raj Ghat memorial to Mohandas Gandhi, Qutab Minar, and the India Gate. In Chandni Chowk in Old Delhi, we had been driven in pedicabs to find tunic tops and trousers known as *salwar kameezes*, the driver darting scandalously through meandering cows and throngs of people surging into every available space. The silk shop was squeezed between two leaning buildings and beneath a huge tangle of haphazard electrical wires hanging dangerously low over the narrow lanes. Taken upstairs by the consummately proper proprietor, we sat on silk pillows and sipped tea in tiny cups. We oohed and aahed over hundreds of silks tossed in the air and floated before our eyes, each of us (hardy mountain women sitting in the garden of silk in our rough-and-ready hiking wear) envisioning ourselves as beautiful, enigmatic Indian women gliding beneath mosaic arches.

On day six of our trip, however, while we waited to pass through security and fly north to Bagdogra in the Darjeeling district of West Bengal, a main travel hub in the region, three of us became violently ill: stomach, bowels, severe headache, shaky limbs. With silent-movie quickstep, we ran for the nearest restrooms. Hiding our plight from security officers, we boarded the plane and instantly hung our heads over brown paper bags for the duration of the gratefully short flight. We transferred to two Tata Jeeps for the bumpy, twisting trip to Darjeeling and the hill country, which was nothing more than a gelatinous mix of blue and brown while I rested my head on the dashboard and free-floated away from real life. Dr. Naushad Siddique (who had attended NYU "before I got fed up with New York and returned to my homeland") came to the rescue at our lodging, the Cedar Inn. One woman rebounded quickly; but for Meg and me, he ordered bed rest for three days. "High fever and dehydration must be treated with the greatest respect. You are very ill."

While everyone else shopped the markets of Darjeeling and visited the Himalayan Mountain Institute to meet with Jamling Tensing Norgay, the son of Tensing Norgay, who had climbed Mount Everest with Sir Edmund

Hilary, I had no choice but to stay in bed, sipping tepid tea and reading when my head stopped aching. In the mornings, my roommate, Leslie, opened the window curtains of our step-down sitting room to try to catch a glimpse of Kanchenjunga—Sikkim's highest mountain and, eighty-two feet shy of Everest's summit, the third-highest mountain in the world—which could be seen occasionally from Darjeeling. It was the mountain our trekking group would view up close after four days of hiking if, and only if, the clouds would allow.

On the last night at the inn, my fever subsided and, after joining everyone for dinner, I sat up in bed reading the guidebook again. The aboriginal Lepchas had worshiped Kanchenjunga, naming it the Curtain of Snow and the Highest Screen. They even staged annual dances in its honor. Because of its sacred status, after the first successful climb in 1955 by a team of British mountaineers who stopped a few meters short of the summit in deference to the wishes of the chogyal, the local monks prayed that any subsequent attempts would fail. The next expedition did fail, miserably. Out of respect for the Buddhists, the government forbade subsequent climbs.

On the day of departure for the trek, Leslie and I rose before dawn and opened the curtains to try one last time for a glimpse of Kanchenjunga. We ordered room service and sat in high-backed chairs to watch for a break in the ever-present clouds. After half an hour, we wondered if such a glimpse was even possible. We took turns as lookouts. While I showered, she watched clouds. She showered while I watched. Half an hour turned into an hour of surveillance. Through latticed windows, I could see foothills resembling a jumble of bent teeth on the edge of a saw, but not the mountain itself. Then, suddenly, the clouds stretched open—interlaced fingers parting from prayer.

"Leslie," I shouted. "It's happening." Her shirt half-buttoned, she ran in from the bathroom and grabbed her camera, as if miracles could be caught on a strip of film.

The clouds were flirtatious. They thinned, bunched, then stretched into strings. They stopped. They started. They were coy. In one magnificent moment, they parted their lips to reveal a throaty glimpse of the snow-cloaked mountain. Open-mouthed ourselves, we gaped at the glory of the hidden giant showing its face, the morning sun amplifying its contours. Leslie snapped her camera. I squeezed my eyes shut to impress this view into memory, anything to hold on to this gift from the mountain, from the gods, it seemed. But in less than two minutes, the clouds covered it. Nature's fan dance: now you see it, now you don't. We looked at each other, speechless, and wondered if we had seen what we thought we had seen.

Our group spent an entire day driving into Sikkim, crossing beneath a "Welcome to Sikkim" gate covered with wood-carved flowers painted red, pink, and turquoise; fording waterfalls caused by an unexpected monsoon that flooded the winding mountain roads; dodging gypsy cars and more Tata Jeeps loaded with passengers leaning out windows and standing on bumpers holding on to topside luggage racks. Finally, after at least a hundred switchbacks and delays on ruptured, sometimes boulder-strewn roads, we arrived at Yuksom, a small mountain village where paved roads did not exist.

The next morning when the first cock crowed, I tiptoed past my sleeping roommate on unsure legs. I sat on the balcony to read from Chögyam Trungpa's *Shambhala: The Sacred Path of the Warrior*: "The vision of the Great Eastern Sun is based on celebrating life. It is contrasted to the setting sun, the sun that is going down and dissolving into darkness. . . . The setting-sun point of view is based on fear. We are constantly afraid of ourselves."[3]

Even though skirmishes were still occurring in my intestinal war, I decided to dress. I would press through my resistance. I would not stay behind, though after discussing my plans with Shirley at breakfast, she suggested trying a half day in and a half day out. "A guide has already been hired to take you back, so you can't lose." Our group of nine (Meg had stayed in Darjeeling) posed for a picture, then threaded through the village with its chickens and goats, its magical stupa near a peaceful lake, its everywhere-drifting prayer flags, finally hooking up with the trail into the Kanchenjunga National Park. Facing the deep escarpments and unforgiving steepness of the trail, the group climbed steadily toward Dzongri, Thangsing, Samiti Lake, Gochela, and Tshoka. Sikkim was known as the Valley of Butterflies, and exotic purple, bluish, dotted, and striped butterflies flitted everywhere. After two miles, however, I was perspiring like someone standing beneath a full-bore shower-head. Colette, a seasoned bicycle-tour-guide member of our group, gave me a withering look. "You're asking too much of your body," she said. "You need to go back."

"But," I said.

"I think not." Her final remark left no room for argument.

As much as I did not want to agree, as much as I stared up the trail and envisioned myself trudging ever onward—strong mountain woman that I visualized myself being (*No, not me; I'm not ready for the sidelines; persistence, will, determination, don't give one thought to mortality*), my idea of trekking for two days, even one, had shrunk to a few hours. You are getting old, I reminded myself, but then, oldness happens only when you give up, right? I wondered about that bit of canned wisdom as I felt the reality of the Himalayan foothills sinking into me stone cold, full on, major major league. I watched the last trekker in my group disappear, still trying to transport myself by sheer wishing. Slowly, I turned to face downhill.

I asked Vhichunz, who had been hired to take me back to Yuksom, if he would wait. He was agreeable in a nonplussed way. Sitting on a bridge and gazing at the treacherous rocks and tumbling mountain stream below, I made a vow. "I will not go gently into that dark night," I whispered fiercely. "I will not go gently." I had given birth to four sons, divorced two husbands and remained friends with them both, given piano concerts, learned belly dancing, clicked the staccato heels of flamenco shoes, gone rock climbing on my fiftieth birthday, hiked the Grand Canyon, bicycled from Colorado to Illinois, and . . .

This time, however, was something else.

II. The First Monk: Losang at the Dubdi Monastery

The morning after our visit to the Coronation Throne, I am sitting on a plastic chair on the hotel balcony, waiting for Vhichunz. A taut line of red, blue, yellow, and green prayer flags in a neighbor's yard lifts and settles in a fragile dance, prayers tossed in a hypnotic partnership with the breeze. When he is an hour late, I walk downstairs to consult the manager, who says not to worry. "India Standard Time. Better known as Indian Stretchable Time." And there in the doorway, as if by a magic snap of the fingers, Vhichunz appears, no daughter in tow today. I ask if he can take me to the local monastery and help me find an English-speaking monk.

A torrential rain fell in Yuksom last night, and the footing on the cut-stone path to Dubdi Monastery is treacherous. Vhichunz wears the same soft flip-flops that cling to stones while my hard-soled hiking boots slip constantly. We continue up and up. And up. Sikkim is a country of violent ups and downs, nothing flat in sight. I walk with baby steps, afraid of losing my footing on the mossy, hand-cut-on-the-square stones, afraid of landing on my nose again. I stop at the elbow of every switchback to catch my breath, still feeling weak as a new lamb.

Vhichunz is patient. When we reach the top, he tells me to wait at the main temple while he finds the monk I have asked for. Standing inside a wide doorway flanked by brass-laden red doors, I stare at carousel-shaped round flags, at the large statue of Buddha flanked by dragons with twinkling green lights encircling their tails, and at a mural of a blue-skinned apparition wearing a crown of skulls.

Vhichunz returns with Losang, a monk on meditation leave from Dharamsala. His maroon robe has yellow triangles across his chest and blue piping on the sleeves. He wears Reebok socks and pats his shaved head absentmindedly. After introductions, I explain that I am a Christian by birth.

"Oh, . . ." Losang says, his face suddenly illuminated. "Jesus Christ is an emanation of Mahakala." He points to the blue-skinned creature on the mural, and his enthusiastic words tumble through the air as if they were theological gymnasts. "Christians think God created all things, that God creates a problem, and that God can control me. In Buddhism, God cannot control me. I can control me. Meditation can control my mind and even the cells in my body, the tendons, the red blood cells, even the nerves."

Thinking that maybe he will be talking a long time, possibly stir crazy from too much meditation, I suggest we sit. We sink to our places across from each other—he on a low bench where light slants through a window, me on a staircase step. I observe his beautifully innocent, sunlit face. "I have a science mind, Western mind, and Central Asia mind," he says, throwing his head back in laughter while his vivid teeth catch more light. He is like the Dalai Lama in this way.

We talk of many things—karma, Dharamsala, his decision to become a monk—and I take careful notes, wanting to take his thoughts home to ponder and hoping to break through my ingrained way of seeing the world ("Think differently," the Dalai Lama has said). Then I ask him a question I have been asking others on this trip. "I am very upset with my country right now, with the business of the Iraq War, which I never supported. If you could send a message to the United States," I ask, "what would it be?"

He has a ready answer. "The United States is acting like king of the world. It says, 'I am all-powerful with atomic bomb.'" He flexes his biceps in imitation of this power. "It says, 'I control the world, I am rich, all-powerful.' But for all people it is necessary to have food, clothes, house, and enough. The rich man should help the poor instead of being bigger and bigger."

Losang is making a valiant attempt to communicate in limited English, but then he says something I do not understand. When I tell him so, he asks to borrow my pen and my journal: "Americans and Europeans are not c-r-e-a-z-e or s-t-u-p-e," he writes. Then, he says out loud, "Tension and war are stupid. Dependent arising is an important view—the union of all things. Independent arising is a wrong conception and creates tension."

"I agree," I say as Vhichunz peeks around the broad red doors of the temple. Losang (I check my watch) has gone on for an hour. I thank him for his time, for the blessing of his illuminated energy, and offer him two pairs of flip-flops—a highly prized gift I have carried from the United States. We stand, clasp our hands in front of our individual hearts, and bow to the divine in each other, *namaste*. He takes his leave.

Thinking Vhichunz is ready to go, I am surprised when he directs me to follow him up the steep wooden stairs to the library, where prayer books are bound in wooden covers and wrapped in ochre cloths. "Once a year," he says, "monks go through the village with prayer books on their heads." Then we walk through double doors to a balcony stacked with beehives. Bees buzzing at our backs, Vhichunz explains the painting of another dark-blue, scowling deity with many teeth that covers the wall.

"Painted by a man from Gangtok who specializes in monastery paintings," he says, pointing to the center. "That is the Wheel of Life showing two worlds—white and black: heaven, the world of gods, and hell, the world of animals and humans. Good deeds rise up to the world of the gods. Bad deeds go down. The snake, pig, and chicken are always at the center of the wheel of life. Snake is anger; pig, stupidity; chicken, desire. How you handle these three things decides whether you go to hell or heaven."

Anger, stupidity, and desire. The snake again—an angry one this time. The coiled serpent. Suddenly I feel that anger transferred. My body has failed me. It will not take me to the base of Kanchenjunga with my friends. More anger about needing to be more than I am, constantly frustrated at what I am not. What does this say about my prospects for heaven or hell?

Vhichunz turns to go. It is time to follow, though I dread the treacherous path back to Yuksom. Faced with more pragmatic considerations, such as not breaking my nose again on that unbelievably slippery surface, I leave my anger and my existential questions behind. While my feet mince around a particularly slick turn in the path, Vhichunz tells me that the seventeenth incarnation of the Karmapa presides over the Karma Kagyu sect of Buddhism here in Sikkim. "It is not the same as Gelugpa, which is the Dalai Lama's sect. Both the Karmapa and the Dalai Lama are revered leaders," he said, "but the lineage of the Karmapa continues from 700 BC, three hundred years older than that of the Dalai Lama. It is the most respected lineage."

This is news to me. I had thought the Dalai Lama was the One and Only in the high ranks of Tibetan Buddhism. The idea of sects had not fully registered until this moment, probably because I had been seeing everything with preconceived ideas.

III. Rumtek Monastery, Eastern Sikkim

At midday, Sailesh, my travel contact, and I arrive at Rumtek, the host town to Rumtek Monastery. We climb hill number one to a formidable iron gate and a serious contingent of armed guards. We stop at the checkpoint, no option, where an unusually surly Indian soldier demands my passport. I hand it to him. He dangles it from his fingertips—an untouchable thing. "Country?" he grunts, the word barely recognizable. Two of the guards, jiggling the noses of their automatics, move closer.

In Hindi or Nepalese or Sikkimese, I will never know which, Sailesh reassures the guard. My passport is official. We have connections at the monastery. After much shuffling and frowning, the guard rolls the heavy gate open. Sailesh assesses my overpacked suitcase and the full-to-the-brim shopping bags leaning against it. He knows I have been seriously ill. He motions to two boys standing idly by the barricade and presses rupees in their palms. Loaded down with my bags, they trail us up another hill in this country of endless hills.

"Not many Americans come here." Sailesh's whispery tone of voice suggests intrigue. After checking into a stark room at the bare-bones

Sun-Gay Guest House (where mothballs have been dropped into the wash basin's sink trap to control suspicious plumbing odors), Sailesh leads me up yet another hill. We have an appointment to keep. I have never negotiated such an up-and-down terrain, native desert dweller that I am, accustomed to much flatter, endlessly stretched space. Nausea surges through me, interfering with my curiosity about karma, impermanence, and afflictive emotions that lead to suffering. What can I really find out about Buddhism in five days and in this condition?

Rounding a curve at the top of the final hill, we are face-to-face with the outer wall of Rumtek Monastery. The entryway, built into an opening in a massive, ochre-colored wall and framed with elaborately carved scrolls and boldly imagined flowers, is filled with more armed guards in gray camouflage. Keeping my distance, I strain to see past them into the courtyard. I hear monks chanting inside the main building, which looks like a most exotic layered cake, topped with a gold-colored replica of a bell suspended above a lotus blossom. Its colors are fearless, brash, a gypsy caravan. Banners are stretched across each tier of this four-tiered building set against a steep, pine-covered hill—one emerald-green banner hemmed with an orange stripe, another with long strips of bloodred and peacock-blue cloth, a third ivory-colored one decorated with auspicious symbols of Buddhism.

Just then, Sailesh spots a man waving at us. "That must be," he pauses, checking the note in his hand, "Jampa, the secretary of Karma Shri Nalanda Institute for Higher Buddhist Studies. Your official contact."

I take measure of the man who will be my lifeline for five days—probably a Tibetan, with his full head of black stick-up-straight hair and a face mapped with hard memories. He also has a brusque I-have-many-things-to-do manner. Sailesh introduces us, and without further ado Jampa says, "Follow me." He maneuvers his way past a slow-moving group of Indian tourists and guides us through guards and a metal detector.

The three of us stand in the open courtyard in front of the main building—the Dharma Chakra Center, Jampa calls it, launching into his official spiel. "This is the home of the Karma Kagyu sect. It is a replica of Tsurphu Monastery in Tibet, which was left in total ruin during the Chinese invasion, 1966, to be exact. Tsurphu is still a most important monastery, now partially rebuilt, but Rumtek remains the exile seat of the Karmapa."

On the third tier of the Dharma Chakra Center, I notice more soldiers carrying Uzis and pacing back and forth on the open balcony. Jampa redirects my attention by pointing out the monks' living quarters behind green doors. To no avail. Are the guards here because of the troubles over the Karmapa?

During our hour-long winding drive to Rumtek from Gangtok (the capital of Sikkim until it became a state of India), Sailesh and I had been chatting an amiable stream of small talk when suddenly he leaned close to my ear and spoke in a clandestine voice. He was an informant giving me a state secret.

"There is a major schism over who is and who is not the real seventeenth incarnation of the Karmapa," he whispered, maybe not wanting the driver to hear.

"And who and what is the Karmapa?" I asked in my blissful naiveté of the complexities of Buddhism.

"There are four sects of Tibetan Buddhism, and the Karmapa, head of the Karma Kagyu sect, is as important to this branch of Buddhism as the Dalai Lama is to his. This lineage claims to have started *tulku,* the tradition of the reincarnated lama, and the position of Karmapa is considered older and more important than that of Dalai Lama. I think that by now the monks at Rumtek have accepted the officially proclaimed Karmapa, but there was big trouble here not so long ago. I wanted you to know. Just in case."

But isn't the Dalai Lama the key to what anyone needs to know about Tibetan Buddhism? I want to protest. I have read several of his books. I am familiar with the Four Noble Truths, the way people can enhance happiness by examining the way they think, and what Buddha said about many boats full of different believers headed for the same shore.

"Apparently," Sailesh continues, "the Dalai Lama sanctioned Ogyen Drodul Trinley Dorje as the true incarnation in 1992 and arranged for his safekeeping at Dharamsala, even though his exiled home should have been Rumtek. Some claim that the Dalai Lama does not have the authority to make this decision for another sect and by so doing has divided the Karma Kagyu School for the first time in history."

While we negotiated the serpentine road with its thousands of switchbacks, he elaborated on this complicated history with its foreign rules, names, and concepts.

"Another incarnation is being disputed. His name is Trinley Thaye Dorje. He currently lives about two hours from Gangtok and has gathered a following here and abroad. Unlike the 'official' Karmapa, who is not allowed to leave Dharamsala for any reason because of an agreement with the Chinese government, Trinley Thaye Dorje is free to travel anywhere. His followers do not recognize the official seventeenth incarnation of the Karmapa. There have been bitter feelings," he said, settling in his seat and folding his arms. "You need to know this in case you run into something."

Now, standing inside the monastery close to Sailesh, I realize that Jampa is speaking. "His Holiness the Sixteenth Karmapa asked me to come here to be a schoolteacher for the children in the village. But then he died. In 1981. He was my friend." He pauses, bothered by a harsh thought, then shakes himself from his temporary trance. "The next Karmapa was not enthroned until 1992. Come, come. I will show you the Dharma Chakra Center."

I feel Sailesh's fingers on my upper arm. "Excuse me," he says in another whispered aside, "but I think it is all right for me to go now. You are in good hands with Jampa. I wish you will find what you want to find here, and," he squeezes my arm gently, "may your health return." He turns to go, then spins quickly back on his heel. "Oh," he says, almost apologetically, "your driver will be here Friday at noon." He speaks a wordless goodbye with a straight, cocked hand.

I watch him walk through the throngs of Indian tourists. *Don't leave me. I am not really the adventurer I am pretending to be. I am only me.* I want this sophisticated, vibrant man whose father was the Yale-trained minister of forestry for the last king of Sikkim, this man who cross-pollinates azaleas in his greenhouses at the Wayside Nursery in Gangtok, to call back over his shoulder, "I forgot. You are supposed to come with me." Instead, he disappears through the arch of the entry gate.

I steady myself. Forget yesterday. Trust in the arms of the God you are always talking about. Something besides yourself.

Jampa bows slightly, his hands in prayer pose. He holds out his arm in the direction of the Dharma Chakra Center, then points to my feet. I nod, then sit on the front steps to untie my hiking boots. I need to reboot mentally. There is too much input, too many armed guards everywhere, and too much alien language flooding my brain. I sit with my back to the mural Jampa is describing: "These are the images of the four guardians of the universe. They promised Buddha they would protect all monasteries and temples."

I will understand this later. Tomorrow or the next tomorrow.

Loosening a stubborn knot, I take more notice of the inner courtyard with its ochre walls and green doors, behind which the practitioners of Buddhism live. I hear the sound of deep-voiced chanting. But my thoughts are still on Sailesh—why he had to leave, whether or not he is a Buddhist, and whether all Sikkimese are Buddhist. Why else would he know so much about the trouble surrounding the Karmapa? While my friends are hiking into the Khanchenjunga National Park without Meg and me, I am hoping for the best for all of us. I suspect that I am swathed in an innocence I do not understand—a complete novice having left her school of fish, thrashing for life in a big ocean.

Jampa unfolds his arms. "Come, come," he says impatiently. "*Puja* is over." He climbs the two steps leading to the Dharma Chakra Center. I line up my boots in a tidy twosome, then follow him into this temple with its myriad of thangkas, rows of benches for the monks, long copper trumpets for ceremony, various-sized cymbals, and drums decorated with green drag-ons suspended from finely braided ropes. While a handful of monks dis-semble their instruments and store them in bags and corners, he leads me through the ornate room painted in reds, greens, blues, and always ochre. He explains the round, carousel-like *gyalchens* suspended from the ceiling ("they signify the victory of gods over devils"), the brass bells ("the sound of the bell is for speech; its shape represents the body"), the *dorje* (a brass implement known as the thunderbolt of enlightenment) in the shape of two crowns resting bottom to bottom against each other ("for clarity of mind"), and eleven brass cups filled with water. ("These cups are filled with clear water in the morning, then spilled out at the end of day. Like cups, we must empty ourselves each day after collecting many concerns and troubles.")

Taking me to the back of the room, he points to a particular thangka suspended from the ceiling. "This was painted by the Seventeenth Incarnation of the Karmapa," he says, then bows to the painting with his hands folded against his heart. "The tiger is a ferocious aspect of Buddha. This is a most beautiful painting. Very sensitive." He bows to the thangka again. "It is Karmapa's gift to Rumtek because he cannot be here with us."

I assess the tiger-with-soul in the blurred light of shimmering votives, aware of Jampa measuring my response. Whatever else the offi-cial His Holiness the Seventeenth Incarnation of the Karmapa is supposed to be, he is a gifted artist.

"Come," he says again. He guides me through two doors and up two flights of stairs. Out of my hearing, he speaks to a guard, who hands him a key.

"This place is off limits to tourists," he says, unlocking a stout wooden door, "but I have permission to take you here." The room's centerpiece is an exquisite golden stupa encased in glass, embedded with raw chunks of turquoise and coral, its walls lined with statues in glass cases. This place is a timeless holy of holies.

"Built in honor of the Sixteenth Karmapa." Jampa says, his face that of an impressionable young boy. "It is the receptacle for objects of worship and deep veneration. Look around the walls. These are statues of the first fifteen Karmapas. All are here."

He pauses in front of the stupa, touches his forehead to the glass, and moves his lips in prayer. He walks to the narrow passageway along the wall and touches his forehead to the feet of the first encased statue on the ledge. An adjunct to this monastery rather than a monk or a lama, Jampa is a devout man with respect for everything about this room. Deciding which of the carved figures speak to my sense of Spirit, I imitate him and bow my head at the feet of the Karmapa who appears to be the most benevolent. In the way of a chameleon, I want to turn the color of Buddhism. I want to feel it entering me, turning my insides into water flowing through me. I want it to ignore my boundaries, my judgments, my opinions and beliefs. I want to be filled in whatever way is possible.

Jampa interrupts: "In 1964, the Sixteenth Karmapa blessed Westerners for the first time. He went to United States to pay respects to Native Americans, especially to Hopis, who have a prophecy that when men in red hats come, there will be a bridge between East and West. It is almost time for you to meet your teacher, but come, there is something I want to show you first."

IV. The Second Monk: Shenphendawa in the Tara Temple

We are in the courtyard again, where scattered monks, dressed in their orange robes with the sleeves of their maroon undergarments showing, stand in animated groups talking. Jampa motions me to follow. We climb shallow wooden stairs, walk down an exterior hallway, and turn into a small yellow room with a parquet floor. A monk sits on a low bench in front of a drum frame, striking the drum with a padded gooseneck stick. A small conch shell rests at the base of the frame. Fruit, money, butter lamps, yellow butter roses with orange tops, and another row of brass cups filled with water cover the altar in the center of the room.

Cubicles in the wall behind the altar are filled with hundreds of statues of the same deity.

"This is the Tara Temple," Jampa explains. "Tara is the female aspect of Buddha. Tara means 'Rescuer.'" He points to the largest statue in the room. "This is White Tara. She represents longevity and healing. There is a third eye in her forehead and an eye in one hand and one foot. See that?" He touches the right foot with confidence that it has the capacity to see. Then he points to the smaller statue in a glass case. "The Green Tara represents wealth and compassion. She has regular eyes. That is how you can tell the difference."

The tall, thin lama in his late teens, his head completely shaved, stops striking the drum, stands, and bows. His movements remind me of an autumn leaf floating through the air.

"This is Lama Shenphendawa," Jampa says. "*Shenphen* means 'to benefit others.' *Dawa* means 'the moon.' He is the keeper of this temple."

I bow back to him. I can feel Tara in the room, something with invisible arms perhaps, something feminine being channeled through the almost-ethereal lama. The suppleness of his body reminds me of the tiger thangka, and the word *gentle* comes to mind. Slow inhalation. Is gentleness born or bred into Tibetans? Into Buddhists? How has this refined way of responding come to be?

Back down the stairs and into the courtyard, I trail Jampa through twisting corridors to a dormitory behind the Dharma Chakra Center, where he knocks on a tall door. A five-foot monk answers. I stand quietly, one hand holding the other, while Jampa tells him that the teacher he has arranged to tutor me has disappeared for the holiday and that he needs a substitute for five days. Will he consider? The monk hesitates. He has studies to finish. Exams to take. Jampa persists while I stand there feeling tall, almost a foot taller than the monk, who looks around Jampa at this curious American. "All right," he says, bowing his head to seal the deal, then tells me to return at 9:00 a.m. the next day. "This is Sherab Tenzin," Jampa says. "And this is Mrs. Barber."

CHAPTER 10

V. The Sun-Gay Guest House and the Diamond Way

After two days of lessons with Sherab in which we have discussed prayer and practiced meditation, I sit down for dinner at one of two picnic tables on the Sun-Gay balcony. I order the least spicy dish to keep peace with my still unpredictable stomach—vegetable mo mos—and chat with Rona, a sixty-five-year-old physiotherapist from New Zealand, where she lives in a solar-powered house.

"And why have you come to Rumtek?" I ask.

"I have come to work with the Buddhist nuns, the Ani. The monastic order here has no use for them. My group, which studies the Diamond Way, comes here to improve conditions—remodel buildings, repair steps, make sure the nuns have enough to eat."

"What is the Diamond Way, may I ask?"

"The twenty-five million followers of the Diamond Way are currently led by Thaye Dorje, the other Karmapa. The real Karmapa."

Aha—a piece of the great intrigue over who is and who is not His Holiness the Seventeenth Karmapa. I fold my arms on the table and lean on them.

"Think in terms of a diamond," she says. "When placed on a red cloth, it shines red. On a blue cloth, it looks blue. Regardless of the background, the diamond stays the same. Using this approach, the Diamond Way has adapted Buddhist teachings to different societies and times."

Rona is noncombative and seems earnest in her desire to help the nuns. I say good-night and climb inside my sleeping bag, which is preferable to the oily sheets on the bed. I feel restless spirits everywhere. From a spot just below the guesthouse, a dog barks all night, maybe at the eyes of demons and ghosts floating abroad on thin mountain air. A squeaky pump stops and starts continually. Rumtek is not as peaceful as Yuksom, and in this uneasiness my mind turns to diamonds, which I know can also be pink, blue, champagne, yellow, even green. Would those diamonds look the same on a red cloth as a clear diamond? Diamonds are split, beveled, faceted, and polished for a particular effect. They are manipulated. But they are all pieces of something extracted from circular pipes found in the mouths of extinct volcanoes. Their essence is the same, and they are thus a symbol for the purity of a constant idea. So why this fight over who is the right Karmapa? Doesn't the pure idea of compassion for all sentient beings trump everything else?

When morning finally comes, I unzip my sleeping bag, pad to the window in my socks, and open the curtains. My stomach feels like a spoiled, moldy grapefruit looks, and clouds layer the valleys among a vast array of hills. I yearn to stay in bed, to cease and desist from adventure. Except, watching the blanket of clouds smothering the valleys, I realize that I have only two days left. I cannot waste this time. I will never be here again.

At breakfast, I ask the proprietor for an unadorned bowl of porridge. While I wait, Eva, a lawyer, and her husband, Heinrek, a groundwater engineer in Copenhagen, traveling with their three young children, sit at the next table while their nine-month-old baby boy crawls the cement floor. It does not take long to discover that they are more adamant than Rona about which man deserves the title of His Holiness the Seventeenth Karmapa. "We are members of the Diamond Way group in Denmark led by Lama Olé Nydahl," Heinrek announces.

"Can you explain the controversy about the Karmapa?" I ask, no time to waste.

Heinrek, eager for the opportunity, speaks first. "Many monks were coerced into signing a loyalty oath to Trinley Dorje. The Dalai Lama spoke out for him and said he had had a vision of the land where the new Karmapa had been born. But, trouble is, he endorsed Trinley Dorje while on a trip to South America. He could not have been paying sufficient attention to the importance of the matter. And," he adds with emphasis, "you should know that the supposed Seventeenth Incarnation of Karmapa Trinley Dorje is a puppet of the Chinese government."

"We have just been visiting Thaye Dorje in Kalimpong," Eva says. "We were there for two weeks. He is definitely the one who should be recognized."

However sophisticated and dedicated these people seem to be, this exchange gives me the sinking feeling that when people become attached to their beliefs, violence in the name of those beliefs can follow. This divisiveness is not becoming to the idea of Buddhism, to my way of thinking, which proclaims, "Many Buddhists, one Buddhadharma."

I excuse myself and go to my room to watch the clouds lift from the hills beyond Rumtek. Maybe I have already taken sides with Jampa and the painter of the tiger thangka. But why, if all of the boats are heading for the same shore, does anyone have to take sides? And why am I feeling worse? It is time to be better. Well. Now.

VI. TARA TEMPLE REVISITED

Barely able to pick up my feet, I drag them up the hill toward the monastery complex, where I am supposed to have my third lesson with Sherab. Built on the slant of a hillside, the semipaved road curves through the loosely assembled, haphazard village of Rumtek. My legs are shaking. My lungs are rebelling at having to climb, climb, climb everyday, everywhere. The little white terrier of self-pity (the phrase borrowed from Alison Lurie's novel *Foreign Affairs*, which I am currently reading) is nipping at my heels. I am approaching that place of erasure where fear will be greater than the sum of my parts. I am afraid of my body, which is not getting better. I despise its weakness.

Negotiating past the ever-present guards at the entry to the complex, I wander into the courtyard and listen for the sounds of puja—the horns, cymbals, drums, and conch shells encased in silver. Nothing. No chanting. If only I could sit right here. On the ground. Never have to move again. Dazed and confused, I stare at the Dharma Chakra Center. Four days ago, its graduated tiers were exotic and garishly beautiful. Today, the goats, bells, and swastikas seem bizarre. Dead. Foreign. I have no will. This is the end. The pathetic finish to an unsatisfactory life. Where did I ever get the notion that I could understand anything? How did this arrogance arise in me to think I could discover God's whereabouts? I need my mother to parachute out of the heavens, catch me by the hair, and tell me I have already been taught what I need to know. But she is long gone.

Suddenly, I feel something touching my fingers, then tugging on my left hand. I look down. A young lama about eight years old has appeared out of nowhere. He pulls my arm and says, "Come." Confused, I let this man-child take my hand and lead me to a flight of narrow stairs on the outer rim of the courtyard. We climb the same flight of stairs I had climbed with Jampa and follow a balcony walk. I am being led by a child I have never seen before. He takes me to a small room with a sign in English on the door, which registers in my cotton-webbed brain. It is the Tara Temple. I have been here before. But it is time to meet Sherab, to go to the building behind the Dharma Chakra Center with its stairs, stairs, and more stairs.

Taking no apparent notice of my arrival as he chants and counts prayer beads with his fingertips, Shenphendawa strikes the drum intermittently, then blows on a battered copper horn. He is absorbed in the rituals of his calling, which do not seem to include the distraction of visitors. I sink to the parquet floor, struggle out of the straps of my backpack, and sit with my back to the wall. I gaze at two large statues of the Green and White Taras, the female aspects of Buddha. Even though I am ignorant of the fact that Green Tara is said to protect one from fear and that White Tara counteracts illness and guides one to long life, healing, and serenity, I feel tears ready to overwhelm me. Shelter. I have been granted shelter. I will not succumb to emotion, however. I breathe deeply and concentrate on counting the Tara statues in the glass cases on the wall, all 108 of them.

These Taras, these deified statues so lifeless on their shelves, remind me of an exhibit I have seen at the Denver Art Museum—a host of headless Buddhas. Above their empty shoulders, different doll heads were hung on strings—Wolverine, Howdy Doody, a Little Rascal. Who and what is the Divine? One God is what I have been taught, but what about the Greek, Roman, and Norse gods, the numerous deities of Hinduism, as opposed to the monolithic God of Islam and Judaism, the three-in-one God of Christianity? Is there any truth to differing aspects of the Divine? Or is God one and the same, unchangeable, forever and ever?

The young lama takes his seat on a floor cushion next to where I sit. Like any boy, he fidgets and yet responds immediately when the monk asks him to perform a function at the altar. When Shenphendawa is not using the gooseneck drumstick, the boy traces its curved neck with his finger, then pretends to be a drummer without touching the drum.

Having counted the Taras three times, I turn my attention to the alien objects on the altar: small copper bowls lined in a row; a dorje; a Tibetan bell; yellow roses carved from butter; a plate of rupees; butter lamps on the altar in front of the Taras. Taras everywhere. I recall a dim memory of something I have read: Tara is said to have been born from a tear in the left eye of Avalokiteshvara, the Buddha of Compassion, when he sat on the summit of Red Hill in Lhasa and witnessed the torment of human beings as they burned, hungered, and thirsted in a Hell of Ceaseless Torment.

Tara. Kuan Yin. Karmapa. Dalai Lama. Avalokiteshvara. Buddha. Jesus Christ. Allah. Elohim. All looking out on the sea of humanity, all engaged in whispering to the swimming, thrashing children not to forget the big picture. But why am I so bent on being a spiritual seeker when maybe an answer is only a chip of dried paint beneath a fingernail? I so want to know, to KNOW. And yet, sitting on the floor with my back to the wall, I know I do not know.

Except, even as I think that, I remember the Tao according to Lao-tzu. It speaks about darkness within darkness being the gateway to understanding. This thought calms the furor inside. My backpack lies slack on the floor. I surrender to the sounds of Shenphendawa counting his prayer beads and know that he is aware of my presence. He had probably sent the young lama to retrieve me. I lean farther against the wall and close my eyes. My muscles relax ever so slightly. For a few minutes, I give myself over to this place far away from anything I have ever known, except it feels so familiar, the way this comfort is being offered. After about ten minutes in this trance, I realize that I am almost late. I lift myself from the floor and instruct my legs to carry me to my appointment.

I bow to the 108 plus two Taras who must have heard me feeling sorry for myself in the courtyard. I leave an offering on the altar. In my heart, I thank Tara the Rescuer, Tara the Compassionate, Tara the Merciful, the young boy with the shaved head and too-large robes, and my own God— whoever has brought me to this place for a respite. Backing out the door, I bow to Shenphendawa, who is still chanting, and to his young assistant. They are children. Both of them. Children chanting, performing rituals, doing their duty for all sentient beings.

VII. THE THIRD MONK: SHERAB, INSTITUTE FOR HIGHER BUDDHIST STUDIES

With slightly renewed energy, I am negotiating the maze behind the Dharma Chakra Center, entering a familiar-looking building. The hallways of Sherab's dormitory have no overhead lights, only open ends and patches of indiscriminate sunlight, but here it is, his door. I knock. When the small, full-spirited monk, whose face and body seem both young and old, opens the door, he smiles with a quick dip of his head and seems glad to see me. But the sight of him fills me with both joy and poignancy. I suspect he is not used to the conviviality we have shared. Yesterday, at our lesson, he told me he had been sent away from his family in Bhutan at a very young age and had not seen them for a long time. His present goal is to be a scholar and a writer, but he feels it is competitive to be striving among so many in the monastery and to be a genuine practitioner at the same time.

CHAPTER 10

Surprisingly to both of us, we have had exceptional discussions about the difference between prayer from the heart and prayer from the mind, about Mahayana, the higher path for the benefit of other beings and not for the one saying the prayer, and Hinayana, the less powerful path when offered for one's self. "Prayer is powerful because of its motivation," he had said. So much for God help me do this, protect me from that, I had said to myself.

After he closes the door behind him, he gathers a portion of his robe in one hand and leads me downstairs, then to another building and up more stairs to the library with its crammed shelves, its assembly room, its long and wide hallways. He leads me to our classroom with no carvings, murals, statues, or brass bells. He sinks easily onto a black cushion and, with a sweep of his hand, invites me to sit on a cushion across from him. I remove my backpack and drop onto my seat.

"What questions would you like answered today?" he asks in flawless English. He folds his legs into a full lotus and gazes serenely—a be-here-now man.

I want to ask about the two Karmapas and the inside story of the Diamond Way, but decide that is not a good idea. Instead, I unzip my backpack and procure the list of questions a Mormon friend back home has asked me to ask. It did not occur to me to make my own list, as I usually follow my intuition, but my friend had been curious at the mention of visiting Buddhist monasteries, maybe even concerned for my spiritual welfare.

"I only ask the insignificant questions," I assure him with a grin. He smiles and tips his head to one side. "So," I read from my list, "how do Buddhists perceive good and evil?"

He hesitates a moment, rocking back and forth, his hands flattening against his thighs, his elbows akimbo. "Virtuous and nonvirtuous actions." He adjusts his robe back onto his shoulder. "Nonvirtuous actions come through the body (killing, adultery, and stealing), through speech (lying, slander, harsh words, and gossip), and through the mind (evil thoughts, covetousness, and erroneous views). Abstain from ten nonvirtuous actions, and you have ten virtuous actions."

His words start floating over my head. There is a small riot happening in my stomach. Stay, I tell myself as if I were my pet dog. How can I ever find God if I cannot stay here and listen? My finger moves down the tangible list. "How do Buddhists conceive of God?" I ask, trying to keep my legs folded in a half lotus, though my bum knee is complaining. *So much moaning today. Lighten up, girlfriend. Be grateful for what you have.*

"We believe in God, but not as a creator," he says.

"And why is that?" Taken aback, I immediately remind myself to set aside my Christian point of view. Just listen. Do not try to fit his thoughts into your established notions. Listen.

"God is someone who has been liberated, who is realized and beyond this world. We are in a confused dimension, struggling to be a god, but the finite mind cannot understand the infinite mind. The unrealized mind cannot understand the realized mind. Yet we still hope."

Realized or unrealized, my mind is turning to Jell-O, Utah's "state food."

"When we understand our own selves, we can understand other human beings. And all beings are similar in that they wish for happiness, not unhappiness."

Happy to receive these gems that keep dropping from his mouth and yet feeling a power shortage coming, I ask the question I have asked others while trouping through India: "What wisdom would you have me take back to the United States?"

He leans on his lotus knee with one elbow, one finger long against his cheekbone. "Because the United States is a power country, jealousy from other countries arises. Ignorance, desire, jealousy, and ego arise naturally, even if there is no wish for that. What the United States lacks is a genuine—that is an important word—spiritual approach. Unable to understand inner happenings through material advancement, it lacks a genuine spiritual approach and therefore is not a powerful country. Self-realization is what transforms our original thinking."

Suddenly I need to lie down, to curl in a fetal position on my side, and to think of something besides my rebellious stomach, maybe a planet whose people are fully aware that killing each other is no solution to its problems. "I hope you don't mind," I say, hiding my panic. "I will be all right if I can just lie down. But," I tell him as I rearrange the contents of my backpack so it can serve as my pillow, "please continue. I want to learn everything I can. I want to know why you choose this life. Why it is important to you."

I am shivering. I grab my coat, pull it over me, and try to find a comfortable position for my head on my lumpy backpack. *I will not go gently. Breathe.* He rises from his lotus position, rolls up a blanket he takes from a pile of mats. "Here." He kneels by my side. "For your head. More comfortable." He is now towering over me, this wise monk, regal in his small body as he returns to his cushion and sits effortlessly while I am sinking into a waking dream of lotus petals enlarging as they open.

"I am curious," I force myself to ask another question. "How do you deal with the wider community when you are sequestered in the monastery? Do you have contact with people living outside? Is there any kind of involvement?"

"We help others through our efforts toward enlightenment."

"But you have no interaction with everyday people?"

"Only on ceremonial days. We prepare ourselves always, but, no, that is not our way."

That concept is alien. I have been raised with an emphasis on serving others directly. Suddenly, I want to laugh at the idea of this way and that way. I want to hear laughter. Does Sherab ever laugh, I mean *really* laugh? I want to read his insides to find out what makes him feel alive, and yet, I am coming from an entirely foreign sensibility. I have no way of understanding what makes him tick. Truth be told, maybe I am the one who is subdued, with so many of my own points of reference blocking my sight. The better question may be, why do I take everything so seriously?

"Do you like being a monk?" I say on an impulse.

"I have many studies. Many conferences to attend. I have never been good with social things. I have much to learn in that way."

From where I am lying, my head on the blanket, my gaze at him skewed by ninety degrees, he seems a lonely, though not unhappy, man. I feel thin threads of a web being spun between us, though what do I really know of this Buddhist from Bhutan, of what has shaped him, of what has brought him to this place across from me? I check my watch. Even if our two hours is not close to being up, I need to leave.

"I thank you for your time," I say, but as I sit up, I feel a whiteness drawing down my cheeks. *Breathe.* You can do what you need to do. I find a way to my feet and fold my arms into the straps of my backpack. "And thank you for this," I say, handing Sherab the blanket he provided for my head. We chat casually as we walk down the long hallway. He asks if I would like to see what books he studies. I nod. *Breathe.* After perusing the library's complete collection of Chögyam Trungpa's books, I realize that the inevitable is arising in me. Everything is moving up out of my stomach. I run for the door. The halls are long, the floors polished to a high sheen. I don't know my way even if I could dash. But Sherab is at my side. He points to a waste receptacle on the wall, which in no way can hold all of what is boiling over inside me.

All of India and the fourteen-hour stuffy airplane ride and wave after wave of security guards and the paneer pakora's rubbery cheese and the breaking of my nose and the medicine I have been taking and the bad-smelling drainpipes in my guesthouse room, all of it comes up and out of me. In the hallway of the Institute for Higher Buddhist Studies, standing on a polished floor and facing a wall with a flimsy stainless steel waste container with a thin, brown paper bag inside, I retch. It keeps coming. My insides are turning inside out.

When an uneasy calm finally returns, I look at Sherab, who has the most peaceful expression on his face. "Please let me take care of this," I tell him, ashamed and embarrassed, knowing my face needs a handkerchief. I have left an untenable mess on this highly polished floor.

"I will take care of it," he says. "Please, do not worry."

He leads me to the monks' private washroom, tells me it is all right for me to wash there, and then says he must take care of the hall floors. After I thank him seven or ten or twelve times, he leaves. I walk across the bare concrete floor to clean my face with water. There are no towels. There is no mirror for double-checking the damage, but I feel better for the first time in a long time.

VIII. Jampa and Old Rumtek

"Today, I will take you to old Rumtek," Jampa says after my fifth and final lesson with Sherab. I have met him at our regular meeting place outside the entry to the monastery. He starts off in a new direction down a road I have not noticed, past a tea stand, past a crowd of Indian tourists still celebrating Dhasara—saris, saris, everywhere. Brilliant lemon, lime green, and shocking pink. A festive atmosphere, a clear sky, and a peaceful stomach today.

"Please tell me more about the Seventeenth Incarnation of Karmapa."

"You want to know?" he asks, tilting his head.

"I do."

I follow him until he stops midway on a steep hill at a gate in a bamboo picket fence. It surrounds a roughly made two-level white stucco house with an outhouse in the side yard.

"This is my home." He opens the gate.

A small woman wearing the traditional Tibetan *salwar korta*, her long black hair tied back from her face, steps into the yard and shades her eyes from the bright sunlight. We exchange introductions while Jampa translates. Then he guides me to his cluttered office, his computer almost buried in papers and pamphlets. He tells me to find a comfortable spot on the sofa. His wife brings tea. He slips a DVD into his old computer.

"*The Making of Living Buddha* DVD," he says, handing me the cover. I read that the DVD is made by Mind Films, Ltd., that it is an "original epic film" by Clemens Kuby. On the screen of Jampa's laptop in his papers-to-the-ceiling office, we watch the story of three rinpoches living in exile in India being given a "red-ink letter" via mysterious sources in the Iron Horse Year of 1990. The letter was considered a sign, and though talismans were not usually opened, this letter was an exception. After reading it, the rinpoches felt sure that the nomadic area of Lhathok in East Tibet was the place where the next Karmapa would be found.

As the story of the three rinpoches traveling incognito into Tibet, the Land of Snow, unfolds on the tiny square of a monitor, I cannot help thinking about Eddie Murphy in *The Golden Child* and Brad Pitt in *Seven Years in Tibet*. The narrator's distorted voice explains that the three rinpoches told others they were going on an inspection trip. They could not divulge their motives to anyone, let alone the eight million new Chinese settlers in Tibet, who would consider this a superstitious act.

From time to time, Jampa watches me watching the search party traveling by jeep, then on small, tough horses across wasteland. Sitting on a cement-like cushion, I hear about the search for the reincarnated Karmapa, who was said to live in a barren nomadic village located at fourteen thousand feet—no mail, no electricity. The area was once a huge forest, the film explains, but during the last decade all trees were cut down and floated to China. Villagers used animal dung for heating their tents; twenty or more cups of yak-butter tea per day were necessary for survival, and four times a year they packed up and moved to new grazing lands.

A Tibetan actress appears on the screen to portray Lolaga, the reincarnation's mother. She was purported to have said fifty thousand prayers before becoming pregnant with this son. Wondrous signs accompanied his birth in the Year of the Ox: a rainbow over the family tent and the sound of conch-shell horns resounding for two hours. The middle son of three boys and five girls born to this exceptionally poor family in Lhathok is now His Holiness the Seventeenth Reincarnation of the Karmapa—the protector of all beings. His success will depend on the power and greatness of his spirit and the degree of his enlightenment.

After Jampa removes the DVD and returns it to its plastic case, I sit in silence. So many stories about the origins of the Karmapa. So many points of view. But then Jampa segues into another story closer to home: "Because of India's political situation with China, I cannot obtain citizenship or a job in India. I have to rely on charity positions to support my family."

"How did you come to Rumtek?" I ask.

"When I was baby in the winter of 1959," he says, "I was sent to Mustang over high mountains on horseback in a blizzard. Tibetan revolutionaries gathered there. I was wrapped in a blanket in a basket on one side of the horse, my brother on the other. Bitter snows. My parents had already fled to Nepal. It was fifteen years before my brother and I saw our real parents again. The Sixteenth Reincarnation of Gyalwa Karmapa brought me here to Rumtek to be a primary-school teacher for twelve years. Now I am the secretary of the institute, though it is not an official job because of India's agreement with the Chinese government."

After we finish our tea, we say good-bye to his wife, and Jampa, who has become a real person to me for the first time—an ordinary man who needs a job, a man trying to make ends meet, a man trying to find safety through devotion, a man wanting refuge from the chaos and sometimes cruelty of his life—leads me up a steep, switchbacked road to old Rumtek. It is a place set apart from the rest of the town on a high point—monasteries always being built on high points in Sikkim, altitude readily available. We follow the dusty road to an unoccupied and lifeless temple. Once–brightly colored banners and gyalchens hang limp from the rafters, as sun barely penetrates the chalky windows. Then we climb a narrow ridge to a crematorium in the midst of juniper trees.

"The Sixteenth Reincarnation of Karmapa designated this as a holy place," Jampa says. "Buddhists bring their dead from great distances to be cremated here." The altar of the crematorium is a high grill built above a pit for wood fires. It is surrounded by three shelters with covered seating. "Lamas sit there to perform puja for the deceased. This is a very holy place," he says again and bows in its honor.

Suddenly, I am humbled by the hundreds of years of Buddhist tradition that this crematorium represents. Jampa has honored me by bringing me here, yet I wince. There has been an arrogance in my visit to Rumtek. I have expected to be taught, no questions asked, expected to be welcomed into this important center of Buddhism—a novice passing through, an interloper looking for something. I feel both small and large, both insignificant and valued in the silence of this crematorium beneath juniper trees.

As we descend that hill in the late afternoon, Jampa pulls a folded piece of paper from inside his vest. He hands it to me in a faltering way, as if I might refuse it. He resembles a torn piece of paper tossed by a stiff breeze, wrinkles around his eyes, weathered with worry. "Please read," he says in a way that makes me want to make the world right for him.

I do not unfold the paper until I return to my room. In a xeroxed 2006 article from *Tibetan World*, Thupten N. Chakrishar wrote that 1.2 million Tibetans had died following the Chinese occupation: 173,221 tortured in prison; 156,758 executed; 432,705 killed in fighting; 342,970 starved to death; 9,002 "suicides"; and 92,731 "struggled to death *thamzing*," whatever *thamzing* means. I refold it. I put it in a zippered pocket, then spend some time thinking about the displaced Aborigines, Maoris, and Native Americans.

IX. JAMPA AND THE SUN-GAY GUEST HOUSE

The next and final morning at Rumtek, Jampa takes me to the monastery courtyard for the last time. He leads me three times clockwise around the periphery of the Dharma Chakra Center. "This will bring good luck in your travels." I follow him through the door of the temple of Mahakala, where, inside a small chapel, a monk hangs the traditional kata around my neck. He points to other white scarves hung above the altar if I want to add my own scarf and its blessing to the collection, then pours water from a holy vessel into my hands. I hesitate, considering whether or not to drink this possibly unfiltered water. Jampa lifts his hands to demonstrate a cup for drinking—a plea for me to accept this holy water. Maybe I will just rub it across my lips. He looks at me, reading my thoughts. "This is what you need," his eyes say. I submit. I let the water of Buddhism slide over my tongue and down my throat.

He then takes me outside through a side entrance to a makeshift tearoom while a group of barefoot and bareheaded teenage monks play hacky sack. We sip tea together at a wobbly picnic table, waiting for an overdue phone call from the driver, who is supposed to be here by now. Watching the young lamas scuffle and laugh, not unlike other young boys do, I know that this encounter with Tibetan Buddhism has changed something in me: a subtle, but definite shift connected to the antiquity of this world, to its traditions. Rumtek is not a place to look for evidence to shore up one's beliefs; it is a place that demands reverence.

"Let's go down to the gate," I say, "and check for the driver." Jampa follows me this time. We walk past the wall of the village temple into which prayer wheels have been built. In single file, people turn the brass cylinders clockwise to accumulate virtue and purify their unholy deeds. I take my turn spinning the wheels and watching them whirl.

"Let's check the guesthouse first," I say. We descend the hill at a brisk pace, but as I turn up the branching road to Sun-Gay, Jampa stops.

"You are staying here?" he asks. I nod. "I will meet you below," he says abruptly. He bends his head down and becomes a man determined to take himself in the opposite direction.

"Don't you want to come with me?" I ask. He mumbles something from which I pick out a few words. "The owners there. The families support . . . the other Karmapa." He makes a wash-my-hands-of-them gesture. His face radiates contempt. "I do not want to see them."

At that moment, the sands of harmony shift. Impermanence reinstates itself. I feel as if I were in the middle of the eternal feuding between the Hatfields and the McCoys or the Israelis and the Palestinians. The all-too-familiar face of duality is alive at Rumtek, too, but then why should I be surprised? Selflessness is no small accomplishment in whatever culture or religion. There will always be opposition in all things, as my own religion professes. But why can't I find a simple, streamlined, clear directive to the Divine not dictated by anyone else?

When my driver backs out of the parking lot, I wave good-bye to Jampa, who stands behind the iron bars at the checkpoint—him locked into his world, me leaving for mine. I think about the timeworn image of ships passing and fog closing over their receding shapes as we descend the hill from Rumtek, climbing another, repeating the same up-and-down process many times to reach Darjeeling, where I will meet up with my friends. Jampa is a good human being. He cares about his family and his roots. But I understand something. I am dealing with human beings born into or claimed by Buddhism, as well as Christianity, Judaism, Islam, Hinduism. All humans, in their reach for perfection, have a need to be right. We need to transcend this tendency to say that God is this or that if peace is ever to return to the earth.

If I had asked Sherab how this feat could be accomplished, he might have quoted something from the Digha Nikaya 12.78: "A certain brahmin said to the Lord [Buddha]: 'Reverend Gautama, it is as if a man were to seize someone by the hair who had stumbled and was falling into a pit, and to set him on the firm ground—just so, I, who was falling into the pit, have been saved by you!'"[4] He would suggest that I follow the way shown by Buddha.

If I asked my Mormon parents, they could have quoted John 3:16–17: "For God so loved the world that he gave his only begotten Son. . . . For God sent not his Son into the world to condemn the world; but that the world through him might be saved." They would insist that Christ is the only way back to God.

Buddha is said to have descended from the realm of the gods. Christ is said to be the Son of God. These saviors seem similar. Why does there have to be my savior and your savior? My way and your way?

Lacy trees arch over the narrow road and cast spiderweb shadows on the hood of the car as we pass a sign that reads "Sikkim: A Land of Peace and Amity. Keep It Neat and Clean." In the middle of the next switchback, the late morning sun strikes the rearview mirror on my side of the car, leaving a stark afterimage on my retina—bright white, red, then dark blue. I blink it away.

The full-blown sun today, the first day in many days. I breathe into it, wishing we could all feel this brilliant, this illuminated, at least once in a while. Nothing else compares with this light, not even the glorified diamond. Even though the root word for *diamond* is *adamas*, Greek for "unconquerable," it seems that diamonds are a paltry metaphor against whatever backdrop—red, yellow, or blue cloth. They are stones found deep in the earth with a few imprisoned shreds of light. A rough block of uncut diamond can be chiseled into a marquise, a full-cut brilliant, a baguette, an oval, or a pear, just as humanity can be shaped into Shi'ites and Sunni, Kurds and Turks, Chinese and Tibetans, the Karma Kagyu and Gelugpa lineages. Southerners, Northerners, Easterners, Westerners, Jampa, and me.

The sun's brilliance on this blue-sky day feels unconquerable, indivisible. No wonder people have assigned God to the skies with their vast blue everywhere, their mirages of horizons, their sense of no-end-to-anything that will always elude capture.

X. Waiting for Kanchenjunga, Once Again

Back in Darjeeling, it is morning. Today, the trekkers return. In an hour, I plan to meet up with Meg and her new friend—a thirty-eight-year old actress named Lloyd (of London, we had laughed), who has committed herself to four solo months in India because she thinks she has not challenged herself in life and wants to prove herself worthy to be called an adventurer. She hopes to find out what she is and is not made of. Over last night's dinner, Lloyd told us that during the first two weeks of her time here, she had been bedridden with dysentery. We soul sisters concluded that beer for breakfast or a nightly shot of whiskey is the only way to kill the messy microbial breeders. India has been a strong-minded teacher. No wimps allowed. The three of us bowed low here. Yet something wordless has happened to who we were and what we were about.

For now, I sit at my window at the Cedar Inn, waiting for another brief glimpse of Kanchenjunga. I ruminate on something I heard yesterday: climbs have begun again because of tourist demand, though trekking companies have agreed to stop six feet short of the top.

Is nothing sacred? Does everything have to be conquered and owned by someone else's flag? Why do all of us come here and try to take something back—a glorious climbing accomplishment to the highest, most dangerous peak or, in my case, a few precious words from a monk? I hate the news about the trekking companies and suspect that the Buddhists do not like it either. They believe in the individual spirits of such things as stones, trees, moths, and lightning. The supernatural is respected here. This mountain is alive. The monasteries are alive with compassion for sentient beings, and I am feeling better. So please, tell me: Is God all of these things?

The mist drifts, settles, and obscures Kanchenjunga. A woman's veil. This mist is the way of things. It is what happens while one waits for God's face to appear. But maybe that happens only when the weather permits—and nobody will be quite sure of what they have seen.

Note: In 2008, Ogyen Drodul Trinley Dorje, His Holiness, the Seventeenth Incarnation of Karmapa, was allowed to travel to the United States.

A REFLECTION OF THE SUN

What is faith? Is it a finger pointing to the moon? A finger pointing to the reflection of the sun? In the spring of 2006, Dan Wotherspoon, editor of *Sunstone Magazine: Mormon Experience, Scholarship, Issues, and Art*, called to propose that I give the "Pillars of My Faith" speech at the magazine's annual symposium—a disparate gathering of active, border-line, and former Mormons, plus any other interested parties. The symposium and the magazine had provided a connection for me after I had decided to leave Mormonism (as if someone can separate so precisely from her roots). They had served as a point of contact for me and others who felt alienated, yet could not disentangle themselves.

But faith . . . , I wanted to say to him. So ubiquitous. So uncatchable. I wanted to laugh, if just a little, that he was asking me to speak on this subject when I often felt miles and even continents away from the condition of being faithful.

"I had better say no, Dan. I will probably be out of town."

But as we were about to end our conversation, maybe worried that a negative response could seal my faith as extinct rather than dormant, I changed my mind. Truth be told, faith was something I desired, hoped for, trusted in. I felt bare at the thought of having no access to it. "Okay, Dan. I'll do it."

Phone in its cradle, I sank into my favorite reading chair, dangled my legs over one arm, and exhaled big air. On one hand, I knew that my mother, God rest her soul, would be comforted if I could stand in front of an audience and express my undying faith in Mormonism. She had taught me five ways to the wind that the LDS church had the answers to life's big questions. But was that faith or faith in Mormonism?

My faith in Mormonism had changed shapes through the years—sometimes round as a full moon, sometimes a sliver of light, sometimes totally absent from the landscape. It had not always been exemplary, if that was what mattered here. Worse yet, there had been those times when I wondered if that religion might prove to be only *one* story about the human need to explain life and its creation, *one of many* stories about people obeying a divinity they could not see. But Dan had not asked me to speak about faith in Mormonism. He had asked me to speak about faith. In the quiet of the morning with my head propped against one wing of the chair with dart holes in the leather upholstery—left by my sons once playing dangerous darts while their mama was not watching—my mind rummaged through its curiosities about faith. I was not sure what it was, what it is.

Not so long before, I had divorced twice, my grown children had scattered, and I was living alone, at times feeling as though I were sinking rather than swimming, succumbing to loneliness rather than a healthy solitude. When I had had trouble finding reasons to keep my personal show on the road, a friend recommended a therapist specializing in clients with strong religious backgrounds. After questioning me for an hour, she commented on what she observed to be my deeply ingrained spiritual feelings. "You need to stop denying your need for their expression."

"Maybe," I told her, "because I have equated spirituality with my particular religious heritage, which I have been battling, I have tried to squash the impulse. Maybe I believe that religion has failed me. Or, maybe," I added, "that I have failed religion."

"You need to differentiate religion from spirituality," she said. "And from faith."

Though I had not been attending Mormon church services for over two decades, I often dressed in my Sunday best to sit on the pews of other churches when Sunday rolled around. I wanted to feel the Spirit. Somewhere. Anywhere. But I had formed no connections, no community, and skated the edges of what sometimes felt like a black hole.

My eyes followed a slash of sunlight moving slowly across the carpet next to the chair where I sat, the way it brightened the reds in the Persian carpet. I continued sorting through my thoughts about faith. As much as I had wrestled with it, tried to bury it under a rock, it had always been with me, persistently alive in my core, a constant companion. My faith *was* like a finger pointing to the moon rather than the sun—more comfortable with reflected, comforting light than with the sun's brutal brilliance (I grew up in the Mojave Desert, after all). My faith liked hanging out in unadvertised, shady spots, where it could flourish without being observed or commented upon. It was more like the tendrils of a bursting seed reaching toward the sun's invitation to come out and grow. And I, human seed that I was, could not tunnel back into the cool soil as a smart earthworm might do.

During a philosophical discussion I was having over lunch with Dan (a cousin through our shared polygamous great-great paternal grandfather, Jonathan Calkins Wright), he suggested a favorite book, James Fowler's *Stages of Faith*. After purchasing a copy on the way home, I settled into my reading chair and bolted down the trail of Fowler's words, especially drawn to his idea of faith as imagination. Referring to the German term for imagination, *einbildungskraft* (literally, the power of forming into one), he writes, "Faith, in its binding us to centers of value and power . . . into communities of shared trusts and loyalties, gives form and content to our imaging of an ultimate environment."[1] As I read late into the afternoon, I was mesmerized by the stages he described that traversed the abstract territory of faith. I scratched some sound-bite notes onto paper:

- The Intuitive-Projective stage, "the fantasy-filled, imitative phase in which the child can be powerfully and permanently influenced by examples, moods, actions, and stories of the visible faith of primally related adults."[2]

- The Mythic-Literal stage, in which the person "begins to take on for him- or herself the stories, beliefs, and observances that symbolize belonging to his or her community."[3]

- The Synthetic-Conventional stage, a "conformist" stage in the sense that it is "acutely tuned to the expectations of significant others and as yet does not have a sure enough grasp of its own identity or the autonomous judgment to construct and maintain an independent perspective."[4]

- The Individuative-Reflective stage, in which the person begins "to take seriously the burden of responsibility for his or her own commitments, lifestyle, the beliefs and attitudes."[5]

- The Conjunctive Faith stage, in which one reclaims and reworks one's past and opens up "to the voices of one's 'deeper self.' This fifth stage understands the sacrament of defeat and the reality of irrevocable commitments and acts. . . . Alive to paradox and the truth in apparent contradictions, this stage strives to unify opposites in mind and experience."[6]

- Universalizing Faith, the fully actualized nature of faith, which is represented by such people as Jesus Christ, Mahatmas Gandhi, Thomas Merton, and Mother Teresa.[7]

I was drawn to Fowler's liberating notion that faith could move beyond an imitative conformity and become something more alive and aligned with one's innate sense of the world. Accepting my own thoughts had been something that felt furtive, almost as if I were unwilling to listen to God if I followed my own promptings. After all, I had laid miles of synaptic tracks through the years: faith was all about believing in the Right Way as prescribed by church authorities, about "holding to the Iron Rod," and about following absolutely every line item of Mormonism, even though some of these items were confusing folkways born of the culture as much as the doctrine. How could I separate the pure from the not so pure? The wheat from the chaff? Faith from faith in Mormonism alone? How could I come to peace with those elements of faith that resonated with me and not be overwhelmed by the rest? Faith, faith, and faith, it seemed, was running out my ears, the word plastered across my eyes. Once again, I wrestled with the old argument: should I return to the ranks of the faithful Latter-day Saints once again? What did that mean?

A few years before Dan's phone call, I had summoned the courage to swallow my pride and darken the door of the local Mormon ward. Yet I still felt like an impostor, an expatriate attempting to live among the Mormons once again. Sometimes I woke at 4:00 a.m. in a panic. *You had better get with the program. Fall into line. Follow the rules. Shape up.* But did going back to church mean heading into a chute and synchronizing one's vision with some kind of LDS checklist? Even Brigham Young said something about not narrowing oneself. Faith was not about being a rubber stamp or playing a numbers game. Christ had condemned praying from housetops or appearing to be a follower when one's heart was elsewhere.

Fowler's writing suggested being fully alive to paradox and to the truth of apparent contradictions. Opposites could be unified, dualities transcended, and one could function apart from either/or, good/bad, black/white through the integration of contradictory ideas. This idea appealed to my imagination—God dwelling in a place transcendent and all-encompassing.

At my writing desk the next morning, I asked myself what could be considered the absolute essence of the terms Latter-day Saint, a Mormon, a Christian? Ever since I was a baby in my mother's arms, I had heard speakers from the pulpit at church reading from the scriptures that "faith in God and in his Son, Jesus Christ" was the ultimate belief for Latter-day Saints and all believers in Christianity. I had underlined those words in my own scriptures. But, paradoxically, the Mormon way contained other requirements, making the Good News of Jesus Christ seem less straightforward.

On the stretch of whiteness on my computer screen, I made a list of "Mormon Requirements for Being Considered Faithful": faith in Christ; repentance; baptism for the remission of sins; service to others—"Charity never faileth"; the health laws of the Word of Wisdom; obedience to the prophet's continuing revelation; ten percent of one's earnings given to the church; sacred covenants to help build the Kingdom of God here on earth. And then my list veered off into subjectivity: women's main calling as mothers, men's as priesthood-holding heads of the home, even though the corollary to mother is father, not priesthood holder. Strictly established patterns of moral behavior, including the length of a girl's skirt or a limit on how many piercings an ear should have . . . Cynicism was creeping into my list. That old bugaboo.

I felt discouraged, stopped typing, sat back in my chair, folded my arms on top of my head, and crossed my outstretched legs. The perennial juke-box in my brain clicked on with the hymn I had sung as a teenager: "And we hear the desert singing, Carry on, carry on, carry on! Hills and vales and mountains ringing, Carry on, carry on, carry on! Holding aloft our colors, we march in the glorious dawn. O youth of the noble birthright, Carry on, carry on, carry on!"[8] I could even hear a few congregational voices trying to hit the high A-flat at the end, sometimes screeching, sometimes hitting the note purely and squarely, idealism intact. How could I ever be that valiant, good soldier for right who sang "Carry on" and who followed everything in precise, lockstep fashion, especially if I was not sure I agreed with the equal importance of all these things? Did I have to fit into one-half inch on the spectrum of humanity if I wanted to be a Saint?

Sitting up in the chair, I poised my fingers over my laptop's keyboard. The white lettering was completely rubbed off of the N key. I stopped to think about how I could not find that letter if I had not typed it for so many years and automatically known where it was. Was this an example of faith?—trusting the N key without seeing it?

"If I have faith," I typed next, "what do I have faith in?" I listed: (1) kindness and an open heart; (2) integrity; (3) sincerity; (4) respect for others as I would want respect for myself; (5) patience, charity, and compassion; (6) inspiration received through prayer and study not only of scriptures, but of great music and literature; (7) the pure laws of God; (8) the belief that I am a child of God.

And what about Fowler's "sacrament of defeat"? I needed to check the context for Fowler's words, which had rung a bell for me on first reading. I stretched from my chair to pull his book from its tight place in my overcrowded bookcase and sat back to thumb through the pages.

I had definitely known defeat in my lean years—point-blank, bottom-line, embarrassingly solid defeat. The bad poker hand. The big blows to sense and sensibility. What descriptions did not manipulate rhetoric in creating effect for this drama? But I had been totally shattered like a Humpty Dumpty who thought she would never find all of her pieces again. Scattered into jagged pieces, I had no ability to resume my arrogant position of knowing my place in the order of things. However, it was a time when the ears that had broken off with the rest of Humpty Dumpty were able to hear, for the first time, what was meant by the words "a broken heart and a contrite spirit." Now, reading about "the sacrament of defeat," rather than mere defeat, I realized this could be the doorway to the reclamation of my spiritual roots.

The open book in my lap, my hand splayed across its pages, I remembered repeating those words as a child, "a broken heart and a contrite spirit," without a glimmer of understanding. Rote words. I had always considered them a quaint figure of speech, something poetic, something abstract, until they actually happened to me. To know brokenness firsthand is a different matter from hearing or reading about it. It is not a place a proud person can inhabit. I had once been proud of my admirable supply of faith and integrity but actually had no idea what that meant until I experienced the full-on wipeout of a broken heart: divorce from a marriage of three decades, a rebound boyfriend with a drug addiction, a second marriage that ended abruptly. I fell to the bottom of the well, looked at the circle of light above, no rope or hand in sight, and begged of whoever might listen, "Help me. I have no answers. I have no idea what to do here." Through that symbolic death, I also discovered that I had no idea what it meant to have courage. I had had to summon all the courage I had ever heard about, which ironically required faith, to emerge from the deep, dank, narrow well.

I held Fowler's book against my chest—an old habit from childhood when I loved the book I had read. However, I could not imagine anyone except a fanatic volunteering to be placed in the refiner's fire to become something more holy, something more exquisite Fire burns. End item. I also felt uneasy when people attributed their troubles, their cancers, their accidents to God's will. It seemed simpler and more rational to say, "That's life. Those are the breaks. We are human."

Whatever the explanation, though, being broken apart and dealing with the bits and pieces of what was and what was not important had been the most valued initiation of my life. I could accept it as a sacred covenant: to lie down in flames while lifting a finger out of the red-hot coals to motion to God for help: "Yes, this proud, proud person needs you, dear One."

I closed my laptop, but before I left the house to run errands, something nagged me to go to the bookshelf again and reread a passage from C. S. Lewis's anthology of readings from George MacDonald, the nineteenth-century writer, clergyman, and professor of English literature at Bedford and King's College in London, whom J. R. R. Tolkien and Lewis claimed as a spiritual as well as a literary mentor. I found the dog-eared place and read out loud: "That man is perfect in faith who can come to God in the utter dearth of his feelings and desires, without a glow or an aspiration, with the weight of low thoughts, failures, neglects, and wandering forgetfulness, and say to Him, 'Thou art my refuge.'"[9]

It is easy to believe in the sun and the moon because they are so visible, but when it comes to knowing how the sun, the moon, and the earth came to be, created by whom or what, then some kind of leap of imagination or reliance on someone else's imagination (call it scientific or mythic, whatever you wish) is the only answer. But, no frills attached, living on earth means going through each night and day with faith that it will keep spinning on its axis. Waking in the morning usually means having faith that we can get out of bed. What is it that gets us out from under the covers? That fills our lungs with breath? Is it God breathing us?

Faith is impossible to capture in one's hands or head. It is a scramble for a foothold in shifting sands. It is a reaching up of one's hand and believing it will be caught, maybe not right away, but when one most needs it to be caught. Faith is like the wind, easy to feel but difficult, if not impossible, to describe. And faith is definitely the finger pointing to the moon rather than being anywhere close enough to touch its rim or feel its shape. The moon is a chameleon, changing shape, hiding in plain daylight. If you stand in Little Rock, Arkansas, and look at the same moon on the same night at the same hour as a friend is looking at it in Salt Lake City—two different lines of sight such as when you close one eye, look at your hand up close, then close the other eye and your hand seems to have moved— you experience a parallax: an angular difference in the direction of that heavenly body as measured from those two different points on the earth's surface. Your fingers will not point at the same exact moon.

When I stood before the Sunstone audience scattered throughout the big box of a room that night in August, an audience willing to sit for an hour to listen to two speakers discussing pillars of faith, I outlined faith's six stages according to Fowler. I spoke of how my own faith grew from an innate sensing that Spirit lived—something I could feel welling inside me at times—an inner, irradiated trembling of sorts appearing in the unexpected and unpredictable.

Spirit manifests itself in beauty, I said, in those things that interrupt your normal breathing pattern and fill you with wonder—like the time I was hiking and happened upon a young moose calmly pulling grass from its roots or the morning a covey of quail waddled through my backyard, their configuration shifting as the chicks trailed behind. You can find it in the clear eyes of someone who trusts you, in that moment when a friend reaches out for your hand, in music that feeds you in ways food never will. Spirit was with me when I had emerged from the bottom of my black-hole well with the conclusion that it was enough to be alive and to appreciate the beauty of this world. That was sufficient reason to live. Mr. Butterfield, my Las Vegas High School English teacher, would have been proud. I had finally understood Keats's "Ode on a Grecian Urn," which we had discussed and analyzed for an entire week. His words had come alive: "Beauty is truth, truth beauty,—that is all / Ye know on earth, and all ye need to know."[10]

Spirit manifests itself in words, I continued, even though I recognized that words were often not strong or large enough to carry what needed to be carried. I confessed to picking up scraps of faith from lyrics of popular songs, such as "Climb Every Mountain" and "It's a Wonderful World," and from words to Mormon hymns: "Love one another" and "All is well, all is well." I was stirred by the faith of writers working for hours and days to say something concisely and essentially, and by their belief that it is possible to do so. I was moved by ecstatic poets who seemed a direct conduit to the Divine, especially Shams-ud-din Muhammad Hafiz, a fourteenth-century Persian poet (1325–1389), a Sufi from the heart of Islam:

> Listen–
> Listen more carefully to what is around you
> Right now.

A REFLECTION OF THE SUN

In my world
There are the bells from the clanks
Of the morning milk drums,

And a wagon wheel outside my window
Just hit a bump

Which turned into an ecstatic chorus
Of the Beloved's Name.

There is the Prayer Call
Rising up like the sun
Out of the mouths of a thousand birds.

There is an astonishing vastness
Of movement and Life

Emanating sound and light
From my folded hands
And my even quieter simple being and heart.

My dear, is it true that your mind
Is sometimes like a battering Ram

Running all through the city
Shouting so madly inside and out
About the ten thousand things that do not matter?
. . . .
. . . O listen–
Listen more carefully
To what is inside of you right now.

In my world
All that remains is the wondrous call to
Dance and prayer

Rising up like a thousand suns
Out of the mouth of a
Single bird.[11]

187

Third, I said, I find Spirit in my Mormon heritage and the determination of my ancestors. I am a product of what they insisted on creating with their irrepressible belief in a Kingdom of God here on earth. Those roots are my roots, and my faith is stronger because those roots have provided a platform of trust in divine guidance. I am inspired and moved by the power of my Mormon community, in which people strive to love with open hearts, even though they struggle with what love means and how best to express it. The good news is that no matter how overwhelming and authoritative my religious community has sometimes seemed to me, there is a built-in elasticity, a give and take, that comes from the desire for a Christlike response to others' needs and fears. That goodness is no simple accomplishment. To love the humble, arrogant, or disenfranchised is a thing of beauty.

I paused and looked out over the audience. They were listening, but there was not enough fire being exchanged here. I was going on too long.

I find Spirit in the faces of my sons, I forged ahead with a growing sense of guilt. Their wives, my grandchildren, my loves, my friends, my neighbors. Even though my children, their father, and I are not configured in the same constellation we once were, we still care for each other's welfare. Family does not have to end at its legal boundaries, and love is there if we allow it to show its face in the way it chooses.

As if I had seen a smoke signal on yonder mountain, I realized that I had been caught up in the mellifluous beauty of my words and phrases, playing the violin *sotto voce*, trying to capture serious beauty with serious music. I leaned my elbow on the podium, feeling the need to be less of a poseur, not so coy or romantic or precious with my pretty words. Forget the lofty ideas about faith. Forget about defining or distilling it for anyone else.

The truth I suddenly wanted to shout like a born-again preacher at the climax of his hellfire and damnation speech, was that I could not have made it out of the well, the fire, the mess I had made of my life, without believing it was possible. Something in me had hoped in "the substance of things not seen." I had not only hoped, but believed. And many in this audience sitting so inertly in front of me, believers and nonbelievers, had been through the same wringer, distillery, or refiner's fire. *What about you?* I wanted to shout. Isn't it furious-making to have to deal with trouble? None of us ask for it. I knew I had tried to be a "good girl"—the noble person my mother had hoped for. And what did I get? The ox's mire. No guarantees. But maybe it was time to admit, my mind stopped its rampage for a second, that whatever it meant to be a sinner, I was one. "None is good save one, that is, God," the New Testament said (Luke 18:19). But simultaneously I felt anger rising that I felt the need to label myself good or bad and play into those binary oppositions I did not believe in. Sure, I was afraid that God did not love me anymore because I had transgressed. Sure, the child in me was hurt to displease her Father, even though the woman I had become hoped that the real, genuine, authentic God was larger than all of this and did not need mollifying. These things were the long and short of what I wanted to shout but did not.

What I did say was that it had been hard to walk back into the Mormon Church after staying away for so long. Swallowing pride was tough, and I did not like hearing people talk about it glibly, as if it were a matter of sipping milk.

And, I added, even though I had walked back into church, I still felt the need for a balance between personal integrity and the desire to be part of the fold. I did not want to live by a flock mentality. Belonging happens to be a temptation for me, but at what price? What do I give up if I am more interested in belonging than in following the dictates of my conscience? Where is that fine balance point between self, which is a creation of God, and God himself?

Bending closer into the microphone, I again quoted George MacDonald: "We are and remain such creeping Christians, because we look at ourselves and not at Christ. . . . [We forget to] lift up our eyes to the glory which alone will quicken the true man in us, and kill the peddling creature we so wrongly call our *self.*"**12**

Midpoint. Speech nearing the finish line. Past the point of scolding myself. Past my born-again-preacher-speechifying urge to undercut everything I had so carefully crafted. Time to explore the sacrament of defeat, the idea that had rung pitch-perfectly clear to me when I had first read about it. The point was the transformation of pain, the moment of being caught in a current of faith that carries you beyond the shore where you have watched and wondered.

I moved to Minnesota in 1998, I launched into my story, knowing everyone's ears would perk up when a story was being told. This was the year after my first divorce was final, and I, a bird without its nest, was casting about to find a place where I belonged. In the process, I had become enmeshed in an obsessive romance, which had taken me out of the West to the foreignness of the Midwest. When the relationship came to the abrupt end to which it was destined, darkest night sucked on my toes, and I could not extract myself from a deepening depression. One morning, I knew I needed to get out of the bleak house where winter still chilled the walls. Because water had always calmed me, I drove halfway to the Mississippi River, bicycled the rest of the way, then walked along railroad tracks on the Wisconsin side. The ground was soggy with spring rain; the flowers had not bloomed, and the day was overcast, but the sound of water calmed the fear in me.

That evening, I said, after I packed my bike in the back of my Ford Explorer and drove toward home, I passed through one especially small town. Everything was closed down for the night. But in the middle of the darkened main street, I saw a lighted store and a man cleaning straw from a window display. Something in me told me to turn my car around and go back to that store. Which I did. The door was ajar. Noticing a box lid full of noisy chicks on the floor and remembering it was the week before Easter, I poked my head inside and asked if I could come in.

I paused, took a breath, surveyed the audience to see if they were with me. This was story time, after all. People's postures had changed. Their expectations were on alert. "I would like to read an excerpt from my memoir, *Raw Edges*":

"Mind if I look around?" I heard myself saying, surprised at the words that came out even though I didn't feel sociable.

"Why not?" the man said, setting the last chick in the cardboard lid. Then he shook his head and put two fists on his hips. "See how they've already messed this cardboard lid? I wanted to keep this display for the kids until the weekend's out, but these chicks might take over the store in the meantime. I wish they weren't such a big Easter tradition around here. Feel free to look around. My wife's in back unpacking a shipment. There's Pepsi and Sprite in the back room if you want anything to drink."

The store: a potpourri of ceramic flowers, cups and beehives, candles, teapots, cards, things I'd seen many times before in small gift shops. But as I approached the back of the store where the man's wife worked at a counter, I could feel something different about this place. Something deep and old. Something contrary to the usual knickknackery. The box the woman was unwrapping had the aura and smell of a faraway place. The cover paper was thick. Woven from something dusky. It had postal markings from another world. Bolder inks.

"I hope I'm not disturbing you."

"Oh no," she said. "The store's closed, but I needed to unpack this shipment." The woman spoke with a Russian accent.

As I eyed the boxes on the floor, the woman bent to retrieve a wrapped parcel, laid it carefully on the counter, unwrapped it, then cradled a nesting doll next to her heart. "*Matryoshka*," she cooed, as if she were holding a small child. "Let's see how many are inside," she said. "There will be seven or nine or eleven. If there are eleven, the smallest one will be like a comma. How anyone could ever paint it is my question. So hard not to lose."

As the woman took the first doll apart, I watched the next and the next and the next doll appear, all painted with winter scenes: a road to a house overshadowed by woods; a snow-topped barn with a picket fence; a Russian Orthodox cathedral with onion-bulb domes. And the smallest of the seven dolls finally appeared. She was painted with a picture of the deep dark woods, that forbidden place where wild wolves and fanged bears lived.

Six dolls were now lined up on the counter, each one issuing from the inside of another, except, of course, the first one—the mother who presented the prime *matryoshka* self to the world. Each birthing, each splitting, had produced another doll wearing the green-painted scarf and the gold-leaf babushka crown, yet each slightly different from the one before. The woman still held the smallest doll in her hand, and I wondered if I was looking at the core of something, except this doll didn't feel like the be-all, end-all essence of anything or anyone. She resembled a hard, darkened, shriveled peanut. A painted chip of wood. Was there something profound about arriving at this last doll? The breaking apart was done, but so what?

Should I make a metaphor with this smallest doll? Was it possible for humans to disassemble themselves and eventually find a pure self? What was the truth of these nesting realities? Was there a seventh, ninth, or eleventh self in each of us that was the real thing? Or were all the selves the real thing? Maybe there was only a mysterious river of divine liquid flowing through the terrain of everything.

Still holding the smallest doll in her hand, she looked at it intently as if it might spring to life. Then she looked up at me as if asking if I thought this thing could be something more than a piece of wood. She smiled over the tops of her thick eyeglasses—a slightly mischievous smile. I felt I was in the middle of a powerful, musky fairy tale—the archetypal wise woman smiling at me, passing on something from the ancients.

"Thanks for letting me look around," I finally managed to say, realizing I couldn't contain my emotions if I didn't hurry out of the store. I needed to go home, even if it wasn't full of children or a husband or a lover or anyone else. It was time to stop entertaining sadness and drama and get on with the business of being alive. Time to know that one can't really know the whys of anything, that one has to put one foot in front of the other and be grateful for the gift of *matryoshka*, the gift of someone changing straw for baby chicks, the gift of light in a store long past its closing hours.[13]

I looked up from my notes in that magic silence when a reading ends and the audience has not responded yet. I wanted to hold on to that piece out of time, chisel it off and take it home in my hand, but the audience needed to be released to their conversations about faith, their cars, the streets, their homes, their hotel rooms. Of course, there was the wrap-up, the thing I had been taught to do in a college speech class and while listening to hundreds of sermons through the years. What I wanted more than anything was to become a song or a whisper from the wind that carried the depth of my feeling about faith, about truth and beauty. The closest I could come were a few lines from "The Layers," a poem by Stanley Kunitz:

> I have walked through many lives,
> some of them my own,
> and I am not who I was,
> though some principle of being
> abides, from which I struggle
> not to stray."[14]

Because of the gift of a broken heart, I have come to know an unexpected wholeness. Because I have known the downside, I savor beauty in a heightened way, similar to an elevated view of a valley after rain. There is beauty in the running from, the rowing toward, and the imagining of God. Amulek had an inkling of this when he said in the Book of Mormon, "Yea, even that ye would have so much faith as even to plant the word in your hearts, that ye may try the experiment of its goodness" (Alma 34:4).

Because of my carved-into-the-bone belief that someone is listening, that something is alive that is greater than the small "I," and that there is meaning to this craziness called life, there is a presence in me willing to bow before this Very Large Presence, to unzip my chest, take my heart out, and put it in God's hand. To trust this exquisite relationship in which I ultimately have no doubt that I and those I love will be guided in the direction we need to be guided.

"The Lord is my light, then why should I fear?"[15] I could have sung at the final moment of my speech, filled with the fervency of Spirit as I have often been in Mormon gatherings. This would have closed the occasion with a burst of faith-promoting, beauteous joy, making everyone glad to have been in the audience and glad that there is such a thing—faith and people who will talk about the pillars that have held theirs up. I had tried my best to put a face on faith, yet I still believed that a major component of faith is *not* knowing, *not* having to know. Maybe the most honest thing I could have done would have been to raise my hand and point my finger at the ceiling in the direction of the moon reflecting light outside the building and hope I was pointing somewhere close to its place in the night sky.

Chapter 12

AT THE CANNERY

I am driving east on I-70, just out of Denver. I am looking for silos. I am also listening to jazz master Herbie Hancock on his new CD, *River,* a tribute to Joni Mitchell. *You have to love that Herbie,* I am thinking. Tina Turner is singing "Edith and the Kingpin," something about victims of typewriters and how the band sounds like typewriters. I laugh to myself. I am one of those victims, who is emerging from my cave where I write every day, to volunteer at the Aurora Cannery, a division of LDS Welfare Services.

Flat roof. American flag. Silos with catwalks against a gem-blue sky. I notice a network of antennae. Probably for shortwave emergency communication with all of Colorado as well as Salt Lake City. When Tina sings her last word, I turn off the engine and the music, then realize that I am fifteen minutes early. I smile at the inverted irony that I had been fifteen minutes late a few weeks ago when arriving at another welfare project in Salt Lake City, a soap factory.

I had called my friend Virginia from Denver to tell her I would be visiting Salt Lake for a few days and to ask if we could get together. She suggested that we do something besides lunch, something more like our normal life together when I had been her neighbor. "I have already signed up for a day at the soap factory when you will be here," she said. "Do you want to come along?" "Yes," I said. "That would be good. Like old times."

She and I arrived at 9:15 rather than 9:00 a.m. We had been looking for 526 South Denver Street, but addresses in the city were usually given in grid terms. We had driven nervously up and down several streets until we sighted the telltale tan bricks of an industrial-looking building in an otherwise residential area. We were definitely tardy when we walked inside the glass door of Deseret Soap & Detergent. Still, we were laughing, full of spring sunshine and exuberance, friends reunited for a few hours. An imposing man with "Larry" embroidered on his blue jumpsuit greeted us. I suspected he had been in charge for a lot of years, the way he rolled his eyes at the dilettante volunteers who had entered his domain without the serious intent to match his. He pointed to a sign: "No jewelry allowed, no watches, no cell phones or purses." He pointed to a row of lockers.

"Are you ready?" He tapped his foot.

"Almost." Both suddenly aflutter, we hurriedly stuffed our purses in the lockers, then pinned the keys to our T-shirts. We followed Larry, who padded down the concrete hall on gummy soles. He opened a heavy door and ushered us into his sacred temple of soap—a huge *Star Wars*-looking warehouse where gargantuan stainless steel contraptions hummed songs of metal on the move and filled boxes of laundry detergent with powder before sealing the cardboard. Solidified ribbons of newly poured soap rolled past on a conveyor belt before being guillotined into rectangles. Everything moved in concert in this factory of mechanical parts and arms.

"You will be working with shampoo today," Larry said.

He assigned Virginia a job taping cardboard boxes with a supersized tape machine. He told me to help George (who was already in place) and keep an eye on the bottles moving down the line toward the spigot dispensing pink shampoo. Then he stood back with his arms folded across the elastic waistband of his jumpsuit to make sure things ran smoothly. But there was trouble in Soap City. When George, the dour man who had been running the operation solo while waiting for us laggards to arrive, launched into his orientation demonstration, there was a snafu. Suddenly shampoo bottles jumped ship, flew through the air and bonked against the shiny concrete floor. Chaos reigned. I wanted to laugh. I could not help my good mood.

The bouncing bottles reminded me of the Three Stooges. I forced down the corners of a breakout grin. We had a Larry, and I felt like a Moe ready to move down the line to where Virginia was taping boxes, elbow her in the ribs, and break into shtick with a "Hey, Curly." But Larry, trusty manager that he was, interrupted that thought. He stepped up to the spigot, jabbed a big red button and caused more bottles to jam into each other. More empties flew through the air and skittered across the floor.

"Give me a minute," he said, grim under pressure.

Virginia took that time to unstick the tape from the roller of the tape dispenser she had been using. I assessed a stack of gigantic cardboard boxes, wandered over to peek into the only open one, then swam my hand through a sea of empty plastic bottles. But the true-north magnet for me was the long ribbon of soap being slashed by paper-thin blades into rectangles. Hypnotic rhythm. Smooth, sharp cuts forming bars that disappeared into a bulky machine. Curious, I walked around to the other side and felt like a kid in the Magical Land of Deseret Soap & Detergent when a newly minted bar of soap popped out, stamped with a beehive.

I once belonged to a church-sponsored class of twelve-year-old girls who were known as Beehive girls in the Mutual Improvement Association (MIA) for teenagers. We were taught about the industry of bees, which worked, worked, worked for the community. (I realized later that no one ever said much about the drones, which worked, so to speak, only for the queen bee.) The traditional hive is the logo for the State of Utah. It ranks high on my list of favorite symbols. Now I see it imprinted on the broadside of a bar of soap—a reminder that in this church industry is a sacred thing. Work, work, work, with joy—a strong Mormon ethic stamped firmly into my own broadside. The key to a good life is service to others.

Now, sitting in the parking lot of the Aurora Cannery not far from Denver International Airport, listening to the peripheral sound of a jet streaming overhead, I check my watch. Ten minutes to go. Time is ticking slower than usual. I find the button to lower the seatback and try to get comfortable while I wait. Larry and Salt Lake still on my mind,

I involuntarily hum "When you're helping, you're happy"—a song learned in Primary before I went to MIA—"And we sing as we go."

Mumbling under his breath after several stops and starts (no expletives—this was a church-run operation), Larry, the old hand in this business, had gotten things under control. The march of the bottles began again. This time, each empty stopped in the correct position for its manually operated fill-up to the right level. Then each was sent on its way to have its top tightened into end-product shape before Virginia hand-loaded them into boxes and taped those shut with her heavy-duty dispenser.

My job was to keep a supply of empty bottles ready for filling and to replenish the bottle-top bin for the man regulating the flow of pink shampoo. As I rushed around trying to be all things to all people, I moved the huge open box of bottles from one spot to another (it was not heavy, but my efforts could make a good impression for anyone who might be watching, maybe Larry) and unloaded it, ready for the assembly line. The man at the spigot kept an eagle eye out to make sure I came nowhere close to being remiss in my duty.

After a few missteps and one reprimand, I synchronized my rhythm with the machines and the process. I felt as if I were a dancer in a mechanical *corps de ballets*. I kept the assembly line supplied before George, the humorless spigot man, could catch me being lax again. I felt a surge of pride in my competence: *Has this soap factory ever had such a fine worker, such an efficient cog in the wheel of industry?* But then I heard George's voice calling out, "Pay attention." I had let the supply of bottles come dangerously close to the red line indicating he would soon be bottleless at the spigot. *Pay attention, Phyllis. Step it up.* Panic hit when I realized that the big cardboard boxes with more supplies were taped shut, the open one empty. I had no knife. Fingernails would not work. *Don't panic. Where's Larry?*

I looked around the concrete warehouse/factory and saw him in the northwest corner directing a forklift operator moving pallets of boxes destined for the Bishop's Storehouse, where those in need could obtain cheese, bread, meat, canned tomatoes, feminine-hygiene products, and soap, of course. I had been to that store without cash registers. But now I needed to get bottles on the assembly line. *Where's Larry?* Luckily, another employee walked by, saw my dismay, pulled a box cutter from his pocket, and sliced the sealing tape. He helped me carry it and pour its contents into a bin. Back in business again.

By now in the cannery parking lot, the sun on the driver's side of my car is heating up the window glass even though it is cold outside. I wish I had a towel to tuck into a crack at the top, something like a maiden's handkerchief signaling that I need the sun to let up. I am ready to go inside for the canning *du jour*. I have heard that the Greeley tomatoes are the A1 product from the Aurora Cannery. It is too early in the season for tomatoes, so I wonder what we will can today. When I look at my watch, it seems as though time has stopped. I shake it, though that is an old-fashioned, useless thing to do with a watch run by batteries. I am still early. I breathe deeply, center myself, ease the tension in my shoulders, slow my overactive thoughts. But they, as usual, keep tramping across the open field of my mind. I cannot believe I am sitting here like a faithful Latter-day Saint, waiting to be a cog in the machine. *Why am I doing this? Am I back on the stage again? I still have my questions. I still have my arguments.* But then, I remind myself, some part of me speaking its truth, that when I hear anyone speaking unfairly about the whole enterprise, I am there. The Defender. There was that difficult evening in 2002 when I lived in Park City . . .

I had been asked to speak to a group of New York socialite women gathered for a week of skiing and après skiing. The acquaintance who had invited me was a part-time resident of New York City and Park City, and her friends had expressed curiosity about Mormonism. Would I please present an after-dinner speech on the culture and a brief overview of the theology?

Having been inactive in the practice of my religion for twenty years, I wondered if I was the best person to speak, but I had, after all, spent the first forty years of my life totally immersed. I had come from a long line of nineteenth-century-pioneer ancestors converted in Wales, England, Denmark, even Massachusetts and Illinois, some bumping across the plains in Conestoga wagons, some pushing handcarts and wearing out their shoes, but all finding something deeply invigorating about the idea of Zion here on earth. It represented something to which they could give their lives, their all, their everything. As they traveled westward, their passion for God became even more thickly mixed with the blood that flowed through their veins and then into mine. Scratch my skin and you would find a Mormon there. I had tried to disaffiliate myself from the religion, frustrated with its challenges to my wide-ranging intellect, spiritual adventurousness, and concern for women's voices being underrepresented outside the domain of homemaking and often unrecognized. However, my Mormon childhood, my roots, tradition, the music, the community, even the language and concepts of the cosmos inhabited much too much of my sensibility for me to think I could make a clean break. I was certainly still Mormon enough to discuss the exotic faith with a group of curious New Yorkers.

The hostess and owner of this never-ending mansion on the side of a hill overlooking Deer Valley had opened her doors with grace. She had shown my sister and me into her breathtaking home, where old money spoke softly from the muted corners of every room. I noticed a copy of one of my books at each place setting, purchased as a favor for each guest. After introductions, I was immediately enamored with the savvy group and their anthropological sensibility: a willingness to learn, to listen, to actually treat Mormonism as a subject worthy of consideration. I had been used to other responses—dismissing Mormons as a quaint/weird anomaly of the other Wild West; decrying the way they sent out their young, naive, robotic missionaries dressed in funereal suits with those grim plastic nametags on the lapels; denouncing them as an insidious cult of long johns–wearing crazies with Stepford wives. While I was still involved with the church years before, a well-known poet had asked me, "How can anyone as smart as you still be a Mormon?" I had surprised myself with the uncharacteristic sharpness of my response. "Do yourself a favor, and don't ask a dumb question like that." Very few outsiders understood the appeal or complex demands of living a life patterned after Christ's teachings in a Mormon format.

But there was an element of surprise that evening in Park City: the inclusion of four guests from Salt Lake, all of whom I had known when I had lived there from 1970 to 1990 and had been involved with community voluntarism. One of the high-profile women was known for her voluble opinions about Utah culture and the ever-present majority population. The divide between Mormons and non-Mormons was a constant topic of newspaper editorials and secretive conversations, and the substance of sniper remarks from both sides of the fence. I wondered if the Salt Lake group would be open to a fresh encounter with an all-too-familiar subject.

I had become accustomed to a wariness around the fact of my Mormonism in Boulder City, where I had spent my early childhood. In that small town of four thousand, my family lived among geologists, engineers, employees of the Bureau of Reclamation, members of Veterans of Foreign Wars, Masons, Catholics, and members of Grace Community Church, all employed in the construction and maintenance of Hoover Dam (called Boulder Dam in those days). There were relatively few Mormons in town. Even though our family was what I thought of as regular as apple pie, with one mother and one father and four kids in a tidy and a tiny white-plastered house with red shutters—a true family of the fifties—my World-War-II veteran father, who had served in the navy, had instructed us children to keep our Mormonism to ourselves. "Too many people do not understand what the religion is all about. They have cockeyed ideas about who we are."

So we learned to keep a tight lip on the subject of our faith. We knew we were viewed as a peculiar people. We knew that our belief in Joseph Smith translating the Book of Mormon from gold plates, in his conversations with the Godhead and angels, and in latter-day prophets who kept our religion current with God's desires and whom we were taught to obey as our consciences allowed, was something that could cause people to raise their eyebrows. And, of course, there was the ever-present topic of polygamy, which everyone loved to seize with canine teeth and roll their eyes about, even though the Manifesto of 1890 had withdrawn official permission for new plural marriages. I could appreciate the difficulty of the topic—both my paternal and maternal great-great-grandfathers had been polygamous—but these things could be skewed and twisted and turned in strangulating, frightful directions.

In that tastefully decorated Park City mansion I spoke for thirty minutes on the bare bones of the theology and on the history, specifically on one of the first United Order experiments in Brigham City, when everyone's crops were taken to the Bishop's Storehouse to be distributed to all. My great-great-grandfather, I added, had played an essential role. I spoke of the paradox of a hierarchical, patriarchal church that was informed with a deep regard for free agency. I spoke of how Joseph Smith, the original prophet, had expressed in his personal writings that "the first and fundamental principle of our holy religion is that we believe that we have a right to embrace all, and every item of truth, without limitation or without being circumscribed or prohibited by the creeds or superstitious notions of men, or by the dominations of one another"—and how this applied to all members, not just to men.[1] The irony, however (which I did not mention), was that this expression of diversity seemed to be on the back burner these days.

The women seemed open-minded. They admitted they knew little about the religion and seemed genuinely curious during the question-and-answer period. After five minutes of questions, the hostess raised her hand. "Why don't Mormons have dinner parties?" she asked. Just as

I was mentally formulating an answer to her what-I-considered-to-be-off-the-wall question, one of the women from Salt Lake City waved her hand impatiently. I called on her, then realized she had raised her hand to ask a question that was not a question. "You are not talking about the reality of the Mormons," she stood to say. "You are not talking about the rednecks from the rural part of the state who have no conception of separation of church and state, who take a lion's share of control over the legislature—the ones who vote for guns to be allowed on the University of Utah campus and think that by their very numbers they can run things however they see fit. You are not addressing the problems in education and in fairly representing the opposing point of view." She seemed a prickly heckler from Hyde Park (the kind I had heard about when speakers in London churches had talked about Mormon missionaries proselytizing) parachuting into this living room in Deer Valley and standing defiantly on her own soapbox.

"I was not asked here to address the problems," I said, trying not to be defensive, my familiar default position. "I was giving an overview of the culture and the theology. Of course there are problems, but that is a subject for another lecture."

I knew the problems well: I had not expressed my concern with the oft-repeated Mormon claim of being "the only true church," a stance that had not seemed so pronounced in Joseph Smith's day. He was too busy making it happen. That posturing made me uneasy because it created an unnecessary divisiveness with other religions, not unlike the insensitivity that occurred when a few ill-mannered Mormon children in Utah taunted non-Mormon children for being blind to their truth. I knew that Utah Mormons were used to being the majority, used to their own language and their own conception of right and wrong. I also knew that they were caught up in the busy and demanding world of their wards and stakes, inadvertently making the uninvolved feel peripheral. Worse yet, many nonmembers felt that Mormons were interested in them only as converts, not as friends. Back in the seventies I had written about this divide in an article for *Utah Holiday* entitled "Culture Shock," observing that a move to Utah challenged Mormon newcomers as well. But please, I wanted to say to that woman, Utah was not the first place in the world having to deal with majority versus minority. Consider Croatia and Bosnia-Herzegovina, India and Pakistan, Northern Ireland, even the entire United States itself.

The fact that people seemed very sure about who and what Mormons were had become a source of irritation. I myself had played that game. For a time, I had tried looking down my nose, not being native to the Utah culture, after all. I had taken a sophisticated, above-it-all stance and sniffed at young couples with overly large families using up the educational resources at the school without paying a fair share of the burden, since there was no tax penalty for large families and I had heard that Utah had one of the lowest percentages of state money spent for education per child. I had groaned over some legislative decisions and liquor laws that ignored people who thought differently. But while I was living in Park City and gradually, subterraneously, reconsidering my roots, I had also been coming to an awareness that I had an immature understanding of my religion and of Jesus Christ. He not only said, "Feed my sheep," and provided fishes and loaves, but also was a source of solace and salvation that I was only beginning to comprehend.

The hostess had raised her hand again. "Please tell us why Mormons don't have dinner parties. I really want to know."

"It is not that they don't have dinner parties," I began cautiously, still torn by the challenge from the Salt Lake woman, her words on the cusp of my mind. "They often have people over for dinner. Mormons are very social, actually, especially among themselves. Their entertaining, however, is done on a practical level, as they are very busy with their families and church service, such as genealogy, working at welfare canneries, and taking food to neighbors with new babies or loved ones who have died." I stalled, trying to stay focused, trying not to short out from the demands on my knowledge and my position of being the authority on a complex subject.

My words began to feel as though they were whirling, going nowhere, unintelligible. "Also, Mormons do not drink alcoholic beverages. Sumptuous dinner parties usually presuppose a familiarity with fine wines. While some Mormons have no objection to providing wine for their guests or telling them to bring along what they want to drink, this still makes for an awkward dinner party."

As I saw a jungle of hands being raised, including the hand of the woman whose comments had worked their way beneath my skin, I felt hunted. I did not want to stand up there anymore. I had subjected myself to old wounds in my psyche long enough. I had left this religion. So why had I accepted the invitation to speak to this group of women, defending it, wanting them to understand something that even I had said did not matter?

"I am sure I have taken more than my time," I finally said. "Thank you for inviting me here tonight and for your interest. If you have further questions, feel free to talk to me afterward."

As I drove home with my sister, who was no longer affiliated with Mormonism, I vowed not to accept that kind of invitation again.

There are still five minutes before I am due to sign in at the cannery and stash my belongings in a locker. I might as well close my eyes for at least three of those minutes. I could turn on the Herbie Hancock CD again, but I am not in the mood. I roll down my window a smidge because the magnifying-glass sun is almost burning my shoulder. The cool breeze helps.

A couple of summers after my speech in Park City, on a hot July day in 2004, I drove through Provo Canyon to Robert Redford's Sundance resort to hear the caustic columnist Molly Ivins speak. I would not want to be on the wrong side of her tongue, though I suspected she was not a total sidewinder beneath the lingo. When I arrived at the Tree Room, I saw the prominent woman from Salt Lake City who had been so outspoken at the Park City dinner two years earlier. We exchanged greetings, though her response still burned hot in my memory. She had seemed so dismissive at the time, sure of her position, even arrogant, and I could be good at holding on to a grudge. I took my assigned seat, which I was grateful was not next to hers.

After a sumptuous brunch at which prime rib was sliced onto plates next to a selection of opulent fruits, vegetables, sauces, and puff pastries, the plates were cleared and the crowd quieted to hear a speech from the lively Molly. Touring to promote her latest book, *Who Let the Dogs In?*, she took us on a brief, wild ride to visit the unruly characters in politics, including the top dog known as Dubya. Afterward, she asked for questions. A man raised his hand and asked, "Is Karl Rove an undercover emissary for the Mormon Church in Washington, D.C.?"

"Hell, no," she said. "He goes to some Presbyterian church, something like that, and doesn't have anything to do with the Mormons. Where did you get that idea?" The next part of her response was something that literally caused me to open my mouth in astonishment. "And furthermore," she said, "I think people say things about the Mormons they would never say about a Jew or a Catholic or whatever they are. There is a lot of disrespect."

Molly Ivins said that? And the woman from Salt Lake heard it too?

Yes! I wanted to raise a triumphant fist. *Yes!*

I had no intention of going back to Mormonism when I bought a house in Salt Lake City in December 2002. I had lived in the city from 1970 to 1990. That was the place where my first husband and I had raised our three sons before moving to Colorado and going through divorce proceedings. But I had been living in sharp contrast to Mormon beliefs for almost twenty years—living with a boyfriend (forbidden), sometimes drinking wine or tea, shopping on Sunday, and never attending church. In one of my moves after my divorce in 1997, I tried Park City so I could be closer to my younger sister but not too entangled in my religious roots. Then, trying to right the ship, I impulsively married a local man. The marriage lasted twenty-one months and was devastatingly disappointing. Not knowing where I belonged, I moved back to Salt Lake to be close to old friends and well-established networks. I needed something when so much else seemed to have failed.

But after ten months of hiking and biking and sometimes attending other churches on Sunday mornings, one day I smelled winter coming, the end of the crisp autumn days. I noticed the change in the light. Sunday mornings had become like other people's Saturday nights for me. The dawning of the Sabbath had always meant it was time to get ready for church. A lifetime of that habit had made its indelible mark. I often felt restless in those early hours.

On that particular Sunday, a neighbor named Belle, another divorced woman, called to invite me to sing in the ward choir with her. "Singing is good for the soul," she said, probably hearing overtones of depression in my voice. On a whim, I decided to go along, possibly influenced by my readings of Carl Jung and the Dalai Lama, who both spoke of reclaiming one's roots. After all, I could keep to myself in the choir and not get caught up in the rigmarole of being called to a church position or answering questions about my worthiness for a temple recommend (Mormons cannot go to their temples without a bishop's interview). I did love music and the chance to sing. But after a few weeks, when we were told we would actually be singing in sacrament meeting, the plan changed.

Walking into that meeting by myself, walking into that lair of "happy families" sitting shoulder to shoulder on the benches, felt like walking the gauntlet—a self-conscious sinner returning to the chapel with a sign around her neck: "I am alone; I am not with my family; I am not like the rest of you anymore."

I walked tall, acting proud, pretending immunity to this all-too-familiar setting with the organ playing prelude music and people chatting amiably before the meeting. I had known what it was like to sit in this particular nest with my own family—secure, safe with my chicks at my side, Mother Hen gathering her polished brood with shined shoes and slicked-back hair close around her, tucking them under her wing during the meeting, urging them to think about Jesus during the sacrament rather than play with a miniature pinball machine or draw giraffes and tigers with crayons.

I walked toward the choir seats on the speaker's stand. I took my seat cursorily, feeling like a displaced person. Facing all of those trimmed and shaved Latter-day Saints in whom, at first glance, I could detect little obvious diversity, I took a deep breath to keep from weeping in front of everyone. As I fought tears, I saw a man who had been sitting behind me in the choir seats making his way out of his row and then walking toward me. He held out his hand. "Hi," he said. "My name is Jim Pearce. I just want to say it is nice to have you with us in the choir. My wife and I have heard you playing the piano when your windows are open and we are out walking. We would love to hear more sometime." "That's nice," I mumbled, feeling as exposed as a snail without its shell. He had picked the perfect, right/wrong moment to approach me, when my protective shell was not in place. Sometimes there are moments when things change, when there is an opening, a little shaft of light, a recognition, moments when the guard is down and when the tide comes in with a wave that curves in a different way than any other wave before it. Jim could have approached me another time and our exchange would have been idle talk, but something about him or something about the moment and its timing caught me by complete surprise.

"I play the banjo," he added. "Maybe you will accompany me sometime." Then it was time for the meeting to start. We nodded to each other as he turned back toward his seat in the tenor section.

After he sat down, the congregation sang the opening song, "Love at Home." I averted my face, tried to stay the tears, though they were coming fast. This was a song I had sung many times. This chapel was my home, my childhood, my family. I surveyed the people when I dared through the wet veil over my eyes, not quite able to focus, but somehow seeing something more than the concrete wall of self-righteousness I had imagined when I first walked in. Those were individuals out there, not just a brick wall of conformity. It was not fair to lump them into one monolithic unit designed to make me feel uncomfortable because I had strayed from the path.

A few days later, when Jim's wife, Virginia, called to ask if they could come by for a visit, I did not quite know what to do with myself. After the meeting at which the choir had sung, Belle had told me that Jim's wife was the daughter of President Gordon B. Hinckley, the current Mormon prophet. I felt briefly like the duck girl from the village noticed by the daughter of the king. I had grown up bearing my testimony of the gospel every first Sunday of the month, saying how I was grateful for a prophet to lead the church. As cynical as I was, I could still be impressed, even touched, by the thought of having the daughter of the prophet grace the threshold of my home. Yet when they came by for the visit, I relaxed immediately, intuitively knowing that these two understood what it meant to live according to Christ's teaching. I felt that I could be myself and that I would not be forced into anything. "We are not here to change you," Virginia said to prove my point. "We like who you are." Before they left that day, Jim and I arranged to practice some Beatles' songs together and work them up to perfection so he could make a recording to give to his grown children and their families.

During the following two years that I lived alone in Salt Lake City, Jim and Virginia were like two patient photographers waiting for an animal to come out of its lair. They never prodded me with a stick. They helped me feel safe by saving a seat next to them on Sundays.

Also during those years, Virginia, another friend named Laurel Olsen, and I volunteered several times together at Welfare Square, one of the church-related services I could render with no hesitation. We bagged bread in the bakery, catching slices after they passed through rows of sharp blades and easing them into a plastic bag. We helped package fruit-drink powder on a day when another machine was acting up and granules of cherry-colored powder sprayed onto the floor, under our feet, so that when we walked we crunched. We toured the cheese factory and were told about atmit, an indigenous Ethiopian porridge of oats, honey, and milk refor-mulated by the Deseret Dairy from oat flour, powdered milk, sugar, salt, vitamins, and minerals. Six hundred tons had been shipped to Ethiopia in 2003 to aid children whose digestive systems had almost completely shut down due to lack of food. Given two tablespoons every two hours about eight times a day by a team of doctors, nurses, and other volunteers, the children graduated to something more substantial. Atmit had also been sent to Uganda, Israel, Sudan, Niger, Southeast Asia, Bangladesh, Chad, and the Gaza Strip.

It is finally time for my shift at the wet-pack cannery. Finally. I raise the back of the seat, grab my purse, and climb out of the car. A few strangers are gathered at the front doors, but no one seems to be going inside. Not in the mood to socialize just yet, I lean back against the cold metal of my car and fold my arms across my jacket. I am living in Denver now, close to my three sons—the Wild Barber Bunch—their wives, my four grandchildren, and my first husband, David, who is, now that the battle cries have faded, a good friend. I am trying to work out what it means to be family again when Mother and Father are not married anymore. But it is not bad. I love my sons too much to be away from them. It is satisfying to feel almost united again. I am still going to church, though I sometimes feel periph-eral, as if I were supposed to be at the center of something and am not. But then I remember how people can feel lonely, and isn't the higher purpose to reach out and be a friend rather than wait for one to come?

The cold from the metal of the hood is seeping through my jeans, making my legs feel like ice, a wake-up call to go inside and practice welfare—something that benefits both the giver and the receiver. I am happy to be here, even though I still feel like a stranger, maybe an impostor, in this role. But as I am walking toward the glass doors, I think of how, just a week ago, I took the bus to my office. That morning it seemed as though all of Africa was aboard, no one speaking a word of English, the aisles jammed with strollers, women with babies in their arms, and tall, thin men. About five stops down the line, in front of the New Covenant Church (which served the Ethiopian Orthodox Church community—Africans dressed in white ceremonial robes sometimes lingered outside the building on certain Sunday mornings), everyone disembarked, the women juggling their babies and barking orders to the willowy men. When they had cleared the exits, a somewhat bedraggled Caucasian man boarded and sat behind me. I surmised that he was en route to the VA hospital not too much farther along the line, probably a Vietnam vet. I had met so many of them on the #10 bus line. "Must be some kind of a church meeting," I said, expressing my curiosity out loud, "but then, it's a Friday morning." "No," he answered. "They've probably come for food."

I had gazed after the last of those Africans streaming across the street and entering the church. Feed my children. Feed my sheep. The loaves and the fishes. Give them this day their daily bread. Feed them. Take care of their hunger, and you will be filled with Spirit.

Spirit shows its face in the most unlikely places and times. I first became acquainted with it as a child when I prayed to God, my Father and Friend. I trusted that he would catch me if I fell, that he cared about my well-being, that each creature was of his making and therefore beloved by him. Beneficence reigned beyond the staging of this world.

I had also heard my father, who served as bishop of the Boulder City Ward (which met in an old wooden church building small enough to be transported on wheels from Las Vegas), talking about stranded travelers he had helped by giving money from the church and from his pocket and arranging shelter. I had accompanied him on Saturday mornings when he directed the building of a brick chapel because he was the bishop, not because he knew the contracting business. Members of the ward came out to help, some of them knowledgeable about construction, most not. He was a good shepherd to his flock, a man who could be filled with Spirit as he tended to their needs for food and shelter as well as the needs of their souls. Once, late at night, I overheard him talking to my mother after he had been gone all evening.

"He shot himself in the head," I heard my father saying. "Do you have any idea what it is like to pick up the pieces of someone who has blown off his head?"

"He's lucky to have you, even if he's gone," my mother said.

"I wish I had known he'd hit bottom," my father said. "I wish he had at least called me first."

I was never privy to the exact details of this story, but I never forgot the image of my father that haunted me before I returned to sleep—him scraping walls and ceilings and trying to gather together a man he had loved and worried about.

And so it is that I am moved to spend a day at the Aurora Cannery, one of a network of over 750 Mormon storehouses, canneries, thrift stores, and family-services providers. The manager directs me to a row of black rubber boots hanging upside down on poles to dry and warns me to be careful stepping over the orange and yellow hoses. Unsupervised, I meander through the facility, surveying large stainless steel baskets next to voluminous pressure cookers, cardboard boxes filled with Ball lids, a row of emergency buttons, a round stainless steel tabletop with twenty round-hole cutouts at its edge.

The six women assigned to the round table, including myself, are short, tall, wide, hefty, wiry. The others could be doctors, lawyers, or Indian chiefs for all I know, their hair and most of their features hidden inside their gauzy shower caps. We stuff mounds of ground beef into tin cans, then send them down the line where lids are sealed and pressure cookers steam. We laugh and make smart remarks. We are sisters. Three hours later, we clean the room with pressure hoses and pressurized hot water. There are squeegees to clean the floor, to push the water and remaining bits of ground beef into a drain in the center of the floor. When everything is spic-and-span and I have retrieved my purse, I take the outside sidewalk to the dry-pack wing to check it out.

"Sister Carlson," her standard plastic nametag reads, is seated at a rectangular folding table in a cavernous warehouse. She greets me cheerfully. I ask her a few questions about the operation, and it is as if I have turned on a spigot. "Mesa, Arizona," she says with high enthusiasm, "has a huge welfare cannery with a monster truck packed and ready to go at all times. When a tornado or hurricane is forecast, a truck will be on the road before the storm even touches the ground. They are ready for earthquakes and tsunamis, too."

Resting her elbows on the table, she grins with delight: "Two churches were listed by the media as being the main source of help to those hit by Katrina, one of them the Mormon Church, the other The Church of Jesus Christ of Latter-day Saints." She laughs a can-you-believe-they-don't-know-it's-the-same-church laugh. "The genius of this system is that there is someone to receive the goods on the other end who knows how to distribute and deliver them where they are needed."

I used to tire of what I considered a certain smugness, this Dudley Do-Right infatuation with one's goodness and accomplishments. Today, though, I respect her pride and dedication. Today, I do not feel separate from, above or below Sister Carlson. Oh so subtly and gradually, I am being folded back into the fold. I have given up resistance somewhere along the way.

As I depart for the parking lot, I read a poster in the foyer, something written by a Sister Jean Christensen while serving a Philippine mission: "Ultimately, I sense I have only . . . been whole when I've divided myself among those who needed me. I've only stood tall when I've stooped to help those that needed lifting." There had been a time when I would have thought, "How saccharine. Give me a break, Mary Poppins," but today

I set my cynicism aside. To be saved spiritually, people need to be saved temporally. Feed my sheep. We are one. Love one another.

As I drive away from the Aurora Cannery listening to Herbie Hancock's incomparable piano accompanying Corinne Bailey Rae, who is now singing the title track, *River*, about Christmas coming on and the upset over lost love, I feel that vulnerable part of myself rising, the part that gets kidnapped by duality, that asks, is this the right way to live life or am I only kidding myself with unreal idealism? Mentally, I scan my emotional interior for that hard edge in myself, the dependable part that will keep me from going too soft. Maybe jazz will save me. Turn up the volume. Blow those horns. "I wish there were a river I could skate away on," Corinne wails. But today I am immune to the sadness those lines have elicited in the past. I have been there, done the blues, and at this particular moment I do not share that sentiment.

Chapter 13

AN UNCERTAIN THEOLOGY

True to the faith that our parents have cherished,
True to the truth for which martyrs have perished,
To God's command,
Soul, heart, and hand,
Faithful and true we will ever stand.

—Evan Stephens

The questions always come when I tell people about my twenty-year hiatus from Mormonism—the Latter-day Saints, the LDS (not the FLDS), the Mormons. They often look at me with the squinted eyes of curiosity. "Hiatus means you have returned. Right? Why did you go back?"

I hesitate. First, I need to explain the prehiatus. In one piece.

Descending from twelve out of sixteen great-great-grandparents who crossed the Great Plains in covered wagons and handcarts in the mid-1800s, I was born into a Mormon family exceptionally proud of its pioneer heritage and devoted to the restored gospel of Jesus Christ. Honest, earnest, and devout, my parents raised their four surviving children to be proud of and to exhibit the same dedication to the faith.

I followed my parents' counsel when I packed my bags for Brigham Young University to find a good husband and get as much education as I could before the wedding bells, not an unusual request for a young girl in the early 1960s. At the end of my junior year, I married a returned missionary in the Mormon temple. I assumed he was "true to the faith" we both shared. I finished my degree in music, gave birth to four sons, and was happy in the church—playing the piano, directing roadshows (short,

215

funny plays produced by Mormon teenagers and their leaders), teaching cultural refinement for the Relief Society (the women's organization), contributing to ward dinners and the community at large.

I also had a wide community of friends who were not Mormon. I loved to read, often wrapping myself in a blanket on a cold day to read the writings of Lao-tzu, the Catholic mystics, Krishnamurti, Yogananda, and the Dalai Lama for inspiration. Blithely rocking along, thinking my husband and I were headed in a good direction, I tried not to open my eyes to the dis-ease in the margins of my marriage. I begrudgingly understood that for my husband, who came from a religiously divided family so unlike my own, the religion was an ill-fitting shoe. He was struggling with wounds he felt he had received from trying to squeeze himself into the Mormon mold. An oil-and-water dilemma. I tried to understand his diatribes as well as his point of view, thus becoming a mental gymnast pretzeling myself around and adapting to his perceptions, wants, and needs. Both of us wanted to keep our family together.

While I likely would have stayed in the church, questioning some of its practices from within and contributing to a deeper spiritual understanding where I could, the nature of our marriage precipitated my journey away from Mormonism. Keeping our family foremost in our minds, we decided to seek elsewhere, to attend other churches, and to consider diverse metaphysical ideas. Thus, I was thrust into a new, even exciting, world, while still honor bound to search for truth and understanding wherever I could. A reluctant theosophist, perhaps, but, above all, I did not want to be accused of possessing a closed, narrow mind or of clinging to an obstinate point of view for no other reason than because it was mine. Eventually, after thirty-three years of challenges to our marriage, not all related to religion, we realized that the chasm was too great to bridge. We divorced. Three years later, I met and married a Jewish man for a brief two years, but was not healed sufficiently for that marriage to work. A year later, I returned to Mormonism, followed by reconciliation with and remarriage to my second husband.

Back to the original question—why did I return? Why back to Mormonism, a religion of certainty, whose members claim they "know" the answers?

This decision may seem incongruous with the me who is often heard saying, "Well, on the other hand . . . ," who realizes that I am hardwired to raise questions, and who even suspects that I am incapable of being a true believer. But as a result of many years of performing gymnastic feats with my mind and stretching it beyond its virgin capacity, I find it difficult to pin down anything with exactitude. I believe that a variety of answers are possible, some of them contradictory, and that there are many possible solutions to any philosophical conundrum. My personal theology has come to resemble something Yogi Berra, the famous catcher for the New York Yankees and an accidental theologian, once said: "If you come to a fork in the road, take it." This is not to say that I believe in murder, theft, cheating, lying, or rape and have given up on charity, kindness, loyalty, or honesty, but rather to say that there are different paths to the destination called Divine.

That said, I realize there is an emotional component to my answer. I would love to tell the people I care about—my parents, the members of my extensive family still deeply involved, dear church friends who have cheered me on and lifted me during those down times—the answers they hope I will give: that Mormonism is the purest path to the truth and to God's presence. I am not a cold, intellectual analyst. I am far from hard-hearted. And, alas, I am not impervious to those people I love. I still want to harmonize with them.

So, get on with it. What is the answer?

Returning to Mormonism—attending church on Sundays, partaking of the sacrament, serving the members of my ward by leading the congregational music or putting the weekly bulletin together, whatever job I am assigned—has been a comforting transition back to the basics I once knew. My Jewish husband tells me that I seem happier since I have begun attending church again and when I am not trying to take on all the possible answers to life's questions. There is familiarity with the scriptures—the King James Version of the Bible, the Book of Mormon, the Doctrine and Covenants, and the Pearl of Great Price, the lay speeches given each Sunday by different members of the ward, the organ music and the hymns, and the sense of community with those dedicated to the teachings of Jesus Christ. But I do not embrace Mormonism in every aspect—either cultural or theological—nor am I sure that this is what is being asked by the religion.

The church's recent political activism against gay marriage in support of California's Proposition 8, for instance, with its subsequent fallout of making a significant portion of the population feel ostracized and less-than, was a stand with which I could not and do not agree. The pre-1978 policy of banning Blacks from the priesthood is another position that troubles me greatly and causes me pain when trying to explain its logic (which I cannot do) to African-Americans. Even though my parents had always been unprejudiced and open armed, as were many other church members, I am wildly bothered by what seems so un-Christian and do not mind saying so. I was not only relieved, but literally exultant when the practice was officially changed. And, while I am not militant about women being given the priesthood, mainly because I know many strong and unoppressed Mormon women who thrive and have thrived within the organization of this church, I am perplexed about why the healing/blessing power of the priesthood has been given to males alone, especially when women in the early days of the church practiced those ordinances now reserved for men. I also like to think that the Holy Ghost—the one who whispers in that still small voice—is actually the female element in the Godhead.

A Mormon friend I was having lunch with recently raised this question: "By attendance at church, are we sanctioning practices in which we don't believe?" That is, indeed, a conundrum—a huge issue, in fact. After some discussion about whether or not a person does more good for an institution by leaving or by staying to help bring about necessary change from the inside, he suggested that no human institution, religious or secular, is perfect. All people need to face and deal with their prejudices, their fears and angers, their quarrels with particulars—inclinations that surface wherever humans gather. Consider the diverse opinions and practices regarding birth control in Catholicism and ritual veiling in Islam.

Granted, with Mormonism we are dealing with an official church that makes proclamations from the top down, but the general belief and trust among the membership is that the leaders, acting on behalf of God's purposes, are worthy of their position despite their obvious humanness and the evidence of personal temperament at play in how and what they teach. The old question that existed long before any religion was organized is, does one need to leave one's tribe because of disagreement, or can one contribute to change by staying and keeping a voice? Does the fulcrum of this teeter-totter provide the necessary balance?

It is true that I sometimes close my ears to things said by some members at church. Very human beings enter through those doors and preach from those pulpits. There are practices, declarations, and much literalism, which I believe will be different given enough time and a deeper understanding. Admittedly, I have an idealistic belief in the ultimate goodness of those who are trying their best to "love one another." Luckily, the teaching to "judge not, lest ye be judged" protects all of us from each other and allows me to let some opinions lie fallow.

When a committed Mormon asks me why I have returned to Mormonism, I am sometimes defensive, feeling that this person might have (1) expectations of my claim of returning to Mormonism, which many believe is an all-or-nothing position; (2) discomfort if I admit to vacillation about what it means to be a Mormon; and (3) possible judgment about my path through life and just why I think I belong with the Saints again. How do I let them know that I really am a good person, even though I have been divorced, even though I have strayed from the path?

Maybe this feeling can be traced back to the time when I lived with a very certain mother. At home and at church, I listened to many voices swearing their allegiance up and down and sideways to the gospel— the teachings of Jesus Christ as interpreted by Joseph Smith and the subsequent Mormon prophets. Mother never mentioned the possibility of gray, even though Brigham Young once said, "Revelations, when they have passed from God to man, and from man into his written and printed language, cannot be said to be entirely perfect."[1] She could be most persuasive in her total certainty of the best way to live and in her unwavering commitment to the truth and nothing but the truth of Mormonism. Maybe she still speaks to me while I sleep, parting the wispy hairs in my ear canal: "You have free agency. But remember, you know the right choice, dear."

Perhaps I am returning to Mormonism to please my mother's departed spirit, knowing the joy it would bring her if I returned to the fold. Maybe I am trying to make it up to her, to show her that her efforts were not without reward. However, I like to think it is more than that, more about the words found in a hymn: "Come unto Jesus, ye heavy laden. . . . He'll safely guide you unto that haven where all who trust him may rest, may rest."[2]

My truth is that I experienced joy, happiness, and fun growing up as a Mormon, participating in dance and speech festivals, talent shows, and bake sales, making scenery for skits, preparing for camping trips, playing softball with the Young Women, accompanying a myriad of soloists both vocal and instrumental on the piano (and being told I was an "amazing" accompanist and pianist, which bolstered my confidence no end). My entire social structure and sense of self-worth were provided for by this community. I felt loved, surrounded by watchful, caring eyes and hands that patted the top of my head. It was here that I learned the importance of serving others and seeing them through the eyes of Christ and his tender mercies. The main reason for returning to Mormonism is this tribal memory, this whole-cloth-way-of-life community that began in the nineteenth century with the early pioneers who attempted to live the United Order. "I, the Lord, have decreed to provide for my saints, that the poor shall be exalted, in that the rich are made low. For the earth is full, and there is enough and to spare."[3]

This ideal was successful in practice for a limited time. In the 1850s, my great-great-grandfather Jonathan C. Wright served on the board of seven directors for Brigham City Mercantile and Manufacturing—a highly successful economic endeavor. Church members produced everything they consumed; merchants united for the common good. In 1874, another group in Orderville, Utah, integrated both communal and economic living—breaking bread together and wearing the homespun cloth they made. No person was left to go without. Ultimately, too much power was placed in the hands of too few men, who had been authorized to decide which members should receive commonly held goods. The enterprise failed. In a letter found in the Scribbling Book of Brigham City, community leader and future LDS prophet Lorenzo Snow wrote: "Concentrating a multitude of individual responsibilities upon one man or a few men . . . is there not danger of getting an elephant on our hands . . . that our wisdom and ability cannot manage or support?"[4]

The practical idea of integrating community and worship, that all are equal before God and that no one should set him- or herself above his or her brother or sister in the gospel, still permeates modern-day Mormonism. Members tithe and also contribute to the church welfare system, which disseminates goods and services not only to members, but to humanitarian efforts everywhere in the world—Hurricane Katrina, the earthquake in Haiti, starving children in Ethiopia, among many others. Granted, many religions provide in a similar way, lest I forget, but it was in Mormonism that I found the web of this sensibility.

When upon life's billows you are tempest-tossed,
When you are discouraged, thinking all is lost,
Count your many blessings; name them one by one,
And it will surprise you what the Lord has done.

—Johnson Oatman Jr. [5]

Nietzsche once said that life without music is a mistake. I agree. During my time away from Mormonism, I felt hungry for the music without even knowing what I was hungry for. I returned over and again to churches with gospel choirs, their singers dressed in red and white or blue and gold robes. These choirs sang as if their music mattered. They sang to connect to God's ear poised just above the church's roofline, believing that he would catch every phrase and maybe even hum along with them. Most contemporary Mormon congregational singing does not rock the rafters and definitely pales next to a good gospel choir. Nonetheless, I am attached to the sweet and quite lovely hymns I still sing. These hymns have been the main vein into the heart of my theology. At odd hours of my life, wherever I have been, whatever I have done, I have heard myself mindlessly humming "Give Said the Little Stream," "Sweet Hour of Prayer," and "I Need Thee Every Hour." Even today, if someone asks me to sing my favorite song, those are the ones that come to mind.

Our family listened to the Mormon Tabernacle Choir singing from Salt Lake City—"the Crossroads of the West"—every Sunday morning. After breakfast, Mother turned the dial to KSL Radio while we children washed dishes and ironed clothes for Sunday school. The music filled every room week after week. We listened to the sonorous tones of Richard L. Evans delivering "The Spoken Word." Duly inspired, we piled into the car and drove off to Sunday school, where we would sing with the congregation and imagine ourselves sounding quite magnificent, just like the "MoTabs."

It mattered, when I was young and impressionable, that we sang these hymns and that our family never missed a Sunday except once when we were quarantined because my sister had smallpox. Music. Every Sunday. Hymns for opening and closing all the meetings. Rehearsals for special music numbers during the week. Music, music, music. If it were not already a factor in my DNA, music imprinted itself on my soul at a young age—music of the pioneers, music of a people that had been martyred and oppressed and chased from one home to another because of their beliefs:

> Come, come ye Saints, no toil nor labor fear;
> But with joy wend your way.
> Though hard to you this journey may appear,
> Grace shall be as your day.[6]

As a Dodger baseball fan (Brooklyn *and* Los Angeles), a student of the bop while listening to Chuck Berry's "School Days," and a skinny girl with braces who conjured up all sorts of bad homemade hairstyles for myself, it felt good to be a "true believer" and to march ahead carrying metaphorical pennants and banners and singing Latter-day Saint songs: "We are marching on to glory," or yet another, "Shall the youth of Zion falter? . . . No!" As a clear-eyed (though substantially nearsighted) youth with all the resolution in the world gathered into my fist and undeveloped bosom, it was glorious, both at the time and in retrospect, to feel my heart beating in my chest and in concert with the others who sang about marching toward the glory of God. What a satisfaction to say, "I know this is the truth." To say it in the company of other assured friends.

Yet, as I grew older, I saw glimpses of shadows flickering in corners—shadows that were not joining in and marching to the same drum. Movement at the periphery. Blurred margins. Was evil incarnate lurking in these shadows? Was it suspicious because it was other than what I believed or who I thought I was? Or was it something else? I listened to some members challenging Mormon doctrine and its claim of embodying all truth. I was party to sacred promises being broken in my marriage, something I never dreamed would happen. I watched the iron rod of my religious passion being bent from straight to curved. I witnessed the slow crumbling of my idealism. In this process, I became marginal myself.

The Church of My Certain Theology dissembled. Even though at church meetings I still sang along with the hymn, "Choose the right, when a choice is placed before you,"[7] I wondered if I really knew what was right and what was wrong. And what was free agency, the teaching that we are free to choose our path and make the right choice for ourselves?

> Know this, that ev'ry soul is free
> To choose his life and what he'll be;
> For this eternal truth is giv'n;
> That God will force no man to heav'n.[8]

After a bumpy and crater-filled personal journey through life's ups and downs, my theology gradually evolved into a plastic and pliable entity—one with the unfettered freedom to question, explore, examine, and doubt. There are many ways to be with God, to find God, to worship God. As the beloved Persian poet Hafiz wrote:

> I am in love with every church
> And mosque
> And temple
> And any kind of shrine
> Because I know it is there
> That people say the different names
> Of the One God.[9]

Ironically, the fact that I am open to a variety of answers may be the pivotal point allowing my return to Mormonism. It is not an either/or proposition for me now. It is not so much about right or wrong. It is more about the deep sensing I have that God is love, not rules, and that I first experienced God's love in this birthplace, this cradle, this home. I was also introduced to the mystical belief in a thin veil between parallel worlds and the all-encompassing possibilities of love.

As a child, I heard stories of the Three Nephites—three disciples who asked Christ if they could live forever on the earth. He granted their wish: "Ye shall never taste of death (or endure its pains); but ye shall live to behold all the doings of the Father unto the children of men, even until all things shall be fulfilled."[10] In the middle of the desert and on lonely roads, these forever-living men appeared out of nowhere to help strangers in trouble, then disappeared without a trace.

At church and in our family, we heard stories of the miraculous: a pioneer man who was awakened in the middle of the night and told to get out of bed and move his wagon before thunder rolled through the night sky. He followed those whisperings of Spirit and the next morning woke to find a fallen tree where the wagon had been parked. We also prayed. Kneeling with my family in the morning before breakfast and at night before bed, I learned to ask for divine help and to expect answers. And I watched my father perform the laying on of hands for people who were sick in their bodies and sometimes in their hearts. I watched him rising, in his most gentle and gracious manner, above his own personal limitations to love and care for people who had fallen behind in one way or another. In these things I believed, these miracles, these prayers: One needs only to knock on God's door, which stands ready to be opened.

Because of these stories and hymns, I sought divinity: "O my Father, . . . when shall I regain thy presence and again behold thy face?"[11] I wanted to know, as everyone does, why we are here on this planet, what is the source of light, what supreme intelligence is guiding the whole show, and whether, indeed, individual spirits lived together in a preexistence and will exist after our physical bodies leave center stage. "In thy holy habitation, did my spirit once reside? In my first primeval childhood, was I nurtured near they side?"[12] I have felt a presence hovering at the edges, a memory of something before this something. I yearn. I enjoy association with others who yearn, in whatever church or gathering they may be found.

Once, while traveling on a deserted highway across northern Colorado, I saw a hawk that had been recently killed, probably glancing off the bumper of a speeding car. Wrapping it in a blanket, I lifted it into the trunk of my car, took it home, and placed its lifeless body on newspapers on my kitchen counter. I wanted to discover something of what it meant to be a hawk. When I lifted its wing from the nest of newspapers, I was startled and amazed at the minuscule gradation of the feathers, their tiny molecular increase in size and purpose, their exquisite symmetry and patterning. Thousands of feathers for flight, for landing, for gliding and catching air, for warmth, for insulation. These feathers may have been created through adaptation of the species, an idea I do not dismiss; Mormons do not have a problem with evolution. But there was the presence of the sublime: the organization and incredible beauty of these feathers witnessed this presence.

I wanted to know about this beauty lying before me, nestled among headlines, week-old news stories, and advertisements for sporting goods. How did this bird come to be? I stepped back, bowed my head in homage to the dead, and withdrew in humility from its sacred geometry.

I, among many others from time immemorial, ask, who and what is God? Is God omnipresent? Is God possible or impossible to imagine? Is God vapor or substance?

In my opinion, no mortal knows this answer absolutely, but I am drawn to the notion of a personal God who not only understands the suffering of those on the mortal coil, but who suffers with us, much as parents suffer for their children presented with difficulty. Mormon authors Terryl and

Fiona Givens write in *The God Who Weeps*: "God has a heart that beats in sympathy with ours. . . . He feels real sorrow, rejoices with real gladness, and weeps real tears with us."[13] These words are similar to the ones I have carried next to my heart since childhood. This understanding, I suspect, is what makes Christianity compelling to me and many others.

There is an innocent in me who likes to kneel in prayer and ask for help to sort through the muddle of the day, to see clearly, and to not be caught up with the worn-out stories of my personal trials. Sometimes I feel that asking the Divine to help me with my problems all the time may be too self-centered compared to the Buddhist idea of praying for all sentient beings, but I want to believe that God will listen and be with me, with you, with all of us, if we will only ask.

Even though I understand that God is not a reality for many people and that there are those who have come to other conclusions in their cosmology, the sense of Divinity feels encrypted in my bones. God is, to me, the one proposed by Joseph Smith when he taught that "God himself was once as we are now. . . . If you were to see him today (the great God who holds this world in its orbit, and who upholds all worlds and all things by His power) . . . you would see him like a man in form—like yourselves in all the person, image, and very form as a man."[14] (Had Joseph Smith been teaching today, I believe his language for God would be gender inclusive, as the Mormon deity is actually believed to be a divine couple.) This is not to say that mortals will ever "catch up" with God, who will always be our God, but that humans have the potential to grow in the eternal scheme of things and become like him. The Almighty is limited in no way, but rather has passed "through the whole of it, and has received his crown and exaltation."[15]

Modern-day Mormons hesitate to engage in public conversations about these teachings, which separate Mormons from the traditional Christian body and have their own logistical challenges. Nevertheless, eternal progression is at the heart of what appeals to me. We are becoming. We are a seed of God capable of full bloom. In this journey on earth, we are here to learn, to be educated in the physical realm, to use what we have learned as our Spirit progresses through the eternities, through whatever realms have been and whatever realms come next and next.

I know that my Redeemer lives,

. . . .

Oh, give me thy sweet Spirit still,
The peace that comes alone from thee,
The faith to walk the lonely road
That leads to thine eternity.

—Gordon B. Hinckley[16]

In the Bible, Jesus Christ was said to have suffered and sacrificed for the world's sins in the Garden of Gethsemane and on the cross on Golgotha. My belief in this atonement did not happen overnight, even though I was taught about Jesus from an early age. An impressionable child, I gave lip service to the fact that he was our Savior, but did not have a clue about the need for redemption, for grace, for forgiveness. It took an experience at Heritage Christian Church, a megachurch in Denver with its outdoor sign "Sinners Welcome Here" to make me realize how much I missed a trust in Christ.

When I walked through the doors into that sanctuary, neon lit up the pulpit with its high-tech tubing. Two huge video screens flanked the stage. A thousand or more people filled the cushioned seats and clapped their hands to the rhythm of a gospel choir. "I am a friend of God, he is my friend," they sang, accompanied by a six-piece rock group of Denver's finest—lead and bass guitars, drums, and a Hammond B-3 organ. Then an immaculately tailored minister came through a door and laid his hands on the what-looked-like-a-rocket-engine pulpit. Religious theater at its best, I mused at the time. I had been here a few times before because of this music, this pageantry, this rock concert early on a Sunday morning. It cheered me when not much else did.

"Glory, hallelujah," he said. "You are a sight for sore eyes, ready to take God into your lives, ready to turn your hearts to the Master. Bless you. Before we get started today," he said, the organist taking a somber turn toward quieter chords, "we have our prayer teams down in front. If your hearts are burdened, if you can't seem to take the right steps in your life, come down here. Allow our Master and Lord Jesus to change you and your life."

Granted, I was at a particularly low place after my brief second marriage had ended, particularly vulnerable with a burdened heart. I rose blindly without thinking about it and made my way across the row and down to the front of the thousand-strong congregation. I did not have much to lose on that particular Sunday in 2002.

A dusky, spindly man with bent shoulders inside a pinstriped suit jacket asked me if I was there to take on Jesus's name. I froze. It seemed too brash, too sudden to just say yes. I had to think about this.

"Jesus loves you," the man said. "Give your burdens to the Lord."

In that moment, I suddenly became my eight-year-old self, standing in the waters of Lake Mead in southern Nevada with my father dressed in white as I was dressed in white. The water came up to my waist and to the tops of his thighs. It was cold in the early part of May, with all the snow runoff from the Rockies draining into the tributaries of the Colorado River. My father held his right arm to the square and said, "I baptize you in the name of Jesus Christ," and then laid me back in the water, making sure my toes and knees did not break the surface. His strong arms held me under water for just a brief second, then pulled me out again. Water rushed over me as I rose, reborn, clean, fresh, free from my sin of stealing a dollar's worth of colored paper from the five-and-dime, which I had already returned.

But even considering that memory, I had not felt an authentically deep connection to Christ before. I had watched an impressive procession of robed and conical-capped Penitentes marching the streets of Quito, Ecuador, seeking forgiveness. I had lit candles in dusky cathedrals throughout Europe and prayed for those in pain. I had borne my testimony of Jesus to a congregation as a child, but knew I had been repeating what others had said. The words of a hymn filled my head:

> The Lord is my Shepherd; no want shall I know.
> I feed in green pastures; safe-folded I rest.
> He leadeth my soul where the still waters flow,
> Restores me when wand'ring, redeems when oppressed,
> Restores me when wand'ring, redeems when oppressed.[17]

"Do you take Jesus Christ as your Savior?" the man asked, standing there, waiting. Something was happening. The weight in my chest was shifting. I felt a lifting, a sense of more air in my lungs. The last few coins in my emotional purse, the base metals of my struggle, were being transmuted like the gold and silver of alchemy, even into a "sacrifice unto the Lord thy God in righteousness."[18]

That kindly lanky man looked at me with tenderness and touched my shoulder lightly. At that moment, I felt that he was Jesus looking at me with liquid eyes and reams of kindness and love and compassion. He had been searching for me, his lamb. My body was filled with a sense of circles and how they connected inside and outside of myself. A sense of threads that were woven into my flesh and bones and heart and mind. I could feel the mercy of Christ, who understood the deepest sludge piles of human error, who had set his heart upon us, upon you and me.

It was at that moment that I knew I could allow religion to be part of my life again. Mormonism did not need to be a perfect church or the one and only church. It could exist with its flaws, its prejudices, its biases. Nor did I have to be a pristine-perfect example held up for all to behold. I was only one of millions of people wending my way through the labyrinth, trying to find the way to something that kept urging me on. I could feel joy in this Christ who loved those inside a Mormon church, a megachurch in Denver, a Tibetan Buddhist monastery in India, a back-woods clapboard church, or in a primeval jungle.

And thus, even though I still squirm in the presence of too much certainty, I have been drawn back into the Mormon fold, uncertain as I confess to being about all of the dos/don'ts, rights/wrongs of this or any other religion.

I suspect that my stance may seem murky or that I do not appear to have a strong moral compass. That is not the case. To say I have returned to Mormonism because it is "the only true church" (a phrase often repeated in the testimonies of individual members), "the only truth," or "the only way," however, is basically not the way I see things.

The story behind the Yogi Berra quote is that to get to Yogi's house, one could take either road at the fork and still arrive there. The divergent roads joined at the end. Either fork would take a person to the same place ultimately. We can learn from a right choice. We can learn from a wrong choice. I suspect that either ultimately leads in the same direction and that God can see the topography with a much keener eye than our own.

I am grateful for the many teachers in my life, found in places large and small, foreign and familiar. To those who understand compassion better than I ever will and to Joseph Smith, the founder of Mormonism and a student of a variety of spiritual teachings himself. I often reread the Thirteenth Article of Faith, which Smith penned to explain Mormonism to a newspaperman and which planted the seeds of larger worlds in my young mind when I memorized these words:

> We believe in being honest, true, chaste, benevolent, virtuous, and in doing good to all men; indeed, we may say that we follow the admonition of Paul—We believe all things, we hope all things, we have endured many things, and hope to be able to endure all things. If there

is anything virtuous, lovely, or of good report or praiseworthy, we seek after these things.[19]

I wish to be honest, true, chaste, and benevolent and to do good to all humans. I wish to love well. Though I have reclaimed Mormonism as my home, I wish to continue seeking after the things that are praiseworthy and of good report, wherever they might be.

Recently, while I was attending Kabbalah class in Denver, David Sanders, our teacher, commented on the sixteenth-century mystic Isaac Luria and his concept of Tzimtzum, saying that humans are in the process of reconnecting the fragments from a "primordial shattering of the vessels." The pieces may be large and disordered or small, fractured splinters. They may be flung far and wide. But in our search for truth, we find only pieces. For me, Mormonism is a piece of this primordial shattering, an essential piece of the puzzle.

To mix metaphors, Buddha is reported to have said of Buddhism, that it is one of the rowboats crossing the channel alongside other boats headed in the same direction. So I return to my familiar piece of the truth, to my boat whose fore and aft are familiar to the touch, to my home place.

Chapter 14

WHO MIGHT WE BE?

On a Sunday morning in Denver, sitting in a wingback chair by a picture window and reading the travel section of the *New York Times*, I read: "I should have gone [to Ireland] a long time ago. . . . But that part of our heritage got lost when [my mother] married an Italian and was swept into his Italian clan, which was so thoroughly steeped in its ethnicity—and so exuberant about it—that none other had any chance. . . . It was like an adult version of that classic children's book "Are You My Mother?" except that I wasn't a lost bird asking a kitten, a dog, a boat. I was a grown man asking a country."[1]

Through the glass, the sun warms my shoulder and one side of my face. *Are You My Mother?* had been one of my sons' favorite books—a newly out-of-the-nest bird asking all the animals just who and where its mother is. And, just like that, I am thinking of my own mother, who passed away more than a decade ago. And her mother before her. Where are they now? In what form do they exist? I have been told there is a hereafter, but what does that mean? And then I am hearing my sons' voices from the past: "Mom. Mo-om," in loud, demanding voices. "Mama," in softer whispers. I am glad I am someone's mother.

Outside the window, I notice an especially orange maple tree against the backdrop of sheer-blue Rocky Mountain sky and a bird diving into the mass of changing leaves. My thoughts keep traversing. I recall a story my cousin told me.

In the 1850s, when a group of Mormon pioneers plodded across the prairies—walking, riding in wagons that creaked, and sitting on horses and carts—a young mother sat in the back of a borrowed barrel-stave wagon. Her shoulders bumped against those of her children, the six of them crowded together inside the rectangular box on wheels. She held tight to the bundle in her lap—a menorah with seven arms.

They must have traveled far in the beginning—carving their route away from the land where soldiers erupted into her family's town and set flame to loose straw. In the middle of the night, she had tied things into bundles. "We are gypsies. Loose threads from the fabric of our homes. Tie knots," her mother must have advised her. "Tie knots to keep your things and yourself together."

This great-great grandmother had carried her precious treasure across borders into Denmark until her family found itself in the company of missionaries for Mormonism. Through the waters of baptism, they had joined the Saints. They sailed. They crossed prairies and rivers and ate dust for breakfast. They were headed to a new Zion. The State of Deseret. And when this young mother climbed from the back of the wagon to take her turn sitting next to her husband holding the reins and the oxen steady, even as he pointed at the hawk floating on air currents above them, I imagine her refastening and resecuring the bundle she carried.

I wonder, what is my ancestry beyond the past few generations, back to the 1800s, even before? If I ran into this particular woman, would I recognize something about her, something *familiar*—that Middle English word from the Old French *familier*, from *familia*, "family"?

I page to another section of the *Times* and read in "The European Left and Its Troubles with Jews," an article by Colin Shindler: "Twitter has shut down a popular account for posting anti-Semitic messages in France. This came soon after the firing of blanks at a synagogue near Paris, the discovery of a network of radical Islamists who had thrown a hand grenade into a kosher restaurant, and the killing of a teacher and young pupils at a Jewish school in Toulouse earlier this year. The attacks were part of an escalating campaign of violence against Jews in France."[2]

This discomfiting news jars me into the memory of a bad dream I had after I had been married to my second husband, a Jew, for fourteen months—I, a Mormon by daylight, possibly a schicksa, but the descendant of a woman with a menorah. In this nightmare, my husband played the part of Asher and I, his sister, Leah:

Someone knocked. This someone, accompanied by other someones who talked as if everyone should be awake, knocked more boldly. It was late, an hour before midnight. Every knock sounded louder than it did in the daytime. The children's mother crept out from under the bedcovers and cupped her hand over Asher's mouth—her son, who slept in a trundle bed pulled out from beneath her higher bed. His sister lay beyond him— sprawled out beside him like a casually thrown rag doll, arms akimbo, mouth wide open.

Asher's eyes opened wide. His mother crossed her lips with one finger. "Hide!" she whispered so quietly that every other sound was an affront to the ears. The tick of the clock. The brush of leaves against the window. The shifting of the cat's tail against the covers—until the sound of knocking rapped against the door again, each knock more demanding.

She heard more voices. Harsh ones. She pointed to the closet they had prepared after hearing whispers about these nighttime visits among their neighbors—the closet with a false wall that opened when someone knew the right panel to push, the place her husband, Herschel, had created by candlelight with his wooden-peg and master-carpentry skills.

Asher, tall for his eight years, slipped from the bed. He had been instructed. He was prepared for this night. His sister, Leah, an undisciplined four-year-old, must not be startled out of her sleep and give their presence away. His mother wanted her children to be safe. As he had been taught, he took a handkerchief from a nearby drawer, soaked it with a blot of liquid from a vial his mother had obtained from the chemist, then put the cloth over Leah's nose and mouth. She relaxed even further into sleep. He lifted her limp body.

His mother closed the trundle bed quietly while Herschel moved toward the door saying, "Coming, coming." Like pieces of a well-crafted watch, each member of the family moved together in prepared symmetry. His father to the door. His mother behind him. Asher to the closet, pressing the middle piece of wainscoting to unlatch the panel, ducking his head to crawl inside, slipping inside the low opening, and placing Leah on a blanket on the floor. He sat on the edge of the blanket. He closed the panel. He listened carefully for the soft click of the lock. He had done all that his mother had asked.

Now the demanding voices filled their front room, his father's voice asking why they had been rudely awakened, his mother saying, "Oy, Gvaldt, God help us." Then Asher could not hear her words anymore. Pushing and shoving and bumping noises. The voices were going away. Fading into the night. And all was quiet. Or at least he hoped all was quiet. His mother had cautioned him to wait for morning light if such a thing happened to their family.

He watched Leah stirring, changing position. He slipped a corner of the blanket over her shoulders, then curled up behind her to keep both of them warm. He stroked her hair and time passed and more time passed, but Asher did not know how late or early it was. He knew only to stay still, to hold his sister close to protect her and warm her. And yet, suddenly, she flung an arm out in her dream. It hit the false panel. A thud. A bump in the night. From the well of her dreams, she said, "Oy, gvalt." Asher put his hand over her mouth to stop a further flow of words, but she pushed it away. "Stop," she said louder.

"Quiet," he whispered. "Now," he commanded. She wriggled out of the cocoon of his arms. "Shhh, Leah. Danger!" These words he spoke into her ear and secured her tighter.

They both heard the sound. Boots crossing the floor. They saw the edges of light through the cracks at the edges of the panel. They heard hands searching the panel, feeling wood, groping, and finally the toe of a boot crashing through the veneer, the wood their father had so patiently fastened together to make their hiding place.

❧❀❧

A nightmare? A past-life experience? Who knows the boundaries between lives or who lives on with us in this gauzy veil between dream and reality?

I finish Shindler's article, which ends with a caution: "The swallowing up of both the Israeli and Palestinian peace camps by political polarization has accelerated the closing of the progressive mind."

It all seems so fluid, even circular—the same mistakes from the past being repeated. When will we get on to more important aspects of our lives, such as greeting each other with no suspicion?

It is time to move on to the book-review section, with writers and their eternal, but somehow comforting, list of book titles—my fellow scribblers writing word after word, salivating with hopes. Turning through captions and headlines—the *Times* as a Rorschach test—I notice a random line from a Robinson Jeffers poem praising "the massive / Mysticism of stone."[3]

Stone. That is a good thing to think about. Massive, silent stone that may not be as mute as we would like. The settling of dust and mire and floods and water and winds. Compressed life. Dead things squashed inside, pressed into silent, layered rock. Compressed history. Headstones that last longer than the remains they mark.

I recall southern Utah, the Red Rock Country—Moab, Arches, the Grand Canyon—then the Rocky Mountains, Kanchenjunga in the Himalayas, Mayan temples in the Yucatan and Chiapas. Suddenly, I am back in Chennai in the south of India, where I had traveled for a month with two friends. Looking at the Hindu temple there—an imposing, steeper-than-a-Mayan-temple structure that towers over the crowded city, no stairs, endless carvings. A behemoth of stone rising out of the valley floor. We had seen this massive temple from our hotel perched on a hill high above the city. We had been wooed by its presence. At dusk, we hailed a taxi and wound around the descending contours of the hill to the main entrance of the temple complex. At the edge of a crowded street, bumping elbows with the washed, the unwashed, the harried, the peaceful, the argumentative, we paid the fee for entering the maze of halls and arches inside the temple. Incense. Smoke. Processions. Women in cerulean veils lined with gold sequins. The blue face of Krishna on statues. The elaborate carvings of Shiva dancing, arms reaching out of the carving, inviting us to dance. An embodiment of Vishnu. Ganesh. Hanuman. Many gods at play on the frieze of stone, colored in bright green, red, yellow, and blue.

Accompanied by tambourines and hand drums, a procession moved amoeba-like past us in celebration, of what we were not sure. We were tourists in this land of the thousand deities. We had read the guidebook explaining that each of these was a different face of the same divinity. We followed the labyrinth of slate stones between intricate columns, brass bells, votive candles lighting the way. I tried to gauge the spirit of this place. I did not feel it in these myriad replicas of red, blue, and yellow gods and goddesses. Still, when I looked again at the carved statues, I wondered what they had seen, what this stone might have witnessed, even before it was carved.

Was reincarnation a reality to which I had not given enough credence? Or were the lives of progenitors encoded in our blood, inhaled from shared oxygen, or carried in the water that has never left the earth's atmosphere? Did I have an ancestor who participated in this ancient religion from which the teachings of Buddha sprang? Had someone related to me walked through these same halls, singing and swaying to the music of a rogue flute? Did any of them embrace this particular path toward God—this religion that does not pass harsh judgment on the phases of humankind: the reality and contours of desire, the striving for power and wealth, the eventual turn toward community, then the acknowledgment of oneness with Atman?

The statues were mute.

Then an oxcart appeared, the spokes of its wheels and the horns of the ox twined with an orange marigold chain. It carried a young almost-woman dressed in bangles and beads. She was wrapped in veils, and her hands were covered with careful designs drawn with henna. A bride. A young man walked to the side, reaching out for the girl's hand while a band of musicians played pipes and drums and dancers arched and bent to one side, then the other. They were laughing, desiring each other, celebrating joy. And, yes, I could not help but think that, yes, I knew them. I felt them. I had been here before. Somehow. As a drifting song of a flute or a dancer.

It is time to put the newspaper away for the morning, but before I refold the pages into their original tidy order, I notice there is a review of Pete Townshend's new book, *Who I Am*. Disregarding the title's play on the word *who*, this sets me to thinking again.

Who I am. Who am I? I Am Who. Am who I?

"Who am I?" I ask the silence of my living room. "Who might we all be?"

If I were to sum up who I am in my usual way, I might say that I am shy or careless or gracious or talented. I would report that I am taller than average, that I am adept at the piano, that I like people. I have spent time reconciling my erratic self with my religious teachings and instructions from various therapists. I have tried to live up to the ideals passed along gently, and sometimes not so gently, by my lioness mother. But what about those before me who are running through my veins, even walking, pacing back and forth inside me, restless for life? Who were we before Mohammed, Moses, Abraham, Jesus Christ, and Buddha were born?

My forebears may have lived in ancient cliff houses dug into the sheer walls of canyons. I may have made bricks out of straw with my bare feet in Morocco. Or maybe I danced in these hallways like a wild fool, abandoning myself to the music and leaping across rooms. I love being captured by a strong beat, a pied-piper tune that will send me into paroxysms of joy and laughter. This rhythm is where I feel part of the body of the family tree that has made me. Child of a shared heartbeat.

And I turn toward the tree outside my window—an exhibitionist every October. Showing off its brilliance, its orange-redness. The morning sunlight illuminates the leaves into gentle fire; it kisses the tops of the Rockies that wait patiently in the distance.

NOTES

Epigraphs: Thomas Merton, *No Man Is an Island* (New York, Harcourt, Inc., 1978), ix. Brian McLaren, *Why Did Jesus, Moses, the Buddha, and Mohammed Cross the Road?* (New York: Jericho Books, Hachette Book Group, 2012), 249.

PROLOGUE

1. Brian McLaren, *Why Did Jesus, Moses, the Buddha, and Mohammed Cross the Road?* (New York: Jericho Books, Hachette Book Group, 2012), 249.
2. Philip Zaleski, ed., *The Best American Spiritual Writing 2007* (New York: Houghton Mifflin, 2007), xi.

CHAPTER 1

1. Hugh Nibley, "Educating the Saints: A Brigham Young Mosaic," in *A Believing People: Literature of the Latter-day Saints,* ed. Richard H. Cracroft and Neal E. Lambert (Provo, Utah: Brigham Young University Press, 1974), 157.
2. William James, *The Varieties of Religious Experience* (New York: Penguin Books, 1985), 337.

CHAPTER 3

1. Quoted in Richard Jackson, "What Are Poets For?" *Mala Revija: A Review of Slovene Art and Culture* (Ljubljana, Slovenia: Spring 1995), 6.
2. Aleš Debeljak, "Public Matters, Private Trials: Slovenian Poets of the 80s," *Mala Revija: A Review of Slovene Art and Culture* (Ljubljana, Slovenia: January 1994), 2.
3. Richard Jackson, "Why Poetry Today?" in "A Brief Poetics," http://members.authorsguild.net/svobodni, 5.

4. Wallace Stevens, "Of Modern Poetry," *Selected Poems,* ed. John N. Serio (New York: Alfred A. Knopf, 2009), 13.

Chapter 4

1. Eliza R. Snow, "O My Father," *Hymns of The Church of Jesus Christ of Latter-day Saints, 1985* (Salt Lake City: Corporation of the President of The Church of Jesus Christ of Latter-day Saints, 1985), 292.
2. First Presidency, "Origin of Man Document," in *Ensign* (Salt Lake City: The Church of Jesus Christ of Latter-day Saints, February 2002), 26–30.
3. Andrew Harvey, *Return of the Mother* (Berkeley, CA: Frog Ltd., 1995), 71.

Chapter 6

1. *Sacred Sites: Places of Peace and Power*, "Jokhang Temple, Lhasa," http://www.sacredsites.com/asia/tibet/jokhjang_temple.html.
2. His Holiness the Dalai Lama, *Becoming Enlightened*, trans. and ed. Jeffrey Hopkins (New York: Atria Books, 2009), 163.

Chapter 7

1. Philip Gardiner with Gary Osborn, *The Serpent Grail: The Truth Behind the Holy Grail, the Philosopher's Stone and the Elixir of Life* (London: Watkins, 2005), 70.
2. Richard A. Kunin, "Snake Oil," in *Western Journal of Medicine*, found on NCBI (National Center for Biotechnology Information), PMC (PubMedCentral), http://www.ncbi.nlm.nih.gov/pmc/articles/PMC1026931/pdf/westjmed00120-0094a.pdf.
3. "Eptifibatide," *Wikipedia*, http://en.wikipedia.org/wiki/Eptifibatide.
4. Jill Bolte Taylor, "Stroke of Insight," *TED*, http://blog.ted.com/2008/03/jill_bolte_tayl.php. Her book about the experience is *My Stroke of Insight: A Brain Scientist's Personal Journey* (New York: Viking, 2008).

5. Keith Plocek, "Eight Ain't Enough for the Rattlesnake King," *The Black Table*, http://www.blacktable.com/plocek050427.htm.

6. Jamie Sams and David Carson, *Medicine Cards: The Discovery of Power through the Ways of Animals* (New York: St. Martin's, 1988), 61.

7. Ibid., 62.

CHAPTER 9

1. Donald R. Wright, "Slavery in Africa," Microsoft Encarta Online Encyclopedia 2000, http://autocww.colorado.edu/~blackmon/ E64ContentFiles/AfricanHistory/SlaveryInAfrica.html.

CHAPTER 10

Epigraph. Oliver Wendell Holmes, Jr., found on *The Quotations Page*, http://www.quotationspage.com/quote/26186.html.

1. Hope Cooke, *Time Change: An Autobiography* (New York: Simon & Schuster, 1981).

2. Sujoy Das, photographs and essays; Arundhati Ray, text, *Sikkim: A Traveller's Guide* (New Delhi: Permanent Black, 2001).

3. Chögyam Trungpa, *Shambhala: The Sacred Path of the Warrior* (Boston: Shambhala, 2003), 46.

4. Marcus Borg, ed., *Jesus and Buddha: The Parallel Sayings* (Berkeley, CA: Ulysses Press, 2002), 85.

CHAPTER 11

1. James W. Fowler, *Stages of Faith* (New York: HarperSanFrancisco, 1995), 24.

2. Ibid., 133.

3. Ibid., 149.

4. Ibid., 172–73.

5. Ibid., 182.

6. Ibid., 198.

7. Ibid., 201–4.

8. Ruth May Fox and Alfred M. Durham, "Carry On," in *Hymns*, 255.

9. C. S. Lewis, *George MacDonald: An Anthology: 365 Readings* (New York: HarperSanFrancisco, 2001), 1.

10. *Poetry Foundation*, "Ode on a Grecian Urn," http://www.poetryfoundation .org/poem/173742.

11. Daniel Ladinsky, trans., "Out of the Mouths of a Thousand Birds," in *The Subject Tonight is Love: 60 Wild and Sweet Poems of Hafiz* (New York: Penguin, 1996), 28–29.

12. Lewis, *George MacDonald,* 19–20.

13. Phyllis Barber, *Raw Edges: A Memoir* (Reno, NV: University of Nevada Press, 2010), 247–50.

14. Stanley Kunitz, *The Collected Poems* (New York: W. W. Norton, 2002), 217.

15. James Nicholson, "The Lord Is My Light," in *Hymns,* 89.

CHAPTER 12

1. Dean C. Jessee, ed., *The Personal Writings of Joseph Smith* (Salt Lake City: Deseret Book, 1984), 415.

CHAPTER 13

Epigraph. Evan Stephens, "True to the Faith," in *Hymns*, 254 (see chap. 4, n. 1).

1. Brigham Young, July 13, 1862, *Journal of Discourses,* 9:310, quoted in Charles R. Harrell, *"This Is My Doctrine": The Development of Mormon Theology* (Draper, UT: Greg Kofford Books, 2011), viii.

2. Orson Pratt Huish, "Come Unto Jesus," in *Hymns,* 117.

3. The Doctrine and Covenants, 104:16–17, *The Church of Jesus Christ of Latter-day Saints, Scriptures*, http://www.lds.org/scriptures/dc-testament/dc/104?lang=eng.

4. Lorenzo Snow, "Scribbling Book" (unpublished manuscript in the possession of Le Roi C. Snow, Salt Lake City, Utah), quoted in Phyllis Barber, "Mormon Manifesto," *City Weekly* (Salt Lake City), March 18, 2004, 23.

5. Johnson Oatman Jr., "Count Your Blessings," in *Hymns*, 241.

6. William Clayton, "Come, Come Ye Saints," in *Hymns*, 30.

7. Joseph L. Townsend, "Choose the Right," in *Hymns*, 239.

8. Anonymous, "Know This, That Every Soul is Free," in *Hymns*, 240.

9. Daniel Ladinsky, trans., "Would You Think It Odd?," in *I Heard God Laughing: Renderings of Hafiz* (Walnut Creek, CA: Sufism Reoriented, 1996), 27.

10. Book of Mormon, 3 Nephi 28:7–8.

11. Eliza R. Snow, "O My Father," in *Hymns,* 292.

12. Ibid.

13. Terryl and Fiona Givens, *The God Who Weeps: How Mormonism Makes Sense of Life* (Salt Lake City: Ensign Peak, 2012), 6.

14. Joseph Smith, *History of the Church*, 7 vols. (Salt Lake City: Deseret Book Company, 1912)*,* 6:305.

15. *Journal of Discourses*, 26 vols. (Liverpool: F. D. Richards & Sons, 1852–86), 11:249; see also 7:333.

16. Gordon B. Hinckley, "My Redeemer Lives," in *Hymns,* 135.

17. James Montgomery, based on Psalm 23, "The Lord Is My Shepherd," in *Hymns,* 108.

18. Doctrine and Covenants, 59: 8.

19. Joseph Smith, "The Articles of Faith of The Church of Jesus Christ of Latter-day Saints," in *History of the Church*, vol. 4 (Salt Lake City: Deseret Book Company, 1976), 535–41.

CHAPTER 14

1. Frank Bruni, "To Ireland, a Son's Journey Home," *New York Times*, October 26, 2012.

2. Colin Shindler, "The European Left and Its Trouble With Jews," *New York Times*, October 26, 2012.

3. Quoted in David Orr, "Daily Devotions: Jack Gilbert's 'Collected Poems,'" *New York Times*, October 26, 2012. The lines are from Jeffers's "Rock and Hawk."

Index

Quest Books

encourages open-minded inquiry into
world religions, philosophy, science, and the arts
in order to understand the wisdom of the ages,
respect the unity of all life, and help people explore
individual spiritual self-transformation.

Its publications are generously supported by
The Kern Foundation,
a trust committed to Theosophical education.

Quest Books is the imprint of
the Theosophical Publishing House,
a division of the Theosophical Society in America.
For information about programs, literature,
on-line study, membership benefits, and international centers,
see www.theosophical.org
or call 800-669-1571 or (outside the U.S.) 630-668-1571.

Related Quest Titles

Beyond Religion, by David N. Elkins

Faith Beyond Belief, by Margaret Placentra Johnston

Growing into God, by John R. Mabry

In Search of the Sacred, by Rick Jarow

Sojourns of the Soul, by Dana Micucci

To order books or a complete Quest catalog,
call 800-669-9425 or (outside the U.S.) 630-665-0130.

More Praise for Phyllis Barber's
To the Mountain

"In her lovely, deeply personal account of her uncommon spiritual journey, Phyllis Barber gives hope to all who would claim the promise: Ask and it shall be given, seek and you shall find. She is a genuine pilgrim on the way. May her journey be blessed, as she has blessed."

—**Scott Cairns**, author of *Slow Pilgrim*

"To travel the spirited world with Phyllis Barber is to dance and sing and play Chopin with the abandon born of a radiance as real as a lithe body and inquisitive mind. She makes the personal universal, a skill reserved for the most competent storyteller. To travel with her is to fall in love with life in its most wrenching, soaring, basic offerings."

—**Emma Lou Thayne**, author of *The Place of Knowing*

"Phyllis Barber is both a gifted essayist and an open-hearted guide to the places of the spirit. To read her essays is to experience vividly the discoveries that are revealed most deeply through reflective travel."

—**Lawrence Sutin**, author of *The Shifting Realities of Philip K. Dick*

"In her particular Mormon-ness, adventurousness, open-heartedness, and soul-inspired creativity, Phyllis Barber's brave confessions unite and inspire us all."

—**Dan Wotherspoon**, PhD, host of Mormon Matters podcast and editor emeritus of *Sunstone* magazine